MATATU WORK

MAKING AND REMAKING THE AFRICAN CITY: STUDIES IN URBAN AFRICA

Series Editors
Taibat Lawanson, Marie Huchzermeyer, Ola Uduku

Series Description

This series is open to submissions that examine urban growth, its delivery and impact on existing and new populations in relation to the key issues of the moment, such as climate control, sustainability, and migration. Showcasing cutting-edge research into how the African city and urban environments are being made and remade across the continent, the books in this series will open up debate on Urban Studies as a dynamic social interaction and urban encounter, and bring a fresh perspective to its exploration. Broad-ranging and multidisciplinary, the series will be mainly monographs, but we also welcome edited volumes that enable a continental, multidisciplinary approach. Innovative, and challenging current perspectives, the series will provide an indispensable resource on this key area of African Studies for academics, students, international policy-makers, and development practitioners.

Please contact the Series Editors with an outline or download the proposal form at www.jamescurrey.com.

Professor Taibat Lawanson, Professor of Management and Governance, University of Lagos: tlawanson@unilag.edu.ng

Professor Marie Huchzermeyer, School of Architecture and Planning, University of Witwatersrand: Marie.Huchzermeyer@wits.ac.za

Professor Ola Uduku, Head of School, Liverpool School of Architecture: O.Uduku@liverpool.ac.uk

Previously Published

1. *Architecture and Politics in Africa: Making, Living and Imagining Identities through Buildings*, edited by Joanne Tomkinson, Daniel Mulugeta, and Julia Gallagher

2. *Migrants and Masculinity in High-Rise Nairobi: The Pressure of Being a Man in an African City*, Mario Schmidt

MATATU WORK

GENDER, LABOR, AND MOBILITY IN NAIROBI

Meghan E. Ference

JAMES CURREY

© Meghan E. Ference 2024

All Rights Reserved. Except as permitted under current legislation no part of this work may be photocopied, stored in a retrieval system, published, performed in public, adapted, broadcast, transmitted, recorded or reproduced in any form or by any means, without the prior permission of the copyright owner

The right of Meghan E. Ference to be identified as the author of this work has been asserted in accordance with sections 77 and 78 of the Copyright, Designs and Patents Act 1988

First published 2024
James Currey

ISBN 978-1-84701-397-2 (hardcover)
ISBN 978-1-84701-413-9 (paperback)

James Currey is an imprint of Boydell & Brewer Ltd
PO Box 9, Woodbridge, Suffolk IP12 3DF, UK
www.jamescurrey.com
and of Boydell & Brewer Inc.
668 Mt Hope Avenue, Rochester, NY 14620-2731, USA
www.boydellandbrewer.com

A catalogue record for this book is available
from the British Library

The publisher has no responsibility for the continued existence or accuracy of URLs for external or third-party internet websites referred to in this book, and does not guarantee that any content on such websites is, or will remain, accurate or appropriate

For My Parents and Steve Langat

CONTENTS

List of Illustrations	viii
Acknowledgments	xi
Conversion Table of KES (Kenya Shillings) to USD	xiii
List of Abbreviations	xiv
Introduction	1
1. Mobile Monopolies: Roots of a Transportation Takeover	38
2. Joyriding: From Placemaking to Publics	68
3. Taking a *Skwad*: The Dangerous Negotiations of Redistribution	88
4. Grubby Bills and Mandatory Gadgets: Financializing Mobility in Kenya	111
5. Paradoxes of Empowerment: Gendered Labor in the *Matatu* Sector	131
6. Feminist Counterpublics: Digital Platforms and Fragile Networks of Solidarity	162
Conclusion. Roundabouts: Kenya's Transportation Futures	187
References	197
Index	211

ILLUSTRATIONS

Figures

1. "The Jam" on Moi Avenue, in Nairobi, which includes over 10,000 *matatu* vehicles and an increasing number of private cars. (Photo courtesy of Claudia Pursals Claret, 2010) — 2
2. Clay sculpture of *matatu* vehicle with scared faces and the slogan inscribed "one more no problem." (Photo by author, 2024 from her collection in Brooklyn) — 3
3. Two *matatu* workers in Nairobi chatting as they climb aboard their vehicles. (Photo courtesy of Claudia Pursals Claret, 2010) — 4
4. Green *matatu* featuring the face of a smiling Wangari Maathai, Kenyan environmental activist and 2004 Nobel Peace Prize Winner, with the slogan "If you don't take care of Nature." (Photo by author, 2017) — 5
5. Three penny coins, or *mapeni matatu*, one theory for the origin of the name for Nairobi's informal taxis. The coins were gifted to the author by a Kenyan friend. (Photo by author, 2024 from her collection in Brooklyn) — 19
6. The big green board that organizes *matatu* turns. Frost was 215L. (Photo by author, 2009) — 29
7. This small notecard with the contact information for the Housewives was stuck in the files between complaint letters from 1956. (Photo by author, 2010) — 39
8. A *matatu* called Funkadelic, featuring a scene where armed men are shooting at police vehicles and helicopters, wreaking havoc in the city. Elizabeth, a key interlocutor, is featured in the image as well. (Photo courtesy of Elizabeth Njoki, 2023) — 77
9. Two *Mungiki* receipts. One old and one more recently acquired. (Photo by author, 2009) — 107
10. "My 1963" cashless transportation card. (Photo by author, 2017) — 114
11a. Card-reading gadget, unused and collecting dust. (Photo by author, 2017) — 116

ILLUSTRATIONS   IX

11b. A box full of card-reading gadgets in a storage shed. (Photo by author, 2017) 117
12. Elizabeth (circled) featured on a billboard in Nairobi, as an advocate for disability rights. (Photo courtesy of Elizabeth Njoki, 2022) 156
13a. Yo-Yo Ma in a *matatu* with his cello on his Bach tour. (Photo courtesy of Elizabeth Njoki, 2023) 157
13b. Yo-Yo Ma kneeling next to and pointing to artwork on a *manyanga* in Nairobi. (Photo Courtesy of Elizabeth Njoki, 2023) 158
14. Flone Initiative Poster for the "Report It Stop It" campaign showing a passenger "manspreading" while oblivious to the woman sharing the seat with him. (Courtesy of Flone Initiative 2019) 171
15. Flone Initiative Poster for the "Report It Stop It" campaign showing a woman entering a *matatu* with a *matatu* conductor (wearing the red uniform of a conductor) crowding her space and seemingly pushing himself into the vehicle closely behind her. (Courtesy of Flone Initiative 2019) 172
16. Flone Initiative Poster for the "Report It Stop It" campaign showing a woman aggressively asking a female conductor for her change. She has picked up the woman worker off the ground by her shirt, while the worker seems shocked and frightened. (Courtesy of Flone Initiative 2019) 174
17. Flone Initiative Poster for the "Report It Stop It" campaign where a young woman is walking away from a group of men who are calling after her and making comments about her body. The woman has her arms crossed and looks defiant and irritated. (Courtesy of Flone Initiative 2019) 175
18. Woman, a member of Flone Initiative's Women in Transportation Group, with "Better BRT needs women" T-shirt, received earlier that year during an Independent Technical Review Panel (ITRP) workshop to which WIT were invited. (Photo by author, 2019) ... 191
19. Basi Go Electric bus in charging station. (Photo by author, 2023) ... 193

Table

1. List of Pirate taxis captured by Mr. Chun in 1960. 64

Map

1. Nairobi and its environs. (Map by Cath Dalton, 2024)   xv

The author and publisher are grateful to all the institutions and individuals listed for permission to reproduce the materials to which they hold copyright. Every effort has been made to trace the copyright holders; apologies are offered for any omission, and the publisher will be pleased to add any necessary acknowledgment in subsequent editions.

ACKNOWLEDGMENTS

This book would not have been possible without generous funding from the Fulbright IIE Program, the Fulbright-Hayes Fellowship, and the Andrew Mellon Foundation as well as generous grants from Washington University, Grinnell College, and the PSC-CUNY fund.

Countless thanks to all the *matatu* owners and operators who took time out of their busy days to sit and talk with me, teach me new words, answer obvious questions, and take me on grand tours of Nairobi. Special thanks to Elizabeth Njoki, Ruth, Jesee, Charles, Tony, Anthony, Jackson, and especially to my route #48 crew, who taught me everything I know about not knowing anything, especially George, Rasta George, Wilson, and Highway. Most importantly, I would like to thank Steve, my dear friend, key cultural consultant, and trusted co-worker. May you rest in peace and may something good come of the tragedy that was your death. Also to Purity Kiura and Kennedy Gitu, who introduced me to *matatus* in Kenya and who have come to my rescue in more ways than one.

To my academic mentors: Angelique Haugerud, Timothy Parsons, and Sydney Harring. Thank you for always taking my calls, reading my drafts, and answering my questions. Your guidance and friendship throughout the years has been a true gift. A special thanks to John Bowen, who took me in when I was far afield from his expertise, and who taught me that writing can and should be fun. To Sowande Mustakeen, who has been an inspiration ever since we met. Finally, to my first anthropology professor, Gary Swee, who among many other things, taught me that I, too, was a professional stranger.

I must thank my generous colleagues at Brooklyn College: Rhea Rahman, Shahrina Chowdury, Jillian Cavanaugh, Naomi Schiller, Kelsey Pugh, Stephen Chester, Katie Hejtmanek, Crystal Schloss-Allen, and Kelly Britt, and my CUNY Faculty Fellowship Publishing Program group: Katharine Chen, Sarah Saddler, Karen Williams, Yaari Felber-Seligman, Robert Robinson, and Shilpa Viswanath, whose helpful reading and thoughtful discussion made the latter part of this book better than it would have been. I learned so much from you and from our time together. Much love and thanks to Patricia Antoniello, a brilliant colleague, generous roommate, skilled chauffeur, and amazing cook.

A special thanks to Brad Fox for his invaluable proofreading advice. To my writing buddy and accountability partner, Tatiana Thieme, brilliant scholar and generous friend. I could not have done this without you.

Infinite love and thanks to my blood and chosen family who have supported me through this book process in countless ways: Peggy Ference, Drew Brady, Shyla and Connie Dishon, Danielle Silber, Michelle Harring, Colleen Knorr, Lynsey Farrell, David Ference, Ginny Stearns-Rossberg, Claudia Pursals Claret, and Peter and Denise Bloom. To my brother Mark, who has taught me so much about what is important in life and how to live it. To my nieces, Cierra and Marydith, and nephew, Michael, who have been making me smile since the day they were born. Finally, to Brad Helm, thank you for your wonderful support, patience, and humor, which has taught me more about love than anything else – life is always easier and sweeter when you are around.

CONVERSION TABLE OF KES (KENYA SHILLINGS) TO USD

Exchange Rates – Currency Converter

US Dollar to Kenyan Shilling (KES)

Year	Average value of KES for $1 USD
2004	78 KES
2006	73.5 KES
2009	78.5 KES
2011	68 KES
2014	68 KES
2015	97 KES
2019	101 KES
2022	117 KES
2023	139 KES
2024	146 KES

ABBREVIATIONS

BRT	Bus rapid transit
KBS	Kenya Bus Service
KBS Ltd.	Kenya Bus Service Management Limited
KTN	Kenya Television Network
MADCOWA	Matatu Drivers and Conductors Welfare Association
M-PESA	Mobile *pesa* (money)
NCC	Nairobi City Council
NTSA	National Transport and Safety Authority
PSV	Public Service Vehicle
TLB	Transport Licensing Board
TMCs	Transport management companies
SACCOs	Savings and credit co-operatives

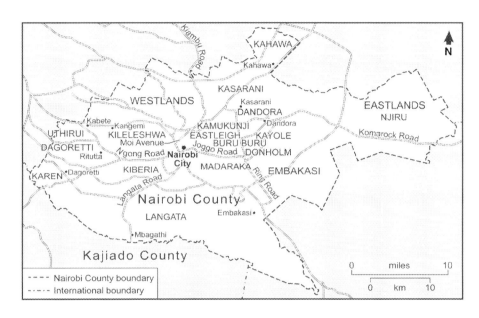

Map 1. Nairobi and its environs.

Introduction

"Utakula nyanya!" (You will eat a tomato!) is a common quip among Nairobi's *matatu* workers. This warning is just one of the many jests one conductor might yell at another, while hanging off the side of an elaborately decorated minivan as it darts in and out of rush hour traffic in a bustling city of nearly four million people. Eating a tomato describes what a *matatu* conductor's face might look like if they fall out of the rapidly moving vehicle that is their workplace. As the conductor's mouth fills with blood, they will appear to have eaten a ripe and juicy tomato. Conductors engage in wide-ranging duties: they shout directions to negotiate merging traffic, collect fares making or requesting change for large denominations of cash, and they constantly discuss current events regarding local politics and celebrity gossip. Through these performances they often literally and figuratively shape Nairobi, setting the pace for the rhythm of life moving through the city with their passengers – about a million people a day.

Matatu minibus taxis range from dilapidated, dangerous, unroadworthy minivans barely creeping along the highway, to vividly decorated mobile nightclubs, their interiors outfitted with ample speakers and large video screens, with exterior flashing lights and musical horns to attract passengers. These vehicles carry anywhere from fourteen to sixty-four passengers at a time, sometimes more. At the time of this research there were around 40,000 *matatu* vehicles operating in Nairobi (Figure 1), providing transportation for over one million people daily (Salon and Gulyani 2019), with figures between 12,000 (Wa-Mungai 2013) and 15,000 (Khayesi and Nafukho 2016) operating in the capital city of Nairobi alone.[1] Paratransit sectors that provide much of the transportation across cities of the Global South, and the *matatu* sector in particular, are often characterized as "chaotic" and in need of improvement (Behrens et al. 2017) and have been said to have a "total lack of adherence to traffic rules" (McCormick et al. 2013: 136), but have also been shown repeatedly to follow the "unwritten rules" of urban life (Fourchard 2023:87, Agbiboa 2022, Ference 2021). Kenyan citizens express deep ambivalence about *matatu* vehicles, simultaneously describing them as "death traps" and "works of art," but for most Kenyans, they are simply seen as a "necessary evil" (Figure 2 – note the scared faces of the passengers represented in the sculpture).

---

[1] Figures around *matatu* numbers, including statistics regarding crashes and fatalities are notoriously hard to access (Klopp 2011).

Figure 1 "The Jam" on Moi Avenue, in Nairobi, which includes over 10,000 *matatu* vehicles and an increasing number of private cars. (Photo Courtesy of Claudia Pursals Claret, 2010).

In Nairobi, in 2010, Zakah, a member of a popular Nairobi hip-hop collective *Ukoo Fulani Mau Mau*, captured their ambivalent aesthetics by evoking graffiti: "In the US you put your graffiti on walls. In Kenya, we put our graffiti on *matatu*" (Figure 3).[2] Like graffiti, *matatu* vehicles express social commentary in subversive ways, and like graffitied walls they are often targeted for clean-up and erasure.

In Nairobi, *matatu* vehicles have become prime disseminators of global and local popular culture. The newest music is often played in a *matatu* first, and only after it becomes popular and requested there, is it played on the radio. *Matatu* exteriors have become canvases for talented Kenyan artists to paint in the colors of multinational brands, religious messages, and the faces of global celebrities. In 2005, one popular *matatu* was completely wrapped in the recognizable tan, black, and red plaid pattern of Burberry, while in 2009

---

[2] In consultation with research participants, I have opted not to use pseudonyms throughout this book. All research participants named have given their expressed written or verbal consent to be named in the study and where sensitive information is discussed, names have been omitted in exchange for descriptions of individuals. For a thorough and thoughtful discussion on the ethics of pseudonym use in ethnography see Weiss and McGranahan (2021).

Figure 2 Clay sculpture of matatu vehicle with scared faces and the slogan inscribed "one more no problem." (Photo by author, 2024 from her collection in Brooklyn).

and 2010, Barack Obama's image appeared on many of Nairobi's vehicles, and in 2022 the most popular *matatu* was called Night Nurse, named after the classic reggae song by Gregory Isaacs. Figure 3 features a *matatu* with an image of Kenyan environmental activist and 2004 Nobel Peace Prize winner Wangari Maathai along with the seemingly truncated slogan, "If you don't take care of Nature."

Vehicle interiors are not only decorated visually with stickers and slogans, but also aurally through music, talk radio debates, and bits of conversation. As the newest music videos play in the background, *matatu* workers create, transform, and disseminate Nairobi's popular urban language, *Sheng*, a mix of

Figure 3 Two matatu workers in Nairobi chatting as they climb aboard their vehicles. (Photo courtesy of Claudia Pursals Claret, 2010).

Swahili, English, Kikuyu, and words from any number of the other languages spoken in Kenya, of which there are currently over sixty (Githiora 2018). *Matatu* operators often use "deep *Sheng*," a version of *Sheng* that is only spoken among a few other people (Samper 2002) as a risk management strategy that can be used between drivers and conductors to discuss suspicious-looking passengers or to devise plans for how to avoid trouble with police. Their linguistic practices shape urban space in Nairobi because *Sheng* is *matatu* operators' occupational language, and they circulate and disseminate so much of it that different routes and neighborhoods of the city have different *Sheng* registers, akin to route dialects.

Matatu Work is an ethnography of Nairobi's popular transportation workforce, with a focus on strategies that circulate both economic (cash, vehicle investments) and symbolic capital (new linguistic codes, music, and elements of style in their clothing and corporeal embodiment) in ways that keep the city moving while adjusting to rapidly changing urban and global landscapes. Unlike many studies of popular urban transportation across cities of the Global South that begin from a position of what is wrong with these systems or what they need to change in order to improve (Behrens et al. 2015; McCormick et al. 2013), my approach focuses on what is generated by these systems and how they work for the people most intimately engaged with

Figure 4 Green matatu featuring the face of a smiling Wangari Maathai, Kenyan environmental activist and 2004 Nobel Peace Prize Winner, with the slogan "If you don't take care of Nature." (Photo by author, 2017).

them. Building on Kenda Mutongi's 2017 pathbreaking book, *Matatu*, a social history of the *matatu* sector covering the struggles and successes of *matatu* owners and their business savvy from the 1960s and over five decades, *Matatu Work* takes an ethnographic approach to provide an in-depth examination of gendered work practices, regimes of labor, economic redistribution, negotiated solidarity and the creation and maintenance of various sociopolitical subjectivities that shape the rhythms of daily life for workers.

Like other popular transportation sectors throughout Africa, the *matatu* sector is a male-dominated industry, having employed mostly young, Kenyan men for decades, and the vehicle itself has been described as a masculine and subversive space (Wa-Mungai 2013), but since 2010, the number of women working in the Kenya's *matatu* sector is estimated to have doubled, from 5 to 10 percent (Flone 2020), especially in Nairobi. This is due, in part, because of a 2010 Transport Licensing Board (TLB) rule that required *matatu* owners to organize themselves under either investment groups known as savings and credit co-operatives (SACCOs) or even larger groups called transport management companies (TMCs) (Plano 2022; Behrens et al. 2015; McCormick et al. 2013).[3] This rule shifted *matatu* management from small-scale, individual entrepreneurs to larger investment groups in hopes of improving service quality, although many of the perceived transport problems (poorly maintained vehicles, aggressive driving, overloading of passengers) have persisted under SACCO management (Plano 2022:157). One aspect of the sector that the rule did change, as many whom I interviewed explained, was that women found it easier to gain entry level employment in larger organizations than under the previous mode of individual ownership where personal bias against women as *matatu* workers often presented barriers to accessing work.

This book tracks the men and women who work in Nairobi's *matatu* sector to understand the gendered regimes of labor in which they are participating and constructing, as well as how they navigate everyday stigma in a job seen as both "necessary" and "evil." This stigma has been used by elected officials, investors, development practitioners, and marketing teams as a justification for neoliberal intervention and reform, and also influenced the way that transportation policy facilitated the shift in wealth from small-scale entrepreneurs, who had owned *matatu* vehicles since the 1960s, to wealthy investors who grew fleets of vehicles over the early 2000s and could lobby the city and national government in ways individual owners could not (Mutongi 2017). Transportation is one of the ways urban megaprojects are imported into city budgets and landscapes and often serve the interests of large-scale global interests rather than local lived ones (Rizzo 2017). Ethnographic research, such as that which appears here, is an attempt to counter off-the-shelf narratives that render workers disposable, problematic, and monolithic by providing granular, in-depth representations of complex lives.

---

[3] For the past two decades there have been four dominant TMCs operating in Nairobi (Citi Hoppa, Express Connection, Kenya Bus Services and Citi Shuttle). Although they attempt to set themselves apart from the *matatu* sector, they are still part of the overall popular transportation sector often running their business exactly how other *matatu* operations in SACCOs are run (See Plano 2022: 157).

While the total number of *matatu* workers is hard to pinpoint, in 2009, a veteran Nairobi driver named Jackson calculated that "each *matatu* employs 100 people." His estimate included the large number of people who earn supplemental income from the sector in a variety of ways. Throughout African cities, transportation systems and depots are bustling arenas of sociality, commerce, and exchange (Stasik and Cissokho 2018) as well as staging areas for dangerous negotiations with a variety of actors (Ference 2021) and corruption (Agbiboa 2022). In addition to *matatu* drivers and conductors, there are touts, who call for passengers, there are mechanics who repair the vehicles, managers who attempt to organize the terminals, DJs who sell mixes of the newest songs to play on the enormous *matatu* speakers, and cooks who prepare *chai* and *mandazi* (tea and donuts) in the morning and fruit salad in the afternoon. There are also several groups who subsidize themselves through the *matatu* sector in more nefarious and violent ways. *Matatu* vehicles are targeted as mobile banks filled with cash by both criminal vigilante gangs and police officers (see Chapter 3).

As a solution to the lackluster bus service provided by the Kenya Bus Service (KBS) company, who had held a colonial monopoly on passenger transportation since the 1930s, in the late 1950s, and throughout the early part of the 1960s, pirate taxis (the precursors to *matatu*) appeared (see Chapter 1). But after their decriminalization and proliferation in the 1970s, the *matatu* sector was characterized by speeding, overtaking, reckless driving, and general rudeness, causing *matatu* work to be seen as a problem. Workers developed a reputation for bad behavior that placed some in a category closer to "thug" than "transportation service provider" or "entrepreneur" (Mutongi 2006). This decades-long resentment has resulted in an antagonistic relationship, often with a violent edge, with the public, exemplified in a 2009 column appearing in *The Nation* newspaper, entitled "Disciplining the Reckless *Matatu* Driver." In the column, Sammy Wambua, prompting Kenyans to act with physical violence toward *matatu* operators, described a harrowing transportation experience and referred to the driver as a "lunatic":

> It was just a matter of time before we were transferred to a hearse from the Toyota. But I was not about to be killed by a dread-locked, twig chewing, twit. Good Kenyans, it is incumbent on you to grab any speeding PSV [Public Service Vehicle] driver by the head and twist it until he sees his back. (Wambua 2009)

Matatu workers' uneven reputation has crossed international borders. Consider former Africa correspondent, Jeffrey Gettleman's descriptions of *matatu* operators for *The New York Times* as, "glassy-eyed conductors ... fleas on amphetamines" who "shanghai hapless passengers from the curb into shuddering minibuses that zigzag through lines of cars, even jumping up on the sidewalk" (2014). Many authors repeat similar tropes to describe informal transportation operators as drug-addled thieves who force innocent passengers into life-threatening situations. In 2010, Ed Mwangi, the son of one of the most successful transport duos in Nairobi's history, Mary and John Mwangi, posed a question to me that had been troubling him. Exasperated, he asked: "If *matatus* were here before independence, why do Kenyans hate them so much? They are part of being Kenyan," he explained. For those unfamiliar with Nairobi in particular, it may be hard to imagine this strong disdain for public transportation workers, but even the more sympathetic renderings of *matatu* operators cast them as "transgressive rebels" (Wa-Mungai 2013) and it is well documented that complaining about *matatu* commuting is a common and therapeutic Nairobi pastime (Wa-Mungai and Samper 2006). This ethnography is not an attempt to ignore the dangers of questionable *matatu* driving or to romanticize the unsavory elements of popular urban transportation that have been widely covered by journalists, scholars, and transportation experts, but to probe the lived realities of the large workforce that provides important urban labor in one of Africa's major metropolitan centers.

When the *matatu* sector is framed by what it lacks, instead of what it generates as a social institution, it only increases the risk to the workers and obscures critical aspects of the work itself. Although they are on the cutting edge of popular culture, the *matatu* sector has long been used as a foil for things that are problematically analog in the digital hub of Nairobi. Even the *The Economist*'s 2012 article that popularized the term "Silicon Savannah," referring to Nairobi's booming technology sector, framed the *matatu* sector through stigmatization. The opening story in that article describes visitors to Nairobi as being "horrified by the homicidal minibuses called *matatus*," and ends with a comparison of irate *matatu* drivers with the mobile game Angry Birds, where cranky-faced and destructive fowl hurl themselves into bridges and buildings.

This negative characterization overlooks the humanity of the massive *matatu* workforce whose members have a long history in an urban institution older than Kenya itself. As part of my ethnographic research, in 2010, I worked as a conductor on a 14-seat *matatu* called Frost, driven by a 30-year-old man named Steve. The vehicle was owned and named by a refrigerator repair man who lived in Nairobi. Two weeks after I left Kenya later that same year, Steve was gravely injured in a head-on collision while driving Frost, ultimately dying in the hospital three weeks later. In June 2010 when I learned of Steve's death, I returned to Kenya for the funeral. I discovered that the drivers and conductors on his route contributed toward Steve's medical bills and subsequent burial expenses by giving a portion of their earnings each day to a representative of their route association named Rasta George, who recorded the contributions in a thick logbook. I remember Rasta George showing me the entries and running his hand down the columns of names and donations, communicating to me that these daily contributions, and his diligent documentation, was an act of caretaking in the face of the ultimate risk in their work. Redistributive practices like this provided an economic safety net for *matatu* workers and complicated the view that they were simply dangerous "thugs." These economic practices also provided an example of the circulative mechanisms and "redistributive labor" (Ferguson 2015) that builds what Keith Hart has described as the "social forms of informal work" (2009), and what I, and other scholars, have identified as one of the many innovative economic practices present in the "hustle" economy (Thieme et al. 2021; Thieme 2018).

The *matatu* is a mobile space for discourse and a discourse in itself, and a good example of a "public," which has "qualities beyond printed texts to include parliament buildings," in this case, minivans (Cody 2011: 47). *Matatu* vehicles, as noted earlier, are key economic and communicative infrastructures in Nairobi, circulating both symbolic and economic capital and carving out urban space as they do it. An important feature of the way that *matatu* vehicles work can be understood by examining how the sector organizes urban space linguistically, socially, and aesthetically. For example, *matatu* routes not only provide transportation services, but the vehicles' exterior art and interior stickers, music, and videos act as social infrastructures of moving mass communication. They have been used as a set and plot point for character development in a Netflix series and, just recently, in 2023, by a global music superstar who used one to travel to a Nairobi market. Being a passenger in a *matatu* is like riding inside of a newspaper. As you are transferred from one place to the next you are not only in intimate proximity to a very wide number of strangers but are exposed to spoken and unspoken linguistic codes. *Matatu* vehicles bring Nairobi's mix of diverse urban forms from the city center to ever expanding neighborhoods. Even in the most basic vehicles the space will be filled with the social commentary and messages reflecting everyday life along with performances by operators that are shaped by age, gender, ethnicity, place, and class.

Popular Transportation in the Postcolony

A 2008 World Bank Report, "Stuck in Traffic: Urban Transport in Africa", analyzed transportation data from urban Africa and found that fourteen major African cities used minibus and midibus taxis (MBTs), like *matatus*, to move much of their population (Kumar and Barrett 2008). MBT systems are generally referred to as "paratransit," or "informal transportation," but both terms are often perceived negatively and as undesirable. The "chaos" of these systems is largely an illusion as they have repeatedly been shown to have their own forms of regulation and structure (Agbiboa 2022; Ference 2021; Klopp and Mitullah 2015; Wa-Mungai 2013; Aduwo 1990). Following Klopp (2021) and others (Mutongi 2017), I will use the term "popular transportation" when referring to minibus taxis instead of paratransit. Although similar to paratransit in that the *matatu* sector has flexible routes and even more flexible timetables (Behrens et al. 2015), they are unlike paratransit because *matatu* vehicles are the primary transportation sector in Kenya, not supplements for a larger, more formal transportation system like the KBS colonial bus system that officially ended service in the 1980s (Mutongi 2017) or the Nairobi Commuter Rail that runs from just one to up to seven trips from Nairobi's major commuter neighborhoods to the city center daily.[4]

Urban transportation, like taxis, buses, and *matatus*, has provided an important place for the expression of marginalized perspectives and played a particularly important role in Kenya's decolonial history. An early example from the 1940s was the political activity of the Kikuyu taxis drivers who ferried radical African thinkers, and their ideas, from Nairobi to their homes in the Kenyan highlands and Nairobi's suburbs, ultimately becoming some of the first people to join the Land and Freedom Army and participate in oathing rituals (Furedi 1973). Just a few years later, in 1956, during extreme British colonial violence in Nairobi, African men and women used colonial buses as a place to engage not only in commerce, but small acts of resistance to the everyday violence of European settlers (see Chapter 1). In the late-1980s, under the authoritarian era of Daniel arap Moi's single-party rule, *matatu* vehicles were one of the only places where citizens could gather to consume, discuss, and debate politics as the workers circulated the speeches of the political opposition on cassette tapes (Haugerud 1995). Nairobi's transportation infrastructures have been important sites to stage moments of resistance and develop political and urban identities.

Publics are not simply mass-communicated messages sent through radios or newspapers, they can include a variety of texts circulating on a mass scale (Latour and Venn 2002) and facilitating conversation and debate between strangers (Warner 2002), much like *matatu* vehicles do. Cody, drawing on

---

[4] The Nairobi Commuter Rail was opened in 2020 for transportation on five routes at a variety of intervals each day. The Embakasi Route runs seven trains a day, the Syokimau route runs six, the Ruiru Route runs two trains a day and the LuKenya and Limuru Routes each run one in the morning and one in the evening (krc.co.ke/the-nairobi-commuter-rail).

Latour (2005) and others describes publics as "relations among people who are mediated by material infrastructures of communication, each with its own qualities, extended beyond printed texts" (2011: 46–47).

Zakah's description of the *matatu* as "moving graffiti" aptly captures the way *matatu* vehicles work as publics and counterpublics: a type of circulating media text where strangers can develop social commentary, while performing and debating meanings through communicative infrastructures (Cody 2011; Hirschkind 2006; Warner 2002). Like graffiti, *matatu* vehicles are sometimes linked with circulating subversive messages, which stems from trying to make oneself seen and unseen at different times in different ways across the postcolonial landscape.

Learning through Infrastructures

In the past decade, exciting urban ethnography on infrastructure has emerged from cities throughout Africa and the world. By focusing on an infrastructural system as a socio-material process that produces various political subjectivities, *Matatu Work* draws from ethnographies of infrastructure which use infrastructure as a lens into urban citizenship (Mains 2019; Anand et al. 2018; Fredericks 2018; Anand 2017) and which focus on the ways that roads (Beck et al. 2017; Harvey and Knox 2015; Lee 2012), bus stops (Stasik and Cissokho 2017) and mobility more broadly shape life and development in the cities of the Global South. Due to the combination of archival analysis with ethnography, *Matatu Work* may most closely align with Brian Larkin's *Signal and Noise* (2008), where Larkin discusses colonial media as a type of mobile infrastructure building a national subject, while this book takes transportation infrastructure as media publics and counterpublics circulating urban political identities, discourses, subjectivities, and debates.

Infrastructures, like water, waste, electricity, and roads, are material forms that allow for exchange over space. *Matatu Work* casts Nairobi's transportation infrastructure of *matatu* vehicles through the lens of infrastructure as "technical and cultural systems that create institutionalized structures whereby all goods of all sorts circulate connecting and binding people into collectives" (Larkin 2013: 6). More specifically, the vehicles are prime spaces for the circulation, debate, and development of ideas and urban subjectivities. *Matatu* vehicles act simultaneously as transportation infrastructures carving their urban paths, but also as media infrastructures that facilitate "flows and create unique aural and perceptual environments, everyday urban arenas, through which people move and work" (Larkin 2013: 3). Transportation infrastructure in Nairobi is both an important avenue for neoliberal governmentality and a communicative infrastructure that provides spaces for shared public intimacy that is productive and generative. It has and will continue to serve as an important place of performance and protest in Nairobi.

Because the sector pre-dated an independent Kenya, it was one of the early arenas where ideas about safety, responsibility, efficiency, discipline, risk, competition, and being a "proper" Kenyan were explicitly debated throughout the 1960s (see Chapter 1). Using mobility as a proxy, Kenyan citizens began publicly asking questions about what kind of nation they wanted to be. Often parliamentary debates pitted ideas of safety and efficiency on the side of the rational and modern Kenya Bus Service, against the pirate taxis' drivers who embraced risk, criminality, and chaos, but who were offering citizens the services they needed. At one point in their history, Kenyans needed the pirates because the colonial infrastructure that was left to them was completely unable to render services at the level needed. By the 1970s, during an intense period of urbanization that the government could not provide for, nor support, the informal economy supplied the services needed to fill the gap left open by the state. *Matatu* vehicles were, and still are, a substantial portion of the informal economy, which in the face of mounting urban struggle was embraced, leading Kenya's first president, Jomo Kenyatta, to finally decriminalize the sector on Madaraka Day, in 1973 (Mutongi 2006: 553).[5]

In the 1980s, during the rise of neoliberal economic policy and structural adjustment programs, Kenyan citizens were increasingly left to fend for themselves, as state services were cut and their currency lost value (King 1996). During this era, the second president of Kenya, Daniel arap Moi, ruled Kenya with an authoritarian regime that crushed dissent (Cheeseman et al. 2020; Throup 2020; Branch 2011) and was known to torture people in the basement of government buildings (Wrong and Williams 2009) and send spies into college classrooms to report back on any opposing political views being disseminated to young people. Under this regime, associations between people and interactions were limited; groups of any kind were difficult to form and any meeting of more than two or three people required permission from the government (Chege 2020).[6] During this time *matatu* vehicles became one of the only spaces where Kenyans of all kinds could interact with each other out from under the dangerous eyes of the Moi regime. While Moi

---

[5] Madaraka Day is a national holiday celebrating the transfer of governmental powers and offices from British control to Kenyan control. It is often described as Kenya's independence day.

[6] Institutions such as churches required permits that were, however, rarely ever given, which then in turn put people at risk and also had the added effect of causing ever-present fear.

was silencing people by tactics like slum demolitions, *matatu* vehicles were playing and passing cassette tapes with political speeches, music, and sermons, commenting on the politics of the day from demolitions to ethnic violence (Haugerud 1995).

Throughout Moi's era the *matatu* sector almost uniformly resisted any type of reform and grew to dominate the transport market with an aura of machismo, danger, risk, and criminality (Mutongi 2017). The 1990s saw a series of street battles over *matatu* territory staged by vigilante groups who were terrorizing the sector and the public at large (Anderson 2002; Heinze 2018). A massive change in policy occurred in 2004, after the first peaceful transfer of power in Kenya in 28 years. In February 2004, John Michuki, longtime Kenyan politician and acting Minister of Transport and Communications in the popularly elected National Rainbow Coalition (NARC) government, passed a bylaw, officially known as Legal Notice #161, which was a set of safety regulations meant to reform the infamously stubborn *matatu* sector (Lamont 2013). Michuki was riding on the momentum of Mwai Kibaki's election. The NARC administration's commitment to transport reform and their conclusions about how to improve the system pivoted on restructuring the "undisciplined" minibus sector (Mitullah and Onsate 2013). When *matatu* owners said they would strike to protest the new regulations, Michuki held his ground, and on the first day of February 2004, the regulations took effect. That first week, there were hardly any *matatu* vehicles on the roads. Instead, the roads were full of private cars and throngs of people walking. From the first week, and in the months following, the *matatu* sector was a constant topic of conversation.[7]

Since 2004, these rules, encompassed under Legal Notice #161, have come to be known as the "Michuki Rules." The regulations called for several new mechanical changes for vehicles and changes for personnel in the vehicles including the installation of speed governors, a paint job, and seatbelts. The personnel regulations required drivers and conductors to wear uniforms and to obtain several government certificates. They were unprecedentedly successful as far as transportation regulations have gone in Kenya, which had during previous iterations been quickly ignored, forgotten, or dismissed by police, passengers, and owners (Plano 2022; Mutongi 2017; Mitullah and Onsate 2013). The Michuki Rules made a lasting impact and many of the elements

---

[7] I remember looking out from the truck I was in at the people walking in the rain in their suits and ties, soaked to the bone the first few days of the regulation. From that time until the time I left in June of 2004, I spoke to people about the *matatu* sector daily and it dominated local and national news.

of the rules were still mostly in place nearly two decades later with speed governors, uniforms, licensing, and seatbelts all present in the *matatu* sector of 2024. Additionally, over this time, many of the new policies have reregulated the transportation sector in a way that has transferred the ownership and wealth of the sector to a smaller group of powerful and elite politicians and business owners, who increasingly adopt large-scale megaprojects or technological solutions while simultaneously putting Kenya's largest, and in some respects most vulnerable, workforce at risk.

The more problematic popular transportation sectors seem, the easier it is to get people to agree and invest in changing them, without understanding the ways in which they work well. Focusing on the negative aspects of the sector like the lack of safety, poor working conditions, poor accessibility for marginal groups and pollution is often preferred over discussing the positive ones like the low cost to public expenditures, adaptability, resilience, and the frequent service that provides transportation in ways in which the government is unable (Klopp et al. 2019: 2). There has been an increasing focus on reforming transportation sectors across the Global South, namely, to invite large-scale urban megaprojects that include bus rapid transit (BRT) systems, which have been successful in Latin America and Asia, but less so in African nations. In some African cities, the BRT is seen as a revival of oppressive colonial policies surrounding the question of who is allowed to provide transportation for which populations. As some scholars argue, bus upgrades become avenues for wider transformations of society, like wealth transfers and deepening class rifts (Klopp et al. 2019; Dewey 2016). In Johannesburg, the owners of the informal taxi system protested the introduction of the BRT system (Graeff 2008). The collective taxis of South Africa represent a sector that has an important history for the African population. The informal transportation sector in Johannesburg especially enjoys a historical legacy as a particularly African enterprise, operating for the African population during apartheid; they are still referred to as "black taxis" (Blom-Hansen 2006; Khosa 1992). Similarly, in Nairobi, the *matatu* sector remains an important indigenous business, displaying messages of ambivalent aesthetics and providing important public spaces for political debate.

Moving Targets

One of the practices that is broadly criticized by transportation experts and development practitioners is the way that MBT systems use competition and perverse incentives to motivate their employees. The *matatu* sector's dependence on daily cash payouts is perceived by transportation planners as a stubborn roadblock to better and more streamlined transportation for modern

African cities and contributes to bad driving behavior by trying to maximize their trips, and speeding or overloading passengers to do it. Although Nairobi received the Silicon Savannah moniker in 2012 due to the innovation and widespread adoption of the digital money transfer technology, M-PESA, in 2014 and 2015, *matatu* workers and passengers rejected the use of cashless transportation cards (Chapter 4). In 2014, after a Google-backed cashless transportation card, something akin to New York City's MetroCard or London's Oyster Card, failed to launch in Eldoret, Kenya, *New York Times* correspondent Gettleman blamed "analog Africans" for their refusal, and criticized *matatu* workers and passengers for wanting to hold on to their "grubby bills" (2014).

It is not that African workers and commuters are resistant to using digital currency, as Gettleman implies, but there are important reasons that *matatu* operators prefer daily cash payouts. *Matatu* workers' pay is structured by a *target system*. The target amount is calculated and set by *matatu* owners, and the driver or conductor must return each day with that amount in cash and a fully fueled, functioning vehicle. Drivers and conductors split the money that is left over from what they pay the owners, after they refuel the vehicle, fix any damage, pay off the managers, touts, police officers, and gangsters they encounter along their route and repay their own personal debts.[8] On average, *matatu* operators may take home 500 to 800 KES ($5–$8 USD) a day.[9] Owners' targets structure the daily lives of *matatu* operators and dictate the number of trips they make, but daily cash payouts also provide direct access to capital, which is subsequently circulated among workers' larger *matatu* work and personal networks. The circulation of daily cash is an important and valuable aspect of *matatu* work and part of why people put up with the risk and pressure. As some would say, without those "grubby bills" the Kenyan economy would stand still.

I first witnessed the unique economic circulation and redistribution practices of *matatu* workers in Mombasa, in February 2005, during the commute to my Swahili language teacher's house. The road through her neighborhood made a two-kilometer loop that started and stopped at the *matatu* stage. The stage was marked by a small bench where passengers waited for vehicles on the way to and from town. My teacher lived more than halfway around the loop, so I usually stayed on with a few other passengers, listening to the

---

[8] A tout in the *matatu* sector is often used as a synonym for a conductor, but is actually a specific role within the sector that includes calling for passengers and loading the vehicle. At times this is done by the conductor, but it can also be performed by an individual who just touts, and who is not (or not yet) a conductor.

[9] This conversion rate reflects the price of currency at the time of this writing, in 2024. In 2004, the Kenyan Shilling was worth more (KES 200–300: $1 USD).

loud Swahili hip-hop and enjoying not being in the sun. When the vehicle arrived in the neighborhood, I witnessed the circulatory nature of *matatu* work in action – as the passengers got off the vehicle at the *matatu* stage, our driver put the vehicle in park and jumped out as well. The conductor quickly climbed out of the back and got behind the wheel. Seconds later, an entirely new and noticeably younger looking man crawled into the back of the vehicle and slammed the door shut. I decided to ride the entire loop and observe this job rotation.

As our new driver/previous conductor slowly rolled through the neighborhood, seemingly practicing his driving skills with live passengers in the back, the new conductor opened and closed the door, calling "*Beba! Beba! Tao! Tao!*" (Carry! Carry! Town! Town!). Because he was from the neighborhood, he was calling to his neighbors and friends. I would come to find out later that he only received payment if he filled the *matatu* with a certain number of people. The young conductor joked with passengers as they refused his gentle cajoling that urged them to climb in the vehicle, and as we continued along the loop, we gathered the few passengers he needed to get his small payment. When the vehicle returned to the main stage the *matatu* musical chairs started in reverse and as the young conductor climbed out of the back, the original conductor jumped from behind the wheel and handed him a few coins for "filling the vehicle." The young conductor pocketed the coins and returned to his friends, who were sitting on the bench at the stage, waiting for the next *matatu* to arrive. The original driver, who had been having tea, said goodbye to his companions and settled in behind the wheel, readying himself for another trip to town. This on-the-job training exemplified how the redistributive labor and circulatory system of economic and symbolic capital leveraged through neighborhood communities was an important element of *matatu* workers' daily lives and labor practices. These economic practices hold important insights into the changing nature of labor in urban centers across the globe and the way the mobility of transportation work provides powerful strategies for managing risk in an increasingly precarious world.

The target system is just one example of how the experts of development sometimes overlook the way that things already work to sustain people before attempting to solve problems with development projects or technology. The cover image of a brochure for Kenya's National Development Plan, *Vision 2030*, showed a nearly empty street, the sun reflecting off the skyscraper's glass and a glaring absence of pedestrians, hawkers, people of any kind, and traffic jams. In an even more thorough bit of erasure, among the thousands of pages of *Vision 2030* documents, websites, images, and overall content, and among the dozens of mentions of "sustainable urban transportation," the word *matatu* did not appear once (Huchzermeyer 2011). Ethnographic research like this, focusing on the economic strategies in complex workplaces, help us understand the important social intersections and circulatory work that is being done in what seems to be unproductive space or "chaos." This type of work and function happens at the street level in a way that planners can sometimes not see, or simply ignore.

Nairobi's Spatialized Inequality

Nairobi has an enduring politics of exclusion where struggles occur at spatial levels. From the early days of Nairobi's development, belonging to the city has always been about "making, containing and controlling urban space" (Jones 2020: 633). In the first thirty years of the British presence, colonialism was uneven throughout East Africa. Some areas were heavily populated with colonial administrators and European settlers, while the residents in other areas may have had no idea that they had been colonized until nearly two or three decades after the fact (Bravman 1998). Nairobi, however, was one place that was heavily populated with Europeans, Asians, and Africans by the 1930s. There were settlements and African locations, with brothels, kiosks, shops, *dukas* (informal shops), and increasing congestion from the private vehicles crawling all over the city (White 1990). Nairobi's unique urban history of uneven and unplanned settlement provides a context for the emergence of the informal transportation sector. The ways people moved in between places of settlement, the paths and the roads they walked down, became written in the landscape.

Since its inception in 1899, Nairobi was a contested space characterized by its racialized inequality (K'akumu and Olima 2007; White 1990). The city of Nairobi itself, meant to be a European enclave of modern urbanism, quickly became a diverse and plural arena where various interests fought for access to resources, space, and services. But Nairobi was officially off-limits to much of the native African population, enforced by a system of work permits and passes, known as the *kipande* system, that limited the movement of workers from the Native Reserves (Weitzberg 2020; M'Inoti 1997; Berman and Lonsdale 1992). The city of Nairobi was supposed to grow from a railroad camp to a proper colonial "garden city," the modern marvel of urbanity with tree-lined boulevards, plenty of parking, and no native people (Myers 2003). In the colonial ideal, Nairobi would have resembled a European reserve, but by 1906, there were around 9,000 Africans living there (Bujra 1975: 217) and by 1926, there were 18,000 Africans, making up around 60 percent of the city (Hirst and Lamba 1994: 77). It was impossible to completely police the city of Nairobi because people were living and dwelling along the boundaries, the edges, and the cracks of town (Myers 2003; Cooper 1983).

If the colonial government recognized that people were settling around the city, they would have to provide for them or at least do something to make them leave. However, if the administration just largely ignored the people and their problems, they would not have to contribute to their well-being, nor would they have to acknowledge them at all. That is, until the settlements got too big and the people there got too comfortable. When they finally did recognize an informal population growing, especially before 1930 they would just demolish the settlement, forcing people to scatter and rebuild (White 1990). These invisible Africans slept underneath verandahs and in the alleys of Nairobi, while the Indian population was crowded into three hundred acres in the center of the downtown (Hirst and Lamba 1994: 76).

Although much of Nairobi's current traffic congestion is blamed on *matatu* vehicles, Nairobi has long had a traffic issue. By the 1930s Nairobi was not only congested with people, but with cars. In 1928, with 5,000 cars, Nairobi was "the most motor ridden town in the world" (Hirst and Lamba 1994: 65). From 1934, transport, traffic, and parking in Nairobi were becoming problems, and the government started to organize the city center through pushing commuters and bus stops further away from the Central Business District (CBD) (Heinze 2018: 7). At this time, the colonial government paid more attention to parking than to driving or transportation for the masses. There were also more accidents and reckless drivers. By the mid-1930s the idea of investing in the colony looked better to British companies because they were promised monopolies over the business they would start. There were monopolies in a variety of sectors including agricultural exports (Swainson 1980), banking (Velasco 2022), and transportation (Ference 2023; Heinze 2018). In 1934, the monopoly of the KBS and the creation of the powerful TLB, which would oversee licensing all vehicles in Kenya, were put in place. In 1934, as KBS maintained their small fleet of buses and their growing circumference of service, the TLB had little to do and had few applicants. In the 1940s, when veterans who were drivers returned from the Second World War, a popular idea was that the soldier population should get licenses, buy cheap vehicles from the military, and start transport services to supplement the growing number of invisible African residents living in and around Nairobi (Parsons 2003).

This history is why *matatus* have long been treated as an invisible service for invisible people. In the early 1960s, pirate taxis violated the colonial monopoly on passenger transportation by providing rides to Africans from African settlements. These informal taxis that emerged to meet the growing demand of the population in the late 1950s were called "pirate taxis" by the newspapers and in the colonial records because they were operating in direct opposition to the KBS monopoly. These pirate vehicles came to be known

Figure 5 Three penny coins, or mapeni matatu, one theory for the origin of the name for Nairobi's informal taxis. The coins were gifted to the author by a Kenyan friend. (Photo by author, 2024 from her collection in Brooklyn).

as *matatu* over time, as they consistently offered a cheaper fare than KBS – by one penny, a ten-cent piece in colonial Nairobi (Figure 5). KBS charged four penny coins for a ride, or *mapeni manne* (*nne* means four in Swahili). Operating informally, a pirate vehicle charged only three coins, *mang'otore* (coins in Kikuyu) *matatu* (three in Swahili).

For those first several years of *matatu* filling the gap in late-colonial urban transportation, it was standard practice to pay small bribes to the police as pirate taxis carried their customers. *Matatu* illegality was overlooked until it was decriminalized by Jomo Kenyatta in 1973, and, as the city grew, the *matatu* business grew, and as neighborhoods stretched further from the Central Business District and the State House, *matatu* vehicles became the essence of urban life (Mutongi 2017).

Shaping Nairobi through *Sheng*

Along with Kenyan hip-hop artists, *matatu* workers import, create, circulate, and distribute the prime urban linguistic register in Nairobi – *Sheng* (Samper 2002). *Sheng* is defined as "a variety of Kenyan Swahili closely associated with Nairobi's urban youth ... and has evolved into a vernacular of Swahili" (Githiora 2018: 1). It has a Swahili grammatical base with a variety of loan words from English and many of Kenya's multiple ethnic languages. Nairobi

Sheng is developed and used by *matatu* operators to build solidarity, not only among each other but also broadly across the large and growing population of young people who are their customers and neighbors; *Sheng* works as a shibboleth, or a code, to allow admittance to an exclusive group and can be deployed to exclude those who would themselves exclude the *Sheng* speakers, such as members of the upper socioeconomic status who speak English and little or basic communicative Swahili (Githinji 2006:448). What makes knowing and speaking *Sheng* a challenge is that it is always changing. Dr. Paul Ngoza, a sociolinguist at University of Nairobi, described the challenge of writing a *Sheng* dictionary: "Documenting *Sheng* is like trying to draw a cloud." *Sheng* is an important part of *matatu* operators' reputations. Commonly linked to *jua kali* ("hot sun") workers and youth in the 1970s and 1980s (King 1996; Osinde 1987), some sources argue that *Sheng* can be traced to networks of pickpockets as far back as the 1930s (Mazrui 1995), but has more recently been linked to rappers (Samper 2002), *matatu* men (Wa-Mungai 2013), and criminal gangs like *Mungiki* (Rasmussen 2012). To some, *Sheng* is a creative force that reflects the oratory traditions of the region. To others, it works as a symbolic rebellion against the normative sociolinguistics structures that link high achievement to the mastery of standard English or standard Swahili (Wa-Mungai 2013). *Sheng* can therefore be seen to have elements of what are known as "anti-languages" (Githiora 2018:2).

Sheng works on multiple layers in the *matatu* sector. As the occupational language of the *matatu*, it serves many functions. At a basic level, it is, as previously mentioned, a code of inclusion and exclusion. The *Sheng* that *matatu* operators speak is called "deep *Sheng*," which is a collection of code words that only a small number of people know (Samper 2004), which can also be developed and spoken between close friends (Githiora 2018). *Matatu* crews will use *Sheng* to discuss passengers (cute girls/suspect boys/ undercover police) and strategize if police officers pull them over or if they encounter a criminal who wants to hijack the vehicle and rob the people inside, a common risk *matatu* operators face. In the *matatu* sector, "deep *Sheng*" acts as a safety mechanism for workers. The safety of *Sheng* is an important part of how *matatu* operators build bonds and develop solidarity among one another.

Urban youth languages like *Sheng* construct solidarity among their speakers (Githiora 2018; Githinji 2006) through a process by which, "youth build deviant vocabulary on top of existing codes" (Kießling and Mous 2004: 303). This was extremely clear in 2009 when I was in Kenya during the national census. The group of young people I was with, who had all grown up in Buru Buru in Eastlands and who were speakers of *Sheng*, often rehearsed with each other what they were going to say when the census takers arrived at their doors. They would say a version of the following sentence repeatedly over a period of weeks: "*Mimi ni Mkenya, Sina kabila. Lugha langu ni Sheng.*" ("I am a Kenyan, I have no tribe, my language is *Sheng*"). Importantly, this was a few years after the 2007 post-election violence erupted in Kenya, and there were many times over the following years where I saw young people define themselves as urban Nairobians rather than their ethnic identities, finding those identities to be problematic.

In addition to solidarity and unity building, *Sheng* is also used to mark boundaries of class separation. For example, Nairobi *Sheng* as well as another dialect called *Engsh*, are both well documented (Abdulaziz and Osinde 1997); *Sheng* is spoken in the Eastlands part of Nairobi and incorporates more Swahili than English, and *Engsh*, a response to *Sheng*, is spoken by young people living in the Westlands of Kenya. The young speakers of *Engsh* are often wealthier, may be more educated, and incorporate more English than Swahili when they talk, making it a marker of class. *Sheng* and *Engsh* have been shown to promote "covert prestige" among speakers who use the language to exclude others from understanding (Kießling and Mous 2004: 303). Increasingly, different *Sheng* dialects (like *Engsh*) are becoming so idiosyncratic to specific neighborhoods that people often reported that they could not understand the *Sheng* of *matatu* workers in neighborhoods they rarely traveled to in Nairobi. This neighborhood distinction produced, at least in part, by the *matatu* sector workers' linguistic practices, is just one of the ways they impact the social landscape of the city of Nairobi across broad domains.

Feminist Counterpublics

Although *matatu* vehicles have historically been an important space for marginalized people, women experience a high risk of gender-based violence in them, and in public transportation more broadly throughout the world (Williams et al. 2020; Fernando and Porter 2002). Feminist scholars were among the first to complicate Habermas' ideas of the public sphere by pointing out that not all publics were available to all people and that there were pluralities of alternative publics experienced by women and other marginalized groups (Fraser 1990; Felski 1989). These alternative publics, or counterpublics, were characterized by the role they played in constructing and maintaining knowledge shared by members of marginalized communities while simultaneously working to make visible issues specific to marginalized experiences (Asen 2000). Urban transportation like taxis, buses, and *matatu* vehicles have all provided an important place for the expression of marginalized perspectives throughout Kenya's history. Recently, women workers, passengers, and feminist organizations have been using the male-oriented space of the *matatu* to spread feminist messages.

In 2015, a young woman named Naomi Mwaura launched a feminist organization called the Flone Initiative (the organization name is for her parents and not an acronym) to address the violence women face in the transportation sector. She explained to me that the organization grew out of an incident in 2014 where a woman was publicly stripped by *matatu* conductors in Nairobi and afterwards the perpetrators released their own video footage of the assault, which subsequently went viral (Cummings 2014, Warner 2014). In response to this event, as well as other public stripping assaults in 2013 and 2014, feminist activists in Kenya launched several social media actions, and one called "#mydressmychoice" went viral, with women tagging themselves in an outfit of their choice (Nyabola 2018). In 2015, Flone Initiative started to address the role of women working in *matatu* vehicles in safeguarding the safety of women passengers and even gathered fifteen women *matatu* workers and staged a play, *Wamama Wa Mathree* ("Mothers of the *Matatu*"). Since then, they have organized four annual conferences on Women in Transport across Eastern Africa with scholars and practitioners from throughout the world. In one campaign, they used music videos and posters that were comic-book-style scenes depicting the dos and don'ts of personal space and sexual harassment (see Chapter 5). For Flone Initiative, and other hybrid institutions of supervision, the *matatu* public is an important space of cultural production of political claims crafted for public circulation (Cody 2011: 47). Flone Initiative uses the *matatu* sector as a feminist counterpublic where they make and distribute posters and place stickers, and create music videos to spread sexual harassment awareness campaigns using media forms and styles commonly found in *matatu* vehicles.

Flone Initiative brought women who work in popular transport together under the group Women in Transport (WIT) and have launched several campaigns to draw attention to the dangers women face on their commutes and in their workplaces (see Chapter 5). Although there are not many women in the sector, they receive a significant amount of publicity and media attention and have been able to gain access to powerful groups and organizations. They have also carved out niches in *matatu* work itself. Take for example a key interlocutor of this study, Elizabeth, a female conductor who makes it her mission to cater to passengers with disabilities in the *matatu* she owns with her husband, which has resulted in her being included in city planning meetings as an advocate for passengers with disabilities.[10] In August 2022, she was featured on a billboard above a Nairobi highway publicizing the need for more attention in catering to

---

[10] Elizabeth has been featured on podcasts, radio and web series interviews as well as written about in news articles (Wikman and Muhoza 2019).

passengers with disabilities in transportation. Additionally, since 2019, Flone Initiative members have been invited to meetings discussing the future of the BRT project in Nairobi, when *matatu* owners and *matatu* management organizations have not been included. *Matatu Work* shows the tactics of women in the male-dominated transportation sector of Nairobi, Kenya and highlights the unique ways that individuals and groups use the sector, a historically male space, as a counterpublic site for feminist ideas to be circulated and potentially impacting Nairobi's future transportation planning.

Contemplating *matatu* infrastructure as moving publics and even counterpublics, we can reconsider how the unproductive time of the traffic jam has become a time filled with consumption, performance, and circulation that shapes the lives of Nairobi residents and how these workers manage risk in their daily lives through placemaking practices using the *matatu*. Through the lens of transportation in Nairobi, this sector provides some insights into the way that Kenya approaches the future of the state and the streets. This ethnography uses *matatu* workers, vehicles, and management institutions to address important issues of urban life today including which urban places count as sites of productive protest and politics, how workers and infrastructures adapt under increasingly precarious and changing regulatory environments, and what kinds of hybrid institutions emerge as transportation becomes a target for development industry technological solutions.

Risk and Responsibility

It is impossible to report exactly how many *matatu* rides I have taken in the twenty years that I have researched this project, but I remember my first one vividly. It was the summer of 2003, and I was returning to Nairobi after a six-week long archaeological field school at the paleontological site of Koobi Fora in Northern Kenya run by Rutgers University. At the time, I was riding with my friend Purity, a Kenyan graduate student at Rutgers who was working as a teaching assistant for the field school. She had invited me to spend my last few days in the capital city with her and her family in the middle-class suburb of Buru Buru. When her car broke down on the way home, she sent me and another Kenyan friend, Ken, ahead telling us that she would meet us at her aunt's house. Ken replied with a gleeful "No problem!" and we darted across several lanes of downtown Nairobi traffic and climbed on to a very crowded, standing-room only, nearly pitch-black *matatu* with painted windows, playing Swahili rap music at high volume. I could feel the bass vibrating my body as I held on to the bar above my head. I kept an eye toward Ken, who I could only catch glimpses of through the bobbing shoulders and heads of the other passengers. After what seemed like a long time, but was probably about 30 minutes, Ken reached over several passengers to tap me on the shoulder, and he motioned that we were getting off. We wormed our way through the passengers, out of the vehicle and into the late afternoon light, squinting like we had just emerged from seeing a movie in the theatre during the day. I realized that those were not the same basic and austere city buses I had grown up taking in central Illinois, and I was excited by the idea that public transportation was not simply a means to an end but was itself an important destination and urban place for the residents of Nairobi.

In January 2004, I returned to Kenya for another field school, this time a semester-long program run by St. Lawrence University that focused on the language, culture, and ecology of Kenya and included an internship with the globally prominent environmental activist Wangari Maathai, known in Kenya and throughout the world for her organization, The Green Belt Movement. In 2004, Maathai won a Nobel Peace Prize for her work.[11] I had decided to focus on environmental anthropology for the semester, but because our arrival and orientation coincided with the implementation of the Michuki Rules in early February 2004, almost all that Kenyans wanted to talk about were the changes to the public transportation sector. Our language teachers, home stay families, and colleagues at internships were always discussing and debating the *matatu*. By the end of that semester, I was even more curious about these mysterious machines called *matatus*, and I was intrigued by the upheaval it would have for the labor force, many who were Kenyans in their early twenties, which at the time was around my own age.

The negative perception and distrust of *matatu* work is pervasive and picked up by local and global institutions. For instance, in 2005, in the orientation for the Fulbright IIE fellowship at the US Embassy in Nairobi, the standard safety protocols for US citizens living in Kenya was to avoid taking *matatu* vehicles for travel. Coincidentally, the very thing the State Department had given me permission and funding to study. As noted above, the general commuting public in Kenya often dehumanizes these workers and understands them as dangerous people, or "thugs" risking their lives along with innocent commuters (Mutongi 2006). The negative perceptions are so strong that complaining about *matatu* and talking about terrible *matatu* rides has been shown to be a bonding and coping mechanism for young professionals, and when they go out at night there is often ample time spent on the topic as part of the conversation

---

[11] For more information on Wangari Maathai's life and work, see her 2007 memoir, *Unbowed*, as well as Namulundah Florence's 2014 examination of Maathai's social and political background in *Wanagari Maathai: Visionary, Environmental Leader, Political Activist*.

(Wa-Mungai and Samper 2006). This speaks to the way that the *matatu* works as a moving public in Nairobi, able to shape life and collectivity in the city long after one has departed the vehicle. Researchers found that "even in stories where the *manamba* (another *Sheng* term meaning *matatu* conductor) plays a central role, the *manamba*'s attitude, behaviors, motives, and character are often neither described or discussed, but assumed" (Wa-Mungai and Samper 2006: 55). In the eyes of the general Kenyan commuting public there is widespread disdain for *matatu* workers, which potentially makes their jobs even more dangerous.

In summer of 2009, I struck up a friendship with a *matatu* driver named Steve who drove on my neighborhood route through the upper-middle class neighborhood of Nairobi called Kileleshwa, which houses a variety of international expatriates as well as many young Kenyan professionals.[12] Steve was driving a small, 14-seater *matatu* called Frost. A polyglot, he spoke near perfect English along with Kikuyu, Swahili, Kalenjin, Kamba, and a little Italian. A month or so later I saw him again as he picked me up on my street in the small Frost *matatu*, and I saved his contacts. Steve saw himself as a "good" driver, as someone who could protect me and other passengers, and someone who felt responsible for the people he carried on the busy and dangerous roads of Nairobi. I would wait for Frost specifically or text Steve to coordinate leaving my house and his path to town.

Matatu operators take on much of the risk of maneuvering a dangerous driving environment and ultimately suffer the consequences. Recalling his early days when he first started driving the Frost, Steve remembered sitting in heavy traffic but choosing not to drive along the steep shoulder of the road to get around the cars ahead. Many of the passengers berated him, sarcastically asking him: "What is wrong with you? How did you get this job? Are you even a real *matatu* driver?" *Matatu* operators are, in practical and symbolic ways, an important representation of a changing urban environment that is steeped in risk and economic precarity. They join other urban transport operators who are increasingly organized and mobilize their unique position as transport operators, who "through filtering mobility ... reclaimed their centrality as owners, transformers, and gatekeepers of both representational and physical spaces of the city" (Sopranzetti 2014:139). Around the 1970s, the perception of *matatu* workers went from "entrepreneurs" embodying many of Kenya's positive values of self-reliance and hard work to "thugs" who simply take what they need from hard working people (Mutongi 2006).

---

[12] Kileleshwa was one of the oldest African settled neighborhoods in colonial Nairobi but was demolished in 1926 only to be rebuilt and resettled by wealthier residents years later (Hirst and Lamda 1994: 64).

There is an understanding that if you are a *matatu* worker you will have to break the law; it will be required of your work. It can play out in a variety of discriminatory actions. Take for example Steve's story of housing discrimination shared with me:

> There was a time I remember, that I wanted to rent a house, independent. So I went to the landlady. She told me there's a room, and it's going for 2,000. And then … before we finalized the deal, she … she asked me, "what do you do?" "Well, honestly…" Ok, I am honest, I … I didn't know, it will cost something. I said, "I work in *matatus*, I'm a *matatu* driver." And that was the end of it. Yeah. She told me "there's no house."

This is part of the reason why Steve and others joined MADCOWA, Matatu Drivers and Conductors Welfare Association, in 2008 when the Kileleshwa route #48, was chosen by the organization as a pilot route. The following excerpt is from one of my earliest conversations with Steve, which we had in 2009 in a private taxi in Nairobi that Steve was driving because *matatu* vehicles were on strike. Steve and I spent almost all day in traffic due to the strike, which prompted many good discussions about the state of urban transportation in Nairobi.

MF: MADCOWA?

Steve: Of which, in my route #48, I am vice-chairman.

MF: Really? [Loudly, surprised]

Steve: Uh-huh. You know when you come up with an idea like that – we want to protest, yeah? – and you send it to the other crews … cause we have one thing in common, whatever the experience of the *matatu* driver on this end, it is the same, same thing, the experience on the other end. Ok, except, not up-country, but in Nairobi we have that one thing in common.

MF: Do you have meetings? [For MADCOWA]

Steve: Yeah! [Voice going way up]. We have meetings! We have, um, we write minutes and what have you. What we don't have, cause we just started the other day after … actually we were trying to find a solution to the … in not coming in conflict with the government, collecting views from the stakeholders actually. We can have a bargain you know, we don't want to be in conflict with … you [meaning the government]. We are encouraging our members to have the proper documents and what have you. So we need your support [again, meaning the government].

So, where do you see us? Where is the problem with us? We want a transparent system. The court fines should be harmonized. The highest offense is not around 60,000, 30,000 [shillings], it should be 5,000. This 5,000, you should be given a ticket, like in your places [to me], you get a tickets. It's OK if you are given a ticket, you are told to go pay this amount to KRA [Kenya Revenue Authority] on whatever day that is. That would be better ... but they are not giving us a chance to talk to them, you see?

One day Steve offered to arrange for me to observe some on-the-job, "conductor training," which he scheduled for a Sunday morning from 7:00am–2:00pm. He thought it was necessary to my research. I ultimately agreed. When he arrived that Sunday morning, I realized he had planned for me to participate more than simply observe as he did not bring along a conductor for me to work with but intended for me to work alone from the get-go. In his mind I had done enough observation as a passenger in the many previous months and did not need to be trained by a conductor that day. The following excerpt from my field notes is a good way to capture the feeling of my first shift as a *matatu* conductor with Steve on the *matatu* Frost.

> I woke up early, at 5:16am, and by 7:00am Steve was calling me, and I was answering. He was in town and coming to Kileleshwa's terminal stage, Othaya, in a half-hour. I agreed and started walking and arrived at Othaya at 7:54am. Most people walking with me at that time were middle-aged men, probably on their way to work or church. When I arrived, I called Steve and he was three minutes away. "Here we go" I thought and immediately started watching the tout and conductor of the other *matatus* thinking, "Am I seriously about to do this?" I looked for the *makanga* (conductor) who would train me and there was no one. Steve immediately recognized my fear and laughed a little, saying not to worry, "it was easy." When I asked where the *makanga* was he replied, "you are my *makanga* for today." Then he pointed to my belly and said, "I see butterflies in there, Meg, don't worry, you have a good driver."
>
> As foot traffic picked up, I saw that a nearby tout was filling Frost while Steve and I talked. Steve told me the going rates to pay the tout for filling the vehicle: "if he fills 5–10 people you give him 10 shillings, if he fills the whole thing, you pay 20 shillings. If there are 4 or less, you tell him, 'I am coming back.'" When we left, I told the tout that I was "coming back," and we headed to town. Before we took off, Maina, Steve's friend and sometimes conductor laughed and jumped in the vehicle saying, "Even me, I'll pay if an *mzungu* (European) is the *makanga* ... and I never pay in *matatu*. I am one of them." Maina got in with me and showed me that the door had a trick ... you must pull the door handle and push the door out with your forearm at the same time.

Once we were on our way and I was picking up people, everyone in the vehicle was laughing and smiling. We had fun. They were shocked that a White lady was working on a *matatu*. Then we picked up another White woman and people were joking that she was my *mwenzako* (relative). She and I both laughed and had a short conversation in English along the way. The trip was 30 shillings to town, everyone paid and when we got close to the stage people started yelling *Shuka*! *Shuka*! Stop the bus! But Steve warned me to keep the door closed until we pulled all the way into the stage and parked. Against their wishes, I did and they waited to get out.

When we let people out at the stage, we chatted for a bit outside the vehicle and fellow workers started coming up to ask us questions and say hello. We looked at the big green board that organizes *matatu* turns (Figure 6). It has about 7 columns and 30 rows and there are number plates in the cells. We are 215L. We had to wait for five cars ahead of us to fill, so we had a cup of tea, and chapati. We talked about our personal lives like we usually did. Our families. When we got back to Frost there was someone sleeping in the van. When the other touts and conductors saw the sleeping man they started yelling and he woke up and went to the next *matatu*. Steve pointed out that some of the guys were hovering around him because they were waiting to rob him if he passes out. Steve said, "some of the friends you have around here…" and raised his eyebrows. We started to fill the car and Steve assured me that going back to the stage was easy because you just drive, and most people get off near the end. Most people on the return route paid with exact change, but when I did have to provide change, it was harder than I thought because I had to remember exactly where people got on.

I made a few classic errors as we went along, I overloaded the vehicle once for just a few meters (the guy insisted and just kind of jumped in) and another time I thought I heard someone bang on the vehicle to stop it, but then no one got out. Embarrassing. When we finished our route, we counted the money. We made 470 shillings. The float was 250 and I made 50 shillings in the end for that one *skwad* (trip). When I told Steve about picking up passengers, he assured me that in a little while I will be able to "distinguish between those who are going to town and those who are just out of the house." He explained that by body movements and clothes you can tell if they are going to town. I started to see the customers in a completely different way after that.[13]

By the last month of my fieldwork in 2010, instead of catching a *matatu* home, I would find Steve and we would ride *mlengo* (out of turn on the board) until my stop. Going *mlengo* meant that we would skip our turn on the board

---

[13] Excerpt from fieldnotes, Nairobi, 23 May 2010.

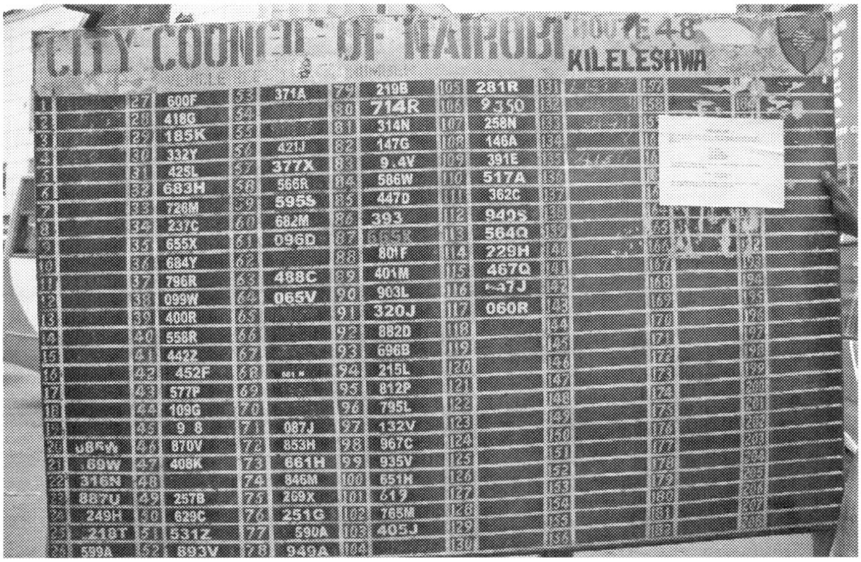

Figure 6 The big green board that organizes matatu turns. Frost was 215L. (Photo by author, 2009).

and leave with a few passengers and pick up more on the way. Working as a *matatu* conductor was not just rare for an anthropologist, up until that point never having been done before, but also rare for women in Nairobi at the time.[14] Something that would change over the next decade.

Anthropologists have described this type of mobile research as conducting "go-along" ethnography, a mixed method of walking or riding with interlocutors as they tell you what the landscape means to them, and they populate it with their thoughts and memories (Carpiano 2009; Kusenbach 2003). This included the months spent at different termini in the city center, where *matatu* workers drank tea, smoked cigarettes, and ate bowls of fruit salad while chatting with other crew members in empty *matatu* vehicles, waiting their turn to be filled again, or, choosing to simply go *mlengo* – out of turn, without waiting or filling up with passengers – collecting passengers along the way. Go-alongs, or in my case ride-alongs, are a unique method because one can "combine participant observation and interviewing ... in order to access some of the transcendental and reflexive aspects of lived experience *in situ*" (Kusenbach 2003: 456, italics original). My fieldwork site is not based on

---

[14] Several years later, in 2013, Daniel Agbiboa worked on a minibus taxi during his ethnographic fieldwork in Nigeria (2022).

any one school, hospital, or neighborhood but on the routes through the city. I got to know the city through the lens of its paths in and out.

A few weeks after I left Nairobi in 2010, Steve was driving Frost through his regular route early on a Sunday morning when he was hit by an SUV. The driver of the SUV was a drunk, twenty-year old who had borrowed his father's vehicle and was leaving a nearby bar after a long Saturday night of drinking. The drunk driver was uninjured in the crash, but Steve's leg was crushed, and he was taken to the nearest hospital. The hospital he was taken to is a private hospital and caters to the upper-middle class residents of the Westlands area. Upon seeing Steve in his driver's uniform, a blue shirt with navy pants and vest, the nurses and administrators at the hospital refused him service, despite his dire need. Steve's ankle was so badly crushed that it was amputated hours later when he was finally seen at the public hospital across town. Steve stayed in the hospital after the surgery for three weeks until he succumbed to preventable complications and died.

The hospital would not release his body to his family and friends for burial until his bill was paid, which was over 600,000 KES ($8,000 USD). A significant portion of the funds for Steve were raised by fellow drivers and conductors on his route, all under the membership of their route organization, MADCOWA. Everyone had been giving donations from their routes (from 50 KES to 200 KES) during the two weeks since he passed. Donations were entered in a logbook. When it came time to pay the final bill, they had raised over 100,000 shillings (around $1,200 USD) for Steve's burial and hospital bills.[15] My research and this book is informed by the work I did with Steve as one of my primary interlocutors and the tragic and too common loss of life of *matatu* drivers. I spent many days over the years of my research in Kenya working with him and other crews as we rode *mlengo* from *tao mpaka mwisho* (from town until the end of the route).

Research on the *matatu* sector in Kenya show that when *matatu* vehicles get into accidents they are almost *always* fatal to the driver (Gladys 2006). In Steve's case, he was not killed in the accident and even his crushed leg could have been saved if he was admitted at the first hospital he went to, the private one that turned him away. The uniform he wore and stigma of being a *matatu* driver helped kill him. Although his leg was crushed and he was no doubt in an extreme amount of pain, when the hospital staff saw that he was a *matatu* driver, knowing that he could not pay and perhaps even assuming it was his fault, they sent him away. This cost him his leg, which eventually cost him his life. This is the type of effect that stigma has, which has been documented as a decrease in life chances (Link and Phelan 2001; Goffman 1963).

---

[15] The rest of the $8,000 dollars was provided by me, and Steve's friends and family.

INTRODUCTION 31

Mobility, Power, and the Foreign Anthropologist

Mlami is the *Sheng* word for White person. *Lami* is the Swahili word for tarmacked roads. The black, smoothly paved roads that link people, commerce, and ideas are the *lami* roads. In Swahili, adding an *m-* to a verb transforms it to indicate the person who acts out the verb. For example, the verb, *-kupenda*, to love, becomes *mpenzi*, a lover. When I first heard the term *mlami* shouted at me as I walked through Eastleigh with my Kenyan friend, I was confused, thinking "*Mlami* ... person of the tarmac?" Several days later I asked Professor Nzuga, a Swahili language teacher and the author of a *Sheng* dictionary, what the history of *mlami* could be. He described a hypothetical scenario where a group of African road workers were talking about their White bosses, and because most White settlers and colonial administrators knew the word *mzungu*, the common Swahili word for White person, they needed to create a new word to talk about their White bosses in front of them.[16] Professor Nzuga explained that because the road workers were using sticky, black tar to cover and finish the road, they must have thought this a fitting misdirection. They could chat about the *lami* in the open, complaining that "this *lami* is difficult, ridiculous, smelly, heavy, or stupid." Any negative feelings could be expressed explicitly if they were framed through the tarmac.

The professor's description could be highly accurate, but another explanation might be a more straightforward example of a *Sheng* style of a play on words. As mentioned above, *mzungu* is the word for White person. It comes from the verb *kuzunguka*, meaning to turn around or go around, usually used in reference to maneuvering a car. An *mzungu* therefore is a person who turns around or goes around, generally meaning a person who travels, or as it has been explained to me, a person who has come from afar and will leave again, coming and going as they please: a tourist; a colonial administrator; a researcher. The link between the movement of the foreigner and the black tarmacked road would not be a major leap in logic. Tarmacked roads are associated with tourists and settlers in Nairobi, so it is not too much of a stretch to think about the same people who "go around" as being people of the road. Another important part of the word *mlami* is that *mzungu* can mean any foreigner, although it is most commonly referring to Whites, but Kenyans also use *mzungu* for Black Americans. The word *mlami*, as far as I have been told, means strictly White person, which could circle back to the professor's discussion of the black tarmacked road being a misdirection. Whatever the unknowable origins of the word, *mlami* links whiteness to roads in a powerful

---

[16] Part of his assertion in this story is to drive home the point that although *Sheng* is associated with youth it is an older urban language that was around at the tail end of colonialism.

way, that can provide some insight into how roads are symbolic and physical manifestations of colonialism that completely transform the landscape (Harvey and Knox 2015).

This link between mobility and power is an important one methodologically, and not just linguistically. The fact that I could simply come and go to Kenya in ways that my interlocutors never could and the ways I struggled and failed to assist them in getting them things that they needed still haunts me. The regulation of whose bodies can move through space are reflections of global economic inequality and throughout Kenya's history, the regulation of movement has shaped not only transportation infrastructure, but the way racial and class hierarchy is experienced. As any person in occupied territory will tell you, mobility is power. Those who could move were higher on the colonial hierarchy than others who were limited in their movement and travel. There are countless examples of the regulation and restriction of movement of Kenyans by the former British Empire, and the relationship persists. More recently, on 18 June 2021, the UK decided not to let Kenyans into the UK who had received the Astra Zeneca vaccine for COVID-19 (Andae 2021). The same week, the US had pledged millions of doses of Astra Zeneca to Kenya and other African nations. The postcolonial system of immobility still shapes the way Africans experience the world.

The ethnographic research was collected during nearly a dozen different research trips spanning the past two decades and across what could be understood as four eras, covering three Kenyan presidents and a range of policy approaches to the "problem" of *matatu*.[17] The first research period beginning in 2004 through 2006 (under the presidency of Mwai Kibaki, elected after the 28-year-long leadership of Daniel arap Moi) was dominated by the reverberations of a heavy set of economic and safety regulations imposed on the *matatu* sector in 2004, commonly referred to as the "Michuki Rules," named after the minister who designed and instituted them. The following period, my dissertation research undertaken from 2008 to 2010 was dominated by the contested 2007 election and recovery from post-election violence and the subsequent development and ratification of a new constitution in 2010 (Cheeseman et al. 2020; Branch 2011). Between the years 2003 and 2010, I conducted 173 semi-structured interviews with participants that lasted from one to three hours. The participants varied due to the large and diverse make-up of the working population. The specific breakdown of participants

---

[17] Research trips consisted of both long and short durations: 2004 (6 months), 2005–2006 (10 months), 2007 (1 month), 2008 (2 months), 2009–2010 (11 months), 2016 (3 weeks), 2017 (1 month), 2018 (2 months), 2022 (1 month), 2023 (1 month).

in interviews is as follows: thirty-seven conductors, thirty-two drivers, and thirty-five owners. The remaining sixty-nine interviews were with a variety of other workers: eleven touts, seven graphic designers, six route or stage managers, three trustees, six clerical workers for *matatu* organizations, two Disc Jockeys, four self-identified "hustlers," and one police officer; I also interviewed twenty-nine passengers including professionals, students, informal workers, joyriders, sex workers, and foreigners.

There were an additional seventy-five survey participants that responded to a short questionnaire and then participated in a short discussion of fifteen to twenty minutes in length. These surveys were administered in the introductory phases of fieldwork when I was gaining entry to a new route. It would typically entail going to different *matatu* stages or terminals at 10am to 3pm, between the morning and the evening rush hours, with a newspaper and some questionnaires. I sat at the terminal and read the paper and inevitably someone would ask me where I was going, assuming I was lost or did not understand how the system worked. I would answer in Swahili that I was studying *matatu* workers and had a questionnaire I would like to get answered. Before long, there was a group of people hovering around, some taking questionnaires and going off to fill them out on their own, and some talking to me while filling them out, while others had me fill them out for them. (This was one of the areas where having a research assistant, discussed in more detail below, was helpful, especially when my Swahili was still limited.)

The questionnaires were short and translated in simple Swahili asking for the worker's name, age, the name and route number of the *matatu* they worked on, years employed in the industry, level of education, and home neighborhood. It also included variations on questions about the positive and negative aspects of the industry and had a place to sign informed consent and provide a phone number if interested. In addition to these participants, I had countless informal and unstructured conversations with people about the *matatu* sector while on and off the vehicle.

The third period began after the 2013 election of Uhuru Kenyatta with additional short trips in 2016 and 2017, where I had to relearn Nairobi due to the new landscape dotted with glass skyscrapers and multiple road construction projects. During 2017 and a two-month trip in 2019, I explored the changes that had taken place in the years since my research with Steve. It included researching SACCOs as the primary *matatu* managers, the creation of the National Transport and Safety Authority (NTSA) and the removal of the TLB after nearly one hundred years, as well as the introduction and failure of cashless transportation cards. The ethnographic surprise from that trip was my realization that women had started to have a strong presence in the sector and that I was able to access the main organization dealing with and lobbying on behalf of this workforce, Flone Initiative. Through the women at Flone Initiative, I was able to hang out at a few meetings and meet up with several of the women, one of them being Elizabeth. By the end of 2019, I had decided that I was going to try and understand how these women were faring in the *matatu* sector ten years after I did my little stint as a conductor. Not long after receiving grants to return to Kenya the COVID-19 pandemic struck, and it would be three more years until I was able to travel back to Kenya in July of 2022.

This pandemic gap in research trips was unlike in my previous trips between 2004 and 2010, where there were few ways to get in touch with people outside of email and expensive phone calls. During the pandemic, there was social media and WhatsApp, which enabled calls and texts for free on Wi-Fi meaning that the years between 2019 and 2022 when I was unable to visit Kenya were some of the most fruitful in terms of longitudinal research, especially with Elizabeth and the women of Flone Initiative. I was able to build rapport, conduct interviews, collect pictures, and trade stories of the previous five years. In 2021 and 2022 I attended and participated in the Women in Transportation conference, held virtually by Flone Initiative, and even during to the writing of this book, Elizabeth and I were in contact nearly every day.

Finally, I was able to return to Nairobi and conduct planned research with Elizabeth in 2022 and 2023. I arrived back in Kenya in July of 2022, just before the election of William Ruto. Elizabeth and I picked up where we left off, interviewing all the women she wanted me to meet and talking to the SACCO leadership on her route. It was during my most recent trip in April 2023, when I sat in and discussed electric buses just as they were coming on the market.

At various points of my research, 2008, 2009, and 2010, for short periods of time, I hired some Kenyan men as research assistants to help me gain entrance to the sector at night and to help translate *Sheng* and Kikuyu during interviews. In each case, I could see that *matatu* workers did not want to talk to the Kenyan researchers because they assumed that they were looking down on them. Ultimately, I gained the most understanding of the *matatus* sector by just hanging out, chatting in Swahili and asking questions. Operators told me that they felt comfortable telling me how things worked because they knew I was not going to start a *matatu* in Kenya and I was not going to look down on them. Discussions with each of the three male research assistants (educated, holding papers, and asking questions in collusion with a White woman) seemed to attract a more macho and aggressive crowd.

I quickly realized that in some ways, it helped to be a woman in this overtly male space. For the most part, people were very happy to talk to me and let me listen in on their political discussions or general discussions about the news of the day. I understood enough Swahili and *Sheng* to hold my own and, like I said, most folks were just happy to have someone around to disrupt the monotony of the day. When I wanted to do a bit of a larger study into the *matatu* sector, I asked Kennedy, my peer from the Koobi Fora field school in Northern Kenya who took me on my first *matatu* ride to Buru Buru to accompany me with surveys and some short, general interviews. He was also training as an anthropologist and was thrilled to be joining me in these research outings. But, when we walked into the stage to do the interviews, the workforce in general was rude to him in ways they were not to me. When we split up it was apparent that people would talk to me, while he struggled to get people to talk to him. We were receiving completely different reactions. The old and young men alike were standoffish and, I came to find out later, suspicious of him. They thought it was obvious – he is a Kenyan trying to start a *matatu* business.

My experience was much more productive. No one was afraid that I was coming to steal their business and they generally took me at my word. I was a student interested in the lives of the people in the *matatu* sector because it seemed like a fun and wild lifestyle. The workers I encountered loved talking about their lives, relationships, families, and politics, but inevitably we would also discuss issues of state violence, police corruption, poverty, moral conundrums, and explicit physical danger they dealt with on a daily basis. Quickly I realized that if I just went to the *matatu* stages by myself, armed with simple survey questionnaires and a notebook, I could gather crucial information. Because I was not perceived to be competition in their eyes, they would tell me about their money and how much they made, stole, redistributed, and gave to cops and gangsters. Further, as a White woman, I was treated differently than a Kenyan woman would have been. Although I did befriend several female conductors during my fieldwork, it was fairly apparent that I was not looking for a husband or even a boyfriend but also that I was not subject to the same power struggles as Kenyan women were, because of my resources and perceived power and freedom. In many ways, the power of an *mlami*, to come and go as they please, refers to my race and class, but it transforms gender and sexuality as well.

Although when I worked as a conductor in a *matatu* in 2010 with Steve it was extremely strange for a woman, especially a White woman, to be taking your money and opening and closing the door for you, by the time I was calling passengers for Elizabeth's bus in April 2023 in Nairobi (Chapter 5), there were five women sitting on the bench egging me on. Although the opposite of unobtrusive participant observation, my experience of being a woman on a *matatu* allowed me to encounter important aspects of solidarity with the women in the sector.

Historical Ethnography

I look at *matatus* as an alternative urban archive with which to engage some classic questions about the nature of empire (the limits of power, control over urban space, resistance, and protest) to gain further insight into the current pressing issues of postcolonial cities. I collected hundreds of documents from newspapers, businesses, personal and government archives as well as from two trade magazines devoted to the *matatu* sector: *Matatu Today* and *Matatu News*.

Between 2005 and 2010, I spent significant amounts of time in the Kenyan National Archives (KNA) located in Nairobi. In 2011, I spent six months in the United Kingdom where I researched colonial records at the British National Archives at Kew, formerly known as the Public Records Office (PRO), and I also traveled to Scotland to meet with the Stagecoach Group and look at their business archives.[18] I contacted several UK bus aficionados in the area who had their own private archives filled with information about changing bus styles, colonial timetables, and media scraps, and had the privilege of meeting one such enthusiast and visiting his personal archive in a small village outside of London. Much of the archival data that I collected does not appear in this book, but it informs what does, which is an in-depth look at the one-class, one-fare rule, a bylaw passed in 1956 that ended the separation of first and second-class seating on KBS buses in Nairobi at the time of the Emergency. The reaction to this bylaw and the way that the scenes on the bus are described offer a diverse glimpse into Kenya's colonial past (see Chapter 1).

Chapter Organization

The first several chapters of this book show how, over time, urban transportation in Nairobi, first through Kikuyu taxis and colonial buses, and later through the *matatu* sector, became an important moving public that provided a space for urban political discussion and debate to unfold and circulate across the city. The Introduction and first two chapters sketch the important symbolic elements of the *matatu* sector – *Sheng*, joyrides, routes, and neighborhoods – that make it central to the way life works in Nairobi for workers, passengers, and owners as both a transportation and communicative infrastructure of media circulation. Chapter 3 continues with concepts of circulation, and sketches the more dangerous landscapes of routes and redistribution that are traversed by *matatu* workers and that complicate ideas of reciprocity, competition, trust, and theft as they function through a byzantine path of linguistic, material, and symbolic capital transfers and sometimes violent exchanges. The chapter

---

[18] The Stagecoach Group were successors to the original companies who exported buses to Kenya and ran them throughout the colonial period.

focuses on the economic circulation impacting *matatu* work on local and global levels, from police corruption to state level reform and regulation to broader global campaigns of transportation as development.

Chapter 4 traces the past two decades of neoliberal reform, disciplinary actions, and increasing technological innovation in the *matatu* sector at the local level. Using the case study of cashless transportation cards launched by Google in 2014, this chapter discusses the potential for surveillance capital firms to make inroads into *matatu* infrastructures through forms of everyday financialization facilitated by neoliberal reregulation (Mirowski 2013, Ven der Zwan 2014, Zuboff 2019). The chapter explores the idea of disciplining *matatu* work regimes through hybrid institutions like SACCOs that supervise structures of labor and how transportation technologies are good avenues to see the lengths and limits of state power.

The fifth chapter and sixth chapters of the book look at other hybrid institutions that have emerged due to women's role in the sector during the past two decades. Flone Initiative and Double M are two organizations that are women-led and successful in the transportation space and used the *matatu* medium as a counterpublic. These final chapters explore the way transportation technologies have changed the nature of work around the world for workers as well as their customers, through Uber and other ride-hailing apps, as well as through large-scale urban megaprojects like BRT, illustrating how mobile workers continue to shape Nairobi in important and telling ways. As women enter the *matatu* sector they are making way for other more marginalized members of society, especially passengers with disabilities, to benefit from the service. Popular transportation in Nairobi is a moving urban public that allows for marginalized voices to be heard and coalesce around issues that dominant institutions often obscure or overlook.

1

Mobile Monopolies:
Roots of a Transportation Takeover

On 7 June 1956, just a few years before the first documented "pirate" taxi (the precursor to the *matatu*) appeared in Nairobi, a group of European women calling themselves "the Housewives" sent several letters to the Office of the Mayor of Nairobi regarding a change in bus policy, proposed by the sole provider of passenger transport in the colony, the Kenya Bus Service (KBS). The Housewives included several documents in the packet: three letters (two long letters from individuals detailing negative experiences with Africans on Nairobi buses, and one cover letter authored by the group listing demands and including suggestions as to how bus services could be improved), as well as one small piece of stationary, an official seal embossed in the corner and the words "*With Compliments from the Housewives*" written in calligraphy across the front (Figure 7).

The overall theme of the letters condemned the new "one-class, one-fare" bus policy that would do away with first, second and third-class seating on Nairobi buses, making the entire bus the same price for anyone riding.[1] The Housewives explained in the letter that they would be willing to pay more if the bus company promised to hire more Europeans to work as inspectors and conductors, although it would have been improbable for KBS to afford European employees on the additional payments of a small number of European riders. At this point, the majority of KBS customers were African workers, not colonial settlers. This did not stop them from closing the letters by providing a suggestive reminder that the KBS is owned by a London bus company, which was also running the buses in Salisbury, Rhodesia, where "they have separate buses for Europeans and Africans and it works very well."[2]

Perhaps on the surface, these letters are filled with the normalized racist settler colonial logic of contagion and exclusion, but there are also insights to be gained from reading against the grain for the actions (and inaction) of

---

[1] Kenya National Archives (KNA). MNR/94601/10. Proposal of Kenya Bus Company to make all buses of one class and one fare. July 1956.
[2] Kenya National Archives, Nairobi, Kenya (KNA) 94601/158, letter from "the Housewives," to Mayor of Nairobi, 7 June 1956.

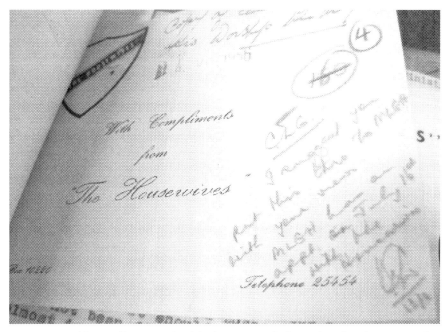

Figure 7 This small notecard with the contact information for the Housewives was stuck in the files between complaint letters from 1956. (Photo by author, 2010)

African bus workers and riders, particularly Muslim women riders, during this time in Nairobi's history. These letters not only present largely unseen perspectives of Nubian women in Nairobi, but they also make a case for urban transportation, specifically the colonial bus, as a unique place for African people to build and perform solidarity during waning settler power in late-colonial Kenya.[3] The case of the bus behavior also addresses an intriguing question Frederick Cooper asked about urban life in colonial Africa – "how are forms of space connected to forms of protest?" (1983). The seemingly innocuous space of the colonial bus can be a lens through which we can witness the racial politics of decolonization in Nairobi unfold, which also give us insights into the ways that urban transportation continued to be an important political space in postcolonial Nairobi. Colonial buses provided a stage for resistance to settler logics of elimination, and an intimate space

---

[3] Nubian Kenyans are descendants of Sudanese soldiers who fought for the British colonial army and were given land in Nairobi on which to settle and live (Balaton-Chrimes 2016; Parsons 1997).

where Africans could build and express solidarity. The letters reveal racist settler colonial attitudes but also give a glimpse of largely unseen behavior and interactions of African men and women, in Nairobi, especially during a highly militarized time in a violent era.

By 1956, while the Housewives were collecting complaints and drafting letters, Nairobi's African, and especially Kikuyu residents, were just emerging from one of the most violent British military exercises of the colonial era conducted in April 1954, Operation Anvil, a screening and detention program (Branch 2009; Anderson 2005). This was just one exercise in a near decade-long insurgency by Kikuyu forest-fighters, which the British called Mau Mau, but which was more akin to a Kikuyu civil war prompted by the European theft of Kikuyu land in what came to be known as the White Highlands (Ogot and Ochieng 1995; Berman and Lonsdale 1992; Kanogo 1987). Operation Anvil saw thousands of Kikuyu, Embu and Meru residents of Nairobi deported and detained (Anderson 2005). Although Kenyan independence turned out to be less than a decade away, the British Empire and European settlers insisted they were in Kenya to stay and, instead of planned decolonization, they touted the development of a "multiracial society built on partnership," which institutionalized the racist colonial hierarchy already in place, with Europeans at the top, South Asian laborers in the middle, and Africans at the bottom (Parsons 2014). It was in this tense and traumatic context that the Housewives' letters reveal an intimate expression of power relations in colonial society, at the end of colonial rule, and an illuminating glimpse into African resistance of colonial power in the intimate environment of the colonial bus. Although there was a tiered price for seating, the letters reveal a porous boundary between first- and second-class seating, with mostly African riders and drivers, while the sheer parameters of the bus itself produced a physical closeness and generated performances of discrimination, discipline, resistance, solidarity, and violence.

The settler women's letters provide insight into two groups of women in late-colonial Nairobi – Nubian women and European settler women. The bus can be interpreted as an extension of domestic territory for both groups of women in Nairobi. Nubian women were known to be empowered in the domestic and economic sphere, many gaining status and wealth through the distilling and distribution of gin (De Smedt 2009). The use of the bus by these European settler women suggests that they were not the aristocratic, wealthy settlers of the 1930s, but members of a poorer and more diverse settler population who poured into the colony after 1939 (Jackson 2013). Like most urban transportation, the intimate space of the bus or train car blurs the boundaries between public and private and brings issues of inequality to the fore. Its intimate, mobile space has long made public buses an important site for making politics personal.

In their letters, the Housewives were employing what scholars of settler colonialism would call "elimination logics" aimed at making indigenous or native people disappear, or at least diminishing them, especially in the most intimate places (Wolfe 2006). There was a significant amount of violence inflicted on African people in Kenya during colonialism, especially in the 1950s, which makes the genocidal-type logic of elimination even more significant in this case. Although Kenya and South Africa, among other African nations, had settler colonial populations, much of the key literature theorizing settler colonialism focuses on the Americas, Australia, Israel, and Palestine; the architect of the field of settler colonialism, Patrick Wolfe, leaves Africa out of his analysis entirely (Kelley 2017). One of the most important conceptual issues in Wolfe's theory of settler colonialism is that, for Americans and others, settlers aim to eliminate people because they want their land, or they eliminate people's land because they want their labor. As Robin Kelley (2017) argues, in Africa, settlers wanted the land and the labor, but not the people and that by ignoring Africa, Wolfe fails to account for labor regimes in which the native is simultaneously eliminated and exploited, like Kenya. Although Kelley agrees that settler colonialism in Africa was also functioning under the logic of elimination, he elaborates, "what was being eliminated was the metaphysical and material relations of people to land, culture, spirit and each other" (2017: 269).

Even though Whites were never the majority in places like Kenya, Algeria and Southern Rhodesia, there was still the logic of elimination at work along with a genocidal impulse (Ginsburgh and Jackson 2018: 78). Take the many public exhibits of torture, hangings and concentration camps committed by the British colonial administration as evidence of these impulses and logics at work (Anderson 2005; Elkins 2005). One of the key features of settler colonialism in Africa, however, is that the genocidal impulse was curtailed by the dependence on indigenous labor, and because of this feature, they also needed strong racial hierarchies and differentiation between White and native, which is reflected in the Housewives' suggestions for segregating the colonial bus, but, because the African population dwarfed settler numbers, they could not maintain these distinctions (Ginsburgh and Jackson 2018: 78). African cases of settler colonialism reflect fragile settler positions and this weakness and anxiety motivates their violence (Ginsburgh and Jackson 2018: 85). Decolonization in settler colonial African states was much more violent and protracted than in non-settler societies, showing how settlers can became even more violent as their position weakened.

Another key feature to the framing of settler colonialism, is continuity through time, which is why Kenya and other African nations are often not included in this analysis, as settlers are not perceived to be in power in these places, however there are still settlers in Kenya who own and control vast tracts of land and businesses and who structure the nature of tourism in the area (Wolfe 2006: 390). This is another reason Kelley argues that it is important to bring African nations back into the analytical frame of settler colonialism because they show that settler societies do indeed fall, and they are not indestructible. He explains that if decolonization is a process, not an event, then "all these struggles can be seen as part of a global assault on settler rule" and the "trace is the refusal to accept the permanence and the terms of settler domination … it is in these spaces that the decolonial imagination lives" (2017: 274). In this way, the letters of the Housewives reveal an important granularity in the global assault on settler rule and a glimpse into the spaces of the decolonial imagination where African women and men stood up for one another in the safety of the bus.

In some ways, the letters show that KBS buses were places where colonial segregation and settler supremacy was explicitly challenged by African residents, during a time when the settlers still considered Nairobi to be the White, colonial garden city of East Africa but when their power was waning. With political organizations outlawed in the years leading up to the particularly brutal assault on Nairobi, along with the violent removal of many Africans from the city, the KBS vehicles that rolled through Nairobi, if not a safe place, were at least a contested space where Africans performed resistance under a particularly violent era of colonial rule in Kenya. In the face of settler colonial logics of elimination, where people were diminished to erasure, their interests ignored, their lives and struggles obscured, the Nubian women on the bus provide an important reminder of the everyday places where the battles of liberation are fought, and where the process of decolonization plays out. Importantly, although Nubians had lost some of their "special African" status among European colonial administrators and settlers, they were still largely unaffiliated with Mau Mau and therefore their conflict with the European women is even more telling in terms of settler colonial control. It was being strongly resisted by those loyal to the Crown.

In this context, colonial buses were intimate battlegrounds, spaces with extremely porous interpersonal boundaries. When asking how forms of space connected to forms of protest, transportation infrastructures are rich sites of state power and socioeconomic circulation as well as political self-making and performances of resistance and solidarity. In buses, eye contact is difficult to avoid and the shared experience of boring commutes and dangerous thrills on the road can bond riders together. It is because of this that transportation vehicles and systems are rich sites of urban life, although often underexplored. As increasing attention has come to mobility studies over time, particularly African mobility, scholars and urban planners, transportation engineers, and labor activists are asking additional, complex questions about how infrastructures facilitate opportunity, operationalize suffering and shape urban space. Histories of urban transportation in colonial Africa are imperative to understanding how popular transportation systems, like *matatu* minibuses, which provide most of the mobility in postcolonial Nairobi, and other paratransit sectors bind contemporary African cities together.

Monopolies of Movement in Colonial Nairobi

Early in the colonial project, to control the African population and direct the flow of their labor, the many different groups of people populating the space between the port in Mombasa and Lake Victoria, the colonial government set up a system of "legibility" that directly linked ethnic identity to space – the Native Reserve system (Scott 1998; Cooper and Packard 1997; Lonsdale and Berman 1979). Racist ideas about African socialization and identity structured colonial protocol that linked identity with space in an ethnic geography (Parsons 2012: 69). Access to land was directly connected to ethnic identity and that identity was then spatialized. The logic of segregation was built on the assumption that ethnicity was the key identifying factor for members of native populations in Africa. African people were believed to be so deeply ethnic or "tribal" that upon too much interaction with Europeans, or people of different ethnicities, they would suffer psychological breakdown; the term for this experience was "detribalization", and "detribalized natives" were a problematic category for the colonial administration throughout their stay on the continent (Balaton-Chrimes 2016; Parsons 1997; Spear and Waller 1993; Berman and Lonsdale 1992; Kanogo 1987). Supposedly, detribalization would eventually lead to violent revolution and rebellion. Native Reserves rested on racist ideologies that ethnicities are bounded groups and was symbolized by their bounded and isolated homelands, and colonial logic followed that interaction between bounded groups was dangerous and movement encouraged interaction, therefore movement was dangerous and had to be controlled.

Their mobility was disciplined by the *kipande* system starting in 1920s, where, under the Native Registration Amendment Ordinance, any male over the age of fifteen was required to carry around their necks a document of their personal details, fingerprints, and employment history to permit their movement throughout the colony (Weitzberg 2020; Anderson 2000; M'Inoti 1997). Africans in the reserves were not allowed to live anywhere but in their own designated area, among their own ethnic group. However, many of the reserves were too small for adequate farming, thus pushing people to other reserves looking for land to farm or other resources (Peterson 2004; Cooper and Packard 1997; Leys 1975). The lack of space, combined with the colonial tax system – the hut tax initiated in 1904, meant to encourage African labor for European settler farms and ranches – motivated movement to other reserves, which could possibly have more land or resources (Spear and Waller 1993; Kanogo 1987). Africans moving into another group's native reserve was illegal and the colonial government termed the offense "infiltration" (Parsons 2012). This illegal movement allowed for some relief from the overcrowding in the reserves. African migrant laborers were expected to return to their native reserve after they completed their work tenure as domestic servants in the White areas or as agricultural laborers on White farms. But ethnic members migrated to other reserves and were often adopted or incorporated to the community. When this practice was discovered to be widespread, the colonial government, unable to stop the practice, renamed it *interpenetration* and allowed it (Parsons 2012).

Although Nairobi was officially off-limits to the native African population, it quickly became a diverse and plural place where various interests fought for access to resources, space, and services. By 1926, there were over 18,000 Africans living in the city, even with the pass system in place (Hirst and Lamba 1994: 77). It was impossible to police settlements throughout the entire city because people were living in its nooks and crannies (Myers 2003). By the 1930s, the population of Africans in Nairobi had grown to over 30,000 (Hirst and Lamba 1994: 77). As the African population grew, the city became a booming, multi-cultural city of Europeans, Indians – who originally came to Kenya as laborers with the railways – and Africans from surrounding farms (White 1990).

By the 1930s Nairobi was not only congested with people, but with cars. At this time, the colonial government paid more attention to parking than to driving, accidents, reckless drivers, or transportation for the masses. In 1938, the Kenya Welfare Association sent a letter complaining about drunk driving on the roads in Nairobi. Reginald Mombasa writes, "It is felt that all citizens of Nairobi of all races have the right to feel assured that the authorities are taking all of the necessary steps to protect them from careless drivers or from drivers incapacitated through alcohol."[4] As the colony grew and was populated the need for a public transportation system was becoming apparent. Not only because of the drunk driving, but also because there was nowhere to park.

By the mid-1930s, the idea of investing in Kenya was looking better to British companies because they were promised a monopoly over any business

---

[4] Kenya National Archive, Nairobi (KNA), "Street Accidents Inquiry," Letter from Reginald Mombasa, President and L.O. Johnes, Secretary, Kenya Welfare Association to Town Clerk, Nairobi. 14 April 1938.

ventures undertaken in the colony.[5] For passenger road service, two institutions were created and discussed at length in the 1936 document laying out the terms of the monopoly of the KBS and the establishment of the powerful Transport Licensing Board (TLB), which would oversee licensing all vehicles in Kenya. In 1936, as KBS maintained their small fleet of buses and their growing circumference of service, the TLB had little to do and had few applicants.

By the 1940s, when African veterans returned from the Second World War, where they had been drivers, a popular idea spread among the returning soldier population that they should get licenses, buy cheap vehicles from the military, and start transport services to supplement the growing number of the underserved, invisible residents of the African settlements in and around Nairobi (Parsons 2003). The TLB Chairman was instrumental in shutting out the African veterans from the transport industry and successfully protecting the interests of KBS. Some returning soldiers ended up driving personal taxis, and Nubian soldiers were absorbed into the ranks of the KBS itself. Throughout the 1940s and 1950s, nearly the entirety of the KBS employee pool was made up of Nubians who were often former drivers in the military (De Smedt 2009).

Kikuyu Taxis: Moving Radical Politics to and from Nairobi

By the mid- to late-1940s Nairobi was changing with the influx of Kikuyu veterans from the Second World War (Furedi 1973). Their idleness fueled growing nationalist and anti-colonial feelings, especially among Kikuyu, who were largely displaced by European settlement just outside of Nairobi (Berman and Lonsdale 1992). Demobilized soldiers came back to a different Kenya, where the war effort had promoted the expansion of settler agriculture, and therefore there was even less land for these returning soldiers than there had been when they left, prompting increasing exodus from the reserves to the nearby city of Nairobi. Only upon marriage and acquisition of land, could a Kikuyu man become an adult (Berman and Lonsdale 1992). This lack of land then, not only compromised their day to day living, forcing them to move to the city, but because they had no land (but money to spend) they were kept from getting married and attaining adulthood, leading to a crisis in the fabric of social obligations or, what Lonsdale described as the "moral economy" of Kikuyu society.

---

5   Kenya National Archive, Nairobi (KNA), K380.5 No. 81–97, "Report of a Committee to investigate considering the desirability of coordinating and regulating all forms of transport in the colony" (1936).

This was the time when soldiers returning with money that they could not spend on wives, land, and children, applied for licenses from the TLB but were rejected. It is important to point out here that the monopoly agreement that KBS held in Nairobi was for passenger transport over eight passengers. The soldiers were attempting to apply for licenses to register lorry vehicles that the army was selling off, to start transport businesses (Parsons 2003). Ironically, many of these Kikuyu men resorted to driving private taxis and subsequently, the Kikuyu taxi association and the Allied Transport Workers Union, formed an important political base for the Land and Freedom Army that depended deeply on their mobility (Furedi 1973).

The Allied Transport Workers Union was the first and largest workers' union in Kenya (Spencer 1985). Throughout the 1940s, leaders used this block of workers to spread political thought and action in Nairobi. This union of taxi drivers, mostly veterans, worked to radicalize the nationalist political movement that was coalescing in Nairobi (Furedi 1973). The importance of movement and mobility cannot be overlooked because the taxis were key in carrying anti-colonial political leaders, and subsequently anti-colonial political ideas, from the city to the countryside throughout the late 1940s and early 1950s, up until the Emergency in 1952 (Ogot and Ochieng 1995). In fact, Kikuyu taxi drivers were some of the first people to participate in Mau Mau oathing rituals, and in turn greatly facilitated the oathing of others in and around the city (Spencer 1985). Using the Kikuyu taxis, radical politics in Nairobi were on the move, and the taxi drivers spread the message.

Eventually the colonial administration recognized the power in the type of mobility Kikuyu taxis provided, because they called for strict controls at the borders of Nairobi for any Kikuyu person traveling in a motor vehicle in the mid-1940s. There were limitations on the number of Kikuyu allowed to travel in motor vehicles, which included a rule that Kikuyu people "coming to Nairobi daily must either walk or use the public transport services."[6] Kikuyu taxis were also forced to put a yellow stripe on their cars, marking them conspicuously.[7] In 2004, under the Michuki Rules, a set of regulations for the *matatu* sector, every *matatu* vehicle was required to put a yellow stripe on the side of their vehicle. This stripe essentially marked both matatu vehicles and Kikuyu taxis as oppositional or rebellious, even dangerous vehicles.

---

[6] The British National Archive, London (PRO), CO822/796, Colonial Office, "Report of the Emergency in Kenya – Operation Anvil and Resulting conditions in Nairobi, 1954–1956."

[7] John Lonsdale, personal communication, 2011.

Multiracial Master Planning

By 1944, with growing unrest throughout the colony, and particularly Nairobi, Sir Phillip Mitchell was sworn in as Governor and he brought with him common paternalist ideas that Africans needed help from the British to become civilized and eventually enjoy some autonomy while the British acted as mere trustees, staying behind to watch over their wards.[8] In order to achieve this, he was armed with the conceptual weapon of "multiracialism" and economic development. Mitchell wanted to override any pesky racial tension between the radical nationalists and the European settlers by focusing on economic production and keeping everyone separate but equal. The colonial landscape was one of inequality, and that inequality and exclusion was built into the environment yet contested at every turn (Yeoh 1996). As noted earlier, Nairobi was officially off-limits to Africans who were not accounted for and employed. The city was not meant to be an integrated, diverse urban metropolis. It was meant to be a White city in the sun. However, urban planners in Nairobi did play lip service to this new realm of tolerance and anti-authoritarian sentiment, which attempted to make colonialism more palatable by introducing the idea of multiracialism.

The concept of multiracialism was built into the environment through the work of urban planners, with the help of sociologists. The sociologist who helped prepare the 1948 Master Plan for the Municipal council was supposed to deal with the social "interactions" in the city. Two reports are of interest for Nairobi's foray into multiracial planning: a 1945 report by the sociologist Mary Parker, and the Master Plan of 1948.[9] The plan called for separate but equal development of city structures. Both Parker's report and the Master Plan called for a multiracialism that allowed the different "cultures" and "races" to have their own separate estates or "locations," self-contained neighborhoods that held everything in one place so that people would not have to leave their area and "interact" with people of a different culture or race.[10] The politics of planning affects who has access to urban space. Who is and who is not represented on a map, and how these representations come to exist, offers important insights into the way the state thinks about its constituents.

---

[8] The British National Archive, London (PRO), CO822/796, Colonial Office, "Report of the Emergency in Kenya – Operation Anvil and Resulting conditions in Nairobi, 1954–1956."
[9] Kenya National Archive, Nairobi (KNA), "Nairobi Master Plan for a Colonial Capital: A Report prepared for the Municipal Council of Nairobi, L. W. Thornton White, L. Silberman, P. R. Anderson. pp. 45–49, 1948."
[10] Ibid.

Violence in Nairobi: Mau Mau and Operation Anvil

As tensions grew, Kikuyu fragmentation became better defined and by the early 1950s, to gain political representation, more moderate Kikuyu politicians like Jomo Kenyatta were spreading their disapproval regarding oathing and violence (Rosberg and Nottingham 1966: 198). The Land and Freedom Army's movement was well underway, and the secret society was growing and gaining momentum, largely facilitated by the Kikuyu taxi drivers who were able to disseminate ideas and messages from the city to the reserves, thus helping to coalesce a somewhat fragmented operation (Furedi 1973). On October 7, 1952, Senior Chief Waruhiru, a Christian and leading government spokesperson, was assassinated. With this news, the colonial administration declared the colony under a "State of Emergency" and referred to the Kikuyu fighters in the forest as terrorists, naming them "Mau Mau."

Nairobi during the Emergency was highly militarized, with soldiers scattered throughout the diverse and growing city populated by Africans, Indians, and European settlers, settlers who were more diverse and less wealthy than the settlers of the 1920s and 1930s (Jackson 2013). Due to thousands of Kikuyu fleeing counterinsurgency campaigns the city was crowded (Branch 2009: 104). In 1952 and 1953, Mau Mau had the support of many Africans in Nairobi, although there were loyalists there as well (Branch 2009). In fact, in 1953, Makadara, the first African settlement in the city, was given to loyal Kikuyu by the Crown (White 1990). By 1956, when the Housewives were writing their letters, most Africans in Nairobi identified as loyalists, but many had also been oathed (Branch 2009: 104).

Only two years before the Housewives' letters were written, one of the largest military operations in Kenya's colonial history, Operation Anvil, a massive screening and detention exercise that violently displaced 24,000 Kikuyu, Embu, and Meru people to drive Mau Mau sympathizers out of Nairobi, was underway (Anderson 2005: 200–212). During the violent oppression that was Operation Anvil, the colonial government descended on the African population of Nairobi and searched their homes and private quarters. They terrorized large portions of the urban African population looking for pass violations among other things. At that time, the daily life of many African people was arduous.

Over time, these demographics, along with the poor treatment of Africans in African settlements, assembled an urban colonial landscape that was not simply "a palimpsest reflecting the impress of asymmetrical power relations undergirding colonial society, but also a terrain of discipline and resistance" (Yeoh 1996: 10). The colonial bus was an important moving public space that shaped and followed the terrain of discipline and resistance in an important and material way. Compared to the other places that European and African women would meet – the domestic sphere, the street, the house, the market – the colonial bus was one of the most intimate and public places in Nairobi. The colonial bus, depending on where one was in Nairobi, was overflowing with African passengers, and very few European passengers. The drivers and conductors of the buses were also Africans. It was an intimate public/private stage where resistance was performed as settler power waned. Perhaps even before the settlers realized it was over, the feelings they had on the buses during the mid- to late-1950s should have alerted them to a changing of the tides. Although, at the same time settlers had little reason to believe that their power was so short lived, because it was only earlier in the year 1956, that Africans had finally gained the right to form political organizations (Furedi 1975: 285).

With Compliments from the Housewives

By the 1950s, KBS was being criticized by everyone, from Africans heading to work, to European housewives going to shop in town. In 1956, KBS executives and Nairobi City Council (NCC) officials started discussing an end to the segregation on Nairobi's buses, making all vehicles "one-class and one-fare."[11] Nairobi's double-decker buses were segregated into three different fare classes. Between 1953 and 1959 the fare for first class was 15 to 20 cents, second-class fare was 10 to 15 cents and third-class fare, called the "minimum fare," was an even lower rate meant for low-income people specifically.[12] At least part of the lower floor for Whites by KBS (Heinze 2018). The segregation of the buses into these classes belied the fact that most of the users of KBS transportation services were Africans and that many times the buses were filled with mostly African people. Most African people would pay second-class seating, minimum rates or, if we are to believe the reports from the Housewives, some would not pay a fare at all.[13]

The one-class, one-fare policy was not a progressive effort put forth by KBS management to recognize the humanity of their African ridership, but an economic decision that intended to squeeze more out of their already burdened African customers. But the policy was surely part of the push by the Colonial Office to adopt a multiracial constitution and is a good example of multiracial

---

[11] Kenyan National Archives, Nairobi (KNA). MNR/94601/10. "Proposal of Kenya Bus Company to make all buses of one class and one fare." July 1956.
[12] Ibid.
[13] Kenya National Archives (KNA). 94601/158. Letter to the Mayor of Nairobi; Kenya Bus Services Ltd. from "the Housewives," 7 June 1956.

logic at work in social policy using urban transportation infrastructure to institutionalize inequality (Parsons 2004). In short, because Africans were most of the riders, and generally paying for second-class seating or even minimum-fare seating, making the fare one-class would likely raise the price on African tickets, even if it was lowering the price for first-class customers.

Thus, it was about raising prices on African consumers, institutionalizing racial inequality under the guise of multiracial living. Multiracialism was popular among Europeans because it granted them the ability to see their future in Africa lasting indefinitely. (In fact, the KBS monopoly over legally permitted passenger transport in Nairobi was lasted until 1985.)[14] Through multiracialism the colonial administration moved away from ideas about decolonization and toward themes of "partnership" in societies that would progress toward nationhood through a series of gradual constitutional reforms. In effect, multiracialism preserved settler privilege and colonial control while creating the illusion of democracy and self-government, and although the imperial administration thought multiracialism would keep them in power, most Africans rejected it, and even when colonial administrators were not listening, ordinary Africans were speaking back to their British Rulers in lots of ways (Parsons 2004). From the Housewives' letters, bus behavior can be read as one of the ways ordinary Africans were speaking back to their "partners" in many subtle, and not so subtle ways.

The European women were loath to lose their segregated and privileged space on KBS buses, indicating settler colonial logic at work insisting on distinct separation and organization into hierarchies, when true elimination cannot be maintained (Ginsburgh and Jackson 2018). Not only did the European women disagree with the proposal, but they argued for completely segregated buses and offered to pay higher fares to keep sitting in their separated, first-class sections. They threatened to stop taking the bus altogether and claimed they would be finding other means of transportation, not that this would matter much to the bottom line of KBS, whose primary customer base were Africans. These letters reflect how little the settlers seem to matter on a bus filled with African riders.

The Housewives' cover letter to the Mayor of Nairobi lays out their case:

> We have had numerous complaints recently about the condition of the Kenya Buses, and the treatment received by passengers. It should be noted that in most cases the complaints have not been directed towards

[14] Kenya National Archive, Nairobi (KNA), K380.5 No. 81–97, "Report of a Committee to investigate considering the desirability of coordinating and regulating all forms of transport in the colony" (1936).

the conductors, but against the almost impossible conditions under which they work. The husband of another member was in an incident on Saturday this week, when the conductor of the bus was quite unable to control the Africans who had been drinking, one of whom hit the face of the European who tried to assist the conductor. We have had several verbal complaints of people who had all seats occupied by Africans not paying the first-class fare and in some cases paying no fare at all who will not allow European first-class passengers to sit in the seats for which they are paying. While the cleanliness of some buses on certain routes improved, we get complaints of dirty floors and seats, particularly on the Ngong Road and Ruaraka routes.[15]

The social situations described in the letters and the way they are written reflect the beliefs, values, and practices of 1956 Nairobi, where European settler women attempted to make their power visible in the city by controlling the public space of the colonial bus, but ultimately documented their own weakness in the waning days of colonial rule. At the same time, the reporting of African drunkenness sits in contrast to the overwhelming reports of settler drunkenness in the Happy Valley (Berman and Lonsdale 1992; Blixen 1937). The letter paints Africans as drunkards while ignoring the drunkenness and rowdiness of settlers on the same buses.

One of the authors of the letters names the East African Women's League (EAWL) as an alternative avenue for recourse when it comes to addressing bus behavior. The EAWL were another, more established and well-documented group of European women who lobbied legislators on behalf of various women's issues (Gorman 2014). Over time, one of the responsibilities that fell to the EAWL in the colony was managing and "correcting" the behavior of poor European women who engaged in intimate relationships with African men (Jackson 2013). Notably, the EAWL published a book in 1962, describing how the group re-inscribed what was to become Kenya into something they could make legible; it is called *They Made it Their Home*, and it is the story of their settlement (1962).

Like the Housewives, the EAWL made it their mission to police urban space, building and renaming streets after notable British people. The emphasis on "home making" by both the EAWL and the Housewives is reflective of the gendered idea of home. The home, the domestic space, is their duty to maintain and run, and can be a point of pride and marker of resilience for settler women (see the Karen Blixen Museum in Nairobi). The emphasis on managing

---

[15] Kenya National Archives (KNA). 94601/158. Letter to the Mayor of Nairobi; Kenya Bus Services Ltd. from "the Housewives," 7 June 1956.

the domestic sphere and "making a home" in a foreign land, especially one where you see yourself as superior, seems like it could prompt action toward various spaces, even only slightly linked to the domestic domain, like the bus you take to do all your domestic chores. These groups were affiliated with things that impacted women's daily lives and it is no surprise that the bus is part of that extended domestic sphere. It is somewhat well documented that, although men provide most transportation services, women use public transportation services more than any other group because they take more trips, more frequently (Fernando and Porter 2002). It makes sense that a bus, then, would be an extension of the domestic sphere for European women who may not have access to a car, but it was also an extension of the domestic realm for the Nubian women mentioned in the letters who were taking the bus as part of their everyday work transporting gin (De Smedt 2009).[16] By looking at the bus as an extended domestic sphere for both African and European women, the activities, interactions, conflicts, and alliances become more complicated and telling.

"Shenzies Kabisa"[17]

One of the two personal letters included in the Housewives' packet along with their stationary card and cover letter, was authored by an elderly man, who was shocked and disappointed that KBS would entertain the interests of their African customers over the preferences of their European clientele. In a telling reference he groups himself with "Housewives and elderly men" in a way that reinforces the idea that the bus is an extension of the domestic sphere where there are vulnerable people and he references the population of poor Europeans who were steadily populating Nairobi throughout the 1940s.[18] He writes:

> The dissatisfaction of the unfortunate Europeans who, of necessity, have to use the buses is very great and with good reason. The dissatisfaction is not only because some buses are dirty and noisy with rattling windows and other parts, but because of the uncontrolled, unchecked behaviors of most Africans who push Europeans out of the way and force themselves onto the bus occupying all seats and leaving European ladies (and elderly men) to stand. Many are extremely rude, dirty and smelly. At peak hours when tired European workers try to get on the bus they are pushed aside

---

[16] Nubian women were also working as brewers, domestic workers, sex workers and landlords (Bujra 1975).
[17] *Shenzies Kabisa* is a Swahili insult meaning, "completely stupid" people.
[18] It is well documented that the European settlers who arrived in the 1940s were significantly poorer than the earlier waves of settlers in Kenya (Jackson 2013).

and if able to get on, left to stand. Seats reserved "for the ladies only" are of no mind whatever as Africans take no notice, and yesterday I saw a well dressed African deliberately pass a seat occupied by one African and occupy one "For ladies only."

This language captures what anthropologist Janet McIntosh, has documented in Kenya as a common settler mindset, whereby: "Most settlers considered Africans to be intellectually inferior, vaguely polluting and potentially dangerous" (2016: 21). The fact that there are still settlers in Kenya who share this mindset, interviewed at length by McIntosh, many of whom are wealthy landowners or business owners, speaks to the "continuity of settler colonialism" as an ongoing process in Kenya.

The letter included more general transportation-based complaints that one may hear in any city in the world across time and place. Examples of bad behavior attributed to young Africans include not offering their seats to older people, loudness, rudeness, and general chaos. As the letter continued, the racist tropes that emerged as the author described Africans using the term "*shenzies kabisa*," signaled racist themes of dirt and contagion. The author described his commute as such:

> Recently I boarded the bus at Kilimani School and had to stand all the way to Nairobi whilst seven African (adults) and five children occupied first class seats. And I am over 70 years of age! Travelling on most buses is becoming a nightmare and unfortunately cannot be avoided by many Housewives and elderly men. To make the buses all one class will allow "shenzies kabisa" as well as all other Africans to sit anywhere and, because of dirt, smell and rudeness, make present conditions more intolerable than ever. The way Kenya Bus Company acts leads one to the conclusion that because they have had a monopoly for several years and because most of their profit is from African passengers, they totally disregard the European public and treat them with disdain.[19]

This elderly settler man specifically condemned the one-class, one-fare policy on physical and moral grounds. As his letter shows, he was irritated at sharing space and offended at the idea that Africans will be able to "sit anywhere" which would be "intolerable." He has some bulleted suggestions at the end of his letter:

> Instead of making conditions worse by creating a one-fare bus, I suggest that —

---

[19] Kenya National Archives, Nairobi (KNA), 94601/158. Letter to the Mayor of Nairobi; Kenya Bus Services Ltd. from "the Housewives," 7 June 1956.

A) The Kenya Bus Company run certain buses for Europeans only; or

B) They reserve special compartments for Europeans; or

C) Other firms and companied be asked and allowed to run buses for Europeans only.

He finishes his letter with the following statement of claims to reverse racism, writing: "The anti-white spirit among the Africans is growing and present conditions of travel in buses is accentuating it. I speak as a resident of over forty years and as someone who worked among them for over thirty years."

The idea that travel in buses, and the condition of that travel exacerbate the racial tension in Nairobi is notable and parallels what psychologists of segregation were observing in the United States at the same time. The materiality of the intimate aspects of the public bus, like the proximity to strangers, the circulation of people and ideas over space and time, and the way that these environments provide opportunities for close observations of inequality, has allowed them to serve as an important urban place where race, gender and power often play out in public struggle. Research on proxemics takes seriously the study of how people unconsciously structure and react to micro-spaces in their houses, buildings, and ultimately towns in ways that reflect and reinforce power hierarchies (Hall 1963). Transportation is no different. In fact, the types of interactions people have on mass transit can be particularly intimate due to the physical closeness to strangers that it produces. Material forms of infrastructure, like a bus, or train car, are ultimately relational and these material spaces frame social interactions. In other words, physical closeness of people in enclosed spaces feels intimate, but the relationship of intimacy is absent, which can make people feel ill at ease and even combative.

The public and proximal nature of mass transportation makes the bus a critical place where social justice issues become visible, especially issues around race, gender, and class, and a historically rich site for protest. In fact, just six months before these letters were written in Kenya, buses were taking center stage in the fight for equality in the Southern United States when Rosa Parks, Claudette Colvin, and others refused to give up their seats to White passengers on segregated public buses in Alabama. Parks' actions are seen to have sparked the Montgomery Bus Boycott, which is often understood as the earliest mass protest of the civil rights era in the United States (Theoharis 2015). In the same year Rosa Parks' refused to move to the back of the bus, Martin Grossack's (1956) study of the outcomes of racial segregation on buses in the United States showed that segregation on buses was detrimental to the mental health of all passengers, Black and White. Many Black respondents pointed to experiences on the bus as pivotal moments in their understanding of their own blackness. As Grossack documents, many Black children, like their White counterparts, wanted to watch the bus driver up-close, but were "yanked away by their mothers" toward the back of the bus where they often explicitly or implicitly understood that they were not treated like their White counterparts (1956). In this way, these type of practices in intimate spaces reinforced and institutionalized racism into public infrastructure.

At the same time as tension builds between the two separate groups, solidarity is also building within the groups, as those who are marginalized commiserate together. Grossack argued that buses were particularly sensitive places in the segregated United States because schools and shops were separated but existed in their own spheres without overlapping. Because the bus is a small, intimate space, when shared between two groups who are treated unfairly in society, the separation and hierarchy between them becomes clear to both groups of people (Grossack 1956: 143–144). In colonial Nairobi, KBS buses were both a site for settler women to exert their power and a place for the staging of resistance to that power. The logic of settler colonialism, founded on the concept of "elimination in order to replace," produces a racialization that "results from colonizers being confronted with the threat of having to share social space with the colonized" (Wolfe 2006: 1). In this light, the Housewives' complaint letters pledging their resistance to new KBS policies that did away with the segregation on city buses can be seen clearly as a warning cry, not about bus service, price, or gender (which it would eventually become), but about the increasing physical and symbolic *closeness* occurring between Europeans and Africans that KBS buses already enabled and were threatening to expand.

Although most African passenger behavior on the bus was probably unremarkable, through the lens of these complaints, the KBS bus emerges as a place where African passengers did transgressive things safely. Outside of a private home, but not in the open street, the bus allowed for Africans to assert themselves with little consequence or qualm. Take for instance seemingly small things like not giving up one's seat for White passengers to larger transgressions like being drunk in public and physically assaulting Europeans. These actions point to passengers who had at least some rapport with African conductors and inspectors on the vehicles or recognized that they would not be held responsible. This solidarity was not lost on the European settlers who called for their own racially segregated buses and staff to service them along every part of the journey.

She Flatly Refused

The other personal letter included in the packet sent to the Mayor by the Housewives tells the story of a European woman's experience on a Dagoretti bus traveling through the Western neighborhoods of Nairobi, one of which would have been Kibera. The author sends the letter because she has heard the Housewives are collecting complaints to send to the bus company, begging questions about the extent of the group's networking and publicity reach.[20]

> I understand that you are working for European women of Nairobi to get better treatment from Kenya Bus Company, and if possible, a bus for Europeans only. I am most grateful to you and your committee and you will receive heart-felt thanks from all the European housewives especially on the Dagoretti route, which runs from Dagoretti corner, the Kibera, the King George VIth and the KAR lines all crowding on about 7th and 8th of the month and Saturday and Sunday afternoons, when so many are drunk.
>
> Perhaps you would care to hear one of my recent experiences on the Dagoretti Bus – I travel on it daily to and from the office. I did report it to the EAWL hoping they would help!
>
> A friend of mine and I were waiting at the Colonial Stores bus stop for the Dagoretti double decker bus one morning last month, and as we boarded the bus a young Nubian woman pushed us aside and put her huge basket of bottles right in the doorway of the first class while she went upstairs. My friend asked her to move it so that we could get in (there is a place for baskets etc. under the stairs) this she flatly refused to do, so we asked the conductor who did not deign to answer, nor did the two African Inspectors help at all.
>
> My friend then tried to move it herself but before she could move it a second and older Nubian woman pushed her way past me and thumped my friend on the back with her closed fist so hard that she nearly fell headlong over the basket but just managed to catch the side of the door in time. Without hesitating, I gave the woman 6 of the best on her back! She turned round and seized me by the front of my blouse and raised her fist to strike me. My friend gave her a good smack. The woman then realized that it would be better to leave me alone and picked up the basket and we were allowed to enter and sit down. We felt so shaky and upset at the whole nasty business and neither the conductor nor the inspectors came to our aid!!
>
> I could tell you _many_ more incidents, most of which I have reported to Mr. Kennard, and on two occasions I have asked the Police for protection on the buses or [to] help us at the Harding Street bus stop at the "peak" hours.
>
> I might add that this Bus Company is owned by a London Bus Company, which also runs the buses in Salisbury, Rhodesia. There they have separate buses for Europeans and Africans and it works very well.

---

[20] Kenya National Archives (KNA). 94601/158. Letter to the Mayor of Nairobi; Kenya Bus Services Ltd. from "the Housewives," 7 June 1956.

These letters clearly show a shift in the reign of settler violence. It was weakening, as Brett Shadle described settler violence against Africans as "the lingua franca of colonial Kenya", just a few decades earlier in the 1920s (2015: 69). Although interpersonal violence committed by settlers against African men was freely admitted to by the perpetrators, they rarely mentioned beatings of women and, disturbingly but not surprisingly, settler violence against women was generally reported as sexual in nature. This letter provides a glimpse into an instance of interpersonal, non-sexual violence *between* settler women and African women, while exposing the limits of settler violence, and the limits of colonial power as it was understood by African residents of Nairobi.

You can read the history of settler violence in the unapologetic way the letter writer described how quickly and violently both European women reacted, "without hesitation" and with a "good" smack. Violence, for settlers, *was* good, and a necessary part of everyday life in Kenya. It was also heavily racialized, meaning that "*all* whites presumed the right to inflict violence on *any* African (and quite often, Indian as well), while intra-white assaults could easily end up in court" (Shadle 2015: 69). In this bus, in 1956, the resistance and reciprocity of interpersonal violence was not one-sided, but crossed age and gender lines, and brought both African women of different ages together as well as African men who were on the bus and in positions of authority. In this letter, one African woman unapologetically refused to obey the European women's demand to move the basket of bottles, and another African woman unafraid to instigate a violent encounter with the White women, thumped one woman on her back and grabbed the clothes of the other.

The Housewives generally stated that "in most cases the complaints have not been directed towards the conductors, but against the almost impossible conditions under which they work."[21] They complained that the KBS employees, who were all African, were incapable of controlling the bus population. In this case, however, the inspectors and conductor of the bus did not aid the European women. The African conductors and inspectors asserted themselves by ignoring the European women, thereby creating solidarity with African women, and in a way rendering the European women invisible.

There may be an additional layer of intimacy at play between the African women on the Dagoretti bus and the African conductor and inspectors who ignored the European women's calls for help in addition to general anti-settler sentiment. There is a chance they were both members of the same community, Sudanese ex-soldiers and their families who settled on what was once a forest patch on the far Western outskirts of Nairobi they called Kibra. Over time,

---

[21] Kenya National Archives (KNA), 94601/158, Letter to the Mayor of Nairobi; Kenya Bus Services Ltd. from "the Housewives," 7 June 1956.

members of this community, marked by Muslim dress, came to be known as Nubians, although they referred to themselves as Sudanese and were most likely a common sight on the Dagoretti bus that passed by what had, by 1956, become Kibera, a bustling, diverse neighborhood of Africans who had a right to live on the land by permission of the Crown and who were protected by their previous military service (Parsons 1997).

The basket of bottles the White women were attempting to move may have contained lots of valuable gin, or at least valuable bottles. Nubian women often transported their home-brewed gin in baskets on KBS buses where the drivers and inspectors were also all Nubian. Nubian gin was the drink of the military and women were the main distillers, making thousands of quarts a day, exporting the gin from Kibera by "delivering gin to customers houses, offices, bars, or shops ... with bottles hidden in baskets or tied around their waists" (De Smedt 2009: 201). During the era of the Emergency, there was more military around who were consuming increasing amounts of gin. De Smedt's Nubian interviewees claim that 70–90 percent of families were involved in gin production at some point and, in a letter to the Superintendent of police, alleged that "the Nubian drivers of KBS are largely concerned with the distribution of Nubian gin" (2009: 201). According to a KBS bus operations account in 1949, the entire workforce of 140 drivers and 140 conductors employed by KBS were "all native," many of whom were probably Nubian.[22]

Nubians in Nairobi

Kibera, located in what is now West Nairobi, was not a hotbed of Land and Freedom Army sympathizers, as the Eastland areas were seen to be, especially in 1956. Instead, Kibera housed a population of Sudanese soldiers and their families who had settled in the area with permission from the Crown (Parsons 1997). In other words, it was not suspected guerilla fighters or Mau Mau oath takers boarding the bus with these settler housewives, but the "good Africans" who were loyal soldiers. Nubians who served as soldiers in the East African Rifles, ended up in Kenya to guard the railway in the late 1890s. By 1902, half of the men in the East African Rifles (later the King's African Rifles (KAR)) were Sudanese due to the fact that "The Southern Sudan was a source of slave soldiers for the independent Sudanese kingdoms of Sennar, Tegali, Darfur and ultimately Egypt" and over time these quasi-slave soldiers developed an ethnic or cultural consciousness through their shared military service, kinship built by adopting orphans and intermarrying other ex-slaves, while also developing

---

[22] Kenya National Archives, Nairobi (KNA), Bus Operating Account – Traffic – Salaries & Wages. Kenya Bus Services Limited, 3 November 1949.

their own distinctive language, dress and cultural practices (Parsons 1997). In fact, some "Nubian" women, in 1956, were likely Kikuyu women married to Sudanese ex-soldiers.

In 1911, the British Crown granted permission for these Sudanese soldiers to settle on a piece of land within the city limits of Nairobi, near the army barracks, but at that time, a significant distance away from the city center, explaining why they called the settlement Kibra, meaning "forest" (Balaton-Chrimes 2013). The place name indicates how far on the outskirts of town and off major paths it was located. By the 1930s, and for the next 30 years, Nairobi grew to meet and then surround and overtake Kibera. The government struggled to evict, remove, relocate, and reorganize Kiberans, who had become a dynamic community of ex-soldiers, their families, and local people (Parsons 1997: 101). When the Second World War erupted, the Sudanese soldiers were able to strengthen their claim to Kibera under their good military service, many of them working as drivers and mechanics, which may explain why some of them took to transportation services in Nairobi.

The war also caused illegal brewing to boom in Kibera and the production of what was called "Nubian gin" became a support system for older women who were denied pensions and "who had no chance of marriage" (Parsons 1997: 101). Throughout the 1940s Kibera shrunk in size as Kikuyu people were removed due to the Mau Mau panic, and it was also targeted for criminal activity due to the production of illegal gin. Perhaps the gin brewing also helps explain the importance of the basket of bottles that the Nubian woman protected on the bus?

The role of Nubians cannot be overlooked in the history of Nairobi as they were and are a particularly unique group of people that were both advantaged and disadvantaged from colonial contradictions and shifting racial and ethnic hierarchies that have increasingly impacted claims to land (Balaton-Chrimes 2013). Similar communities of Africans in other colonial neighborhoods like Kileleshwa and Kilimani with no military connections were bulldozed, while Kibera was perpetually protected by elites in colonial government, like Lord Lugard himself (Parsons 1997: 117). In contemporary Kenya, Kibera residents still constantly battle removal efforts by the government, resisting policies often that are often couched in progressive catchphrases like "urban upgrading," much like the final years of settler colonial rule in Kenya, which were couched in "multiracial partnership" (Farrell 2015; Klopp 2008).

Multiracial Logics and Gendered Public Space

On 19 June 1956, just twelve days after the Housewives' original packet of letters arrived at Nairobi's Mayor's office, the *East African Standard* newspaper reported that women "of all races" in Nairobi were to get "priority seating during rush hours." According to the newspaper, a "Ladies Only" bus stop was going to be set up at peak times in between "4pm and 5:15pm on weekdays and 12:30pm and 1:15pm on Saturdays."[23] The newspaper directly cited letters where "housewives" complained of "scrambles" and about one-class bus service reporting that the same letters from housewives suggested that women would be prepared to "pay more rather than travel on a one-class service" and that "Africans" have "no sense of consideration for other passengers." It is not clear from the newspaper reporting if these letters from "housewives" were the same letters from "the Housewives".

While the Mayor is portrayed in the article to have been swayed by letters from women in the colony, a memo from 20 June 1956, shows that his office is quite dismissive of the Housewives' issues. That memo, from someone who works at the Mayor's office, stated:[24]

> Facts must be faced. Segregation of races or the introduction of buses for one race only would be unacceptable in present-day Kenya. Special buses for Europeans would not be an economic proposition so therefore the bus company should not entertain the idea.
> 2. No one can expect the behavior of the African to conform to that of the British people – ever.
> 3. It would go a long way towards alleviating present discontent if European drivers, conductors and inspectors were employed on those routes where this kind of trouble is being experienced. This would probably involve the Company in a great deal of additional expenditure because not many routes would be involved but possible the European bus users would not object to a small increase in fares to cover the cost of providing European staff.

This reflection sums up overall British colonial policy generally and multiracial logic specifically: that African people and European people were never to be held to the same standards of conduct, while also explicitly recognizing that to allow overt segregation based on race would put the modernity of the Empire into question. Obviously, segregation of ridership by race is unacceptable in a modern society, but racist attitudes toward much of the ridership is standard. In cursive at the bottom of the typed memo, there is a note that says:

---

[23] Although not specified in article referenced here, one might assume that because the priority seating during rush hour was open to women of "all races", so was the "Ladies only" bus stop.

[24] Kenya National Archives, Nairobi (KNA). 94601/161, Memo from the Mayor of Nairobi, 20 June 1956.

> I don't think there is any comment I can usefully make on this question, which crops up again and again. It is a local government problem only. Because the city council may license a company and give them a monopoly, but basically the problem is an economic one.

The next memo from two days later, 22 June 1956, follows with more advice on the issue (perhaps from an assistant) and reminds the Mayor that he has "a meeting with 'the housewives' on the 16th of July to consider this matter."

> The CLG [Commissioner for Local Government] has commented ... but as he points out this is basically a political problem but unfortunately it is the local authority which has to solve it. I do not think you need any briefing from me on a point like this and I would only add my personal view that from the female European point of view us pretty frightful to put it mildly.

Again, in familiar cursive at the bottom of the page, the Mayor issues a handwritten reminder: "Please bring up this file to me on 15th July."

On 28 June 1956, less than thirty days after their letters were first received, the very first "Ladies Only" bus stop went into effect in Nairobi. The *East African Standard* newspaper reports, "Buses on certain routes will be cleared of all passengers ... and only women will be allowed to board them. The scheme is experimental, but there is no time limit." Surely, the settler women were satisfied with their few hours of gender segregation a week because they successfully ended the one-class service proposal. This corresponds to another aspect of settler colonial erasure: "Keeping the dominant minority quiet demanded the appearance of holding the majority down and the reality of retaining its advances under state control" (Wolfe 2006: 387). It is not clear from the archives how long the women's only bus stops and priority seating lasted in Nairobi. Even if it was for a short time, judging by the quick rate of action and the meaningless solution put forward and accepted, what is clear is that although the Housewives wielded some power in the urban space of colonial Nairobi there were hard limits on their power to impact things. These women were able to be publicly placated, presented as more modern and tolerant than they were, while their racist settler views were widely shared and socially accepted, but economically nonviable.

Roots of a Transportation Takeover

Makadara

Pirate taxis emerged out of the Makadara settlement, which was an official African location that housed Kikuyus who had been cleared of Mau Mau influence (White 1990). An important feature of Makadara is that it was developed as a reward for loyal Kikuyus who were displaced and suffered under the Emergency. The scheme included a subsidy for new residents to buy home building supplies from government suppliers at a reduced rate (White 1990). In a departure from other African settlements in Nairobi at the same time, Makadara's residents largely worked in some capacity *outside* of Makadara neighborhood itself. This was in contrast to many of the other neighborhoods where Africans lived at the time (Pumwani, Eastleigh, Buru Buru), which had fully functional internal economies that existed and thrived within the community itself, enabling income to be generated without leaving the settlement. Thus, even though Makadara was a loyal Kikuyu neighborhood, the residents' inability to get to and from work trumped their obedience. Looked at from this angle it is clear to see why pirate taxis, a seemingly heavy-handed label for carpooling, was a logical and completely rational response to colonial inadequacies.

A letter from 21 November 1956, written by W. B. Havelock, the Minister of Local Government, Health and Housing, stated that he was "getting rather worried at the financial burden which the African has to carry in Nairobi" and that he heard "that it costs seventy cents to travel from Makadara to the City Center … and this 1.40 shillings a day adds up to around 35 shillings a month," which "is a very big bite out of the average wage of 120 shillings a month." This letter is written to A. F. Kirby, General Manager of the Railway. Havelock is wondering whether the Railway can offer a service on the Nanyuki line that carries passengers from the outlying Nairobi Estates into the Nairobi Station and if there is any way to reduce the cost. Havelock says that the bus company will not reduce the cost without a subsidy and that he "will be discussing this with the Mayor." When Kirby responded to Havelock's letter, he admits that he is aware of the problems with passenger transport but was not able to take it over at that time. The context within which the *matatu* industry emerged was fertile for action and innovation of this sort.

Pirate Taxis

In 1959, due to several factors, not least the lackluster service the KBS provided for the African residents of Nairobi, just a few years after the one-class, one-fare proposal was abandoned, the first informal "pirate taxis" emerged from these Makadara neighborhoods (Heinze 2018; Aduwo 1990). The pirate taxis started picking up the forlorn commuters waiting for KBS buses, which only came once an hour.[25] Ultimately, these pirate taxis led to the fall of the

---

[25] Kenya National Archives, Nairobi (KNA) POL/128/60, Letter to the Traffic Police from C. E. Chun, Traffic Manager for Kenya Bus Services, 4 April 1960.

KBS because KBS was never meant to serve the entirety of urban residents of Nairobi. Its buses were more like props on the set of a city in a colonial spectacle. It wasn't until pirate taxis emerged, and subsequently the *matatu* sector expanded, that the city got the amount of service an urban center like Nairobi demanded.

In April of 1960, Mr. C. E. Chun, a KBS traffic manager, sent a letter to the Traffic Police stating that he had observed a pirate taxi picking up passengers from the Landies Road bus station in Nairobi at 11:15am.[26] Mr. Chun was irritated at the gall of the operator carrying passengers in total disregard of the KBS transport monopoly and was exasperated that he "actually picked up and set down inside the bus station" in plain sight of KBS management. The next day he wrote a letter of complaint to the Officer in Charge at the Nairobi Traffic Police and copied the correspondence to the TLB as well as the NCC. In a memo to police, the City Council stated that the Bedford van in question was "one of about 12 vehicles that regularly operate from the road reserve opposite to the Machakos bus station" providing unsanctioned transportation.

A few days later, the Chief City Inspector responded to Mr. Chun's complaint. He wrote that "the activities described do not offend the city by-laws" and he regretted to report that the police could not take any action against the pirate taxis. Shortly after this correspondence, Mr. Chun amplified his surveillance and reporting tactics. In his second letter of complaint to the Traffic Police, he wrote that KBS management was "becoming seriously alarmed at the amount of piracy which is occurring" on their Makadara route. These unlicensed vehicles operated throughout the morning and evening peak times and, according to his estimates, had caused the KBS to lose over 2,000 passengers a day. Like his first complaint, this letter was copied to the NCC and the TLB. In his reply, the Inspector explained again that no action could be taken against the unlicensed vehicles because "there are no by-laws to cover it ... the by-laws deal only with vehicles licensed as Public Service Vehicles, which of course the offending vehicles are not."

From the 1960s the pirate taxis gained popularity with the general African population and spread to other African estates. Not only were they more efficient than the KBS, which stuck to timetables and had fewer services, they were also cheaper. The KBS fares increased on 6 May 1960, and on 9 May, just six days later, Mr. Chun reports some "30 cars, taxis, vans and lorries began to operate a service at one-minute intervals from Makadara and Duke Street or Reata Road throughout the morning peak period and almost the same number in the reverse direction in the evening peak period." This letter is written to the Town Clerk of Nairobi and to the Officer in charge

[26] Ibid.

for the Traffic Police and is from KBS. There is a very interesting appendix included in this letter that is a table showing the one-minute intervals and has documented the number plates of the vehicles "carrying over 200 passengers" in that half-hour between 6:30am and 7:00am. At the end of the letter and the report the KBS implies that they will no longer provide service if this illegal operation does not stop. As one can see from the chart taken from Mr. Chun's letter that there are two vehicles that make two trips before the KBS bus returns to pick up more passengers.

Table 1 Chun's list of pirate taxis, including their makes and number plates and number of passengers.

Time	Make/Type	No. of Passengers
6:30 a.m.	Red Lorry	12
6:31 a.m.	Car	6
6:32 a.m.	Car	7
6:33 a.m.	Van	9
6:34 a.m.	Ford Van	8
6:37 a.m.	?	12
6:38 a.m.	Chevy Van	7
6:42 a.m.	Ford Van	11
6:44 a.m.	Van	10
6:45 a.m.	Ford van	7
6:46 a.m.	Bedford Van	12
6:47 a.m.	Austin van	8
6:50 a.m.	Bedford Lorry	15
6:51 a.m.	Ford Consul	6
6:52 a.m.	Morris Van	5
6:53 a.m.	Van	8
6:54 a.m.	Chevy van	14
6:54 a.m.	Ford Consul	7
6:55 a.m.	Car	5
6:56 a.m.	Bedford Van	8
6:57 a.m.	VW Bus	9
6:58 a.m.	Bedford Lorry	12
6:58 a.m.	Pgt. Car	5
6:59 a.m.	Bedford Lorry	12
7:00 a.m.	Pgt. Van	6

Source: Kenya National Archives, Nairobi (KNA) POL/128/60, Letter to the Traffic Police from C. E. Chun, Traffic Manager for Kenya Bus Services, 4 April 1960.

This marks a departure from the radical taxi operators in the 1940s and represents a broader undermining of colonial operations by even loyal Kenyan subjects in the years leading up to independence. At the same time, it shows that the city government, who had a stake in the KBS, as well as the police knew about the pirate taxis but chose not to do anything about them as they were becoming a necessary part of the efficient functioning of the city because as the African population grew they were still largely ignored and denied services by the colonial government. This process has also had long-term effects with regards to police corruption that plagues the industry now because the pirate taxis were not legal but necessary, and therefore paying police to turn a blind eye became imbedded in the industry from its inception.

Unsanctioned or pirate movement was a rational and pragmatic response to the restrictions placed on African movement and mobility by the colonial administration. Transportation, whether in the form of the colonial bus system KBS, pirate taxis, or Kikuyu taxis, represents an important part of Kenya's history. Transportation, movement, and mobility can offer an interesting angle into the things that happen in between the binaries of collaboration and resistance, loyalist and rebel, formal and informal; and thinking of transportation as a world of transition has a sort of ephemeral quality that opens it up as a space of interactions and possibilities. Even the loyal Kikuyu residents of Makadara were not able to survive within the constraints of the colonial bus services that were just not enough. By pushing African urban residents to provide the necessary services for themselves and their associates, the origins of stigma were set in motion.

I offer one last example of how the colonial administration engendered and promoted the proliferation of the pirate taxi sector at the dawn of independence. By using the case of Samuel Githu, a loyal Kikuyu bus owner who had been boycotted since the Emergency and wanted to get his license back and perhaps switch routes.[27] The TLB was not being agreeable. He had voluntarily given his previous license to the administration during the Emergency and surrendered to all the tests to inspect his degree of loyalty to Mau Mau and the Crown. He was found to be loyal to the Crown and not a threat to the colonial regime. He even helped during the campaign against Mau Mau during the 1950s by offering his vehicle over to the use of the home guards. However, when the Emergency ended, he reapplied for his license, but was refused several times.

On one hand, the letters, the cancellation of the one-class bus service in Nairobi, and the subsequent priority seating scheme from the Mayor's office

---

[27] Kenya National Archives, Nairobi (KNA) AA/35/44/12, Letter to Transport Licensing Board regarding the cases of Kiorie Kinyanjui and Samuel Githu, 19 June 1961.

reveal the reaches and limits of settler power in 1956 Nairobi. Read against the grain, these letters show how resistance to settler colonial power can be seen in unexpected places. They help us understand the way that public transportation can become a transformational place for marginalized people to express political will. The letters reveal various levels of solidarity in a tense moment. They also provide a vivid glimpse into the lives of two important groups of women living in Nairobi, vying for control over crucial, but largely overlooked, public spaces like buses and bus stops.

Conclusion

In the past several years, in the United States, there has been a rash of cell phone videos showing White women calling the police to complain and report Black people for a variety of everyday activities as though they are committing crimes such as: Black people barbequing, Black children selling cold water on a hot day, Black women waiting for rides from carsharing apps (Farzan 2018; Jerkins 2018; Mays and Piccoli 2018). The White women on tape calling the police are often dubbed "Karen" or "Becky" throughout the United States, a trend that came from within the Black community, expressed through hip-hop and other popular culture. Although seemingly less alarming than the viral videos of police brutality, the Karen videos are just as insidious when one realizes that these are often two ends of the same nightmare. A White woman's call of distress can easily initiate police brutality and violence, even death.

There is a parallel between the "Karens" all over the United States and "the Housewives" of colonial Nairobi. The Housewives were colonial Karens, which is to say that they used their race and their gender as weapons against Africans in the name of "public safety" and as a way of policing public space. Similar to the viral videos that document injustice and police violence, these letters showed how far they would go and the limits of colonial Karens. The letters give us clues into how KBS buses were places where Africans in Nairobi were able, at least at times, to push back, literally and figuratively, on colonial White supremacy and challenge the settler colonialism logic of elimination and exploitation. It appears KBS buses were one of these places where Africans could give expression to the White supremacy they were experiencing every day, revealing an important place where Africans may have felt able to take up space, to challenge colonial oppression, or just stand their ground, even as it moved underneath their feet.

As we better understand and clarify which urban places are important for the development of political and urban subjectivities, we can use this historical through-line to contextualize the placemaking practices considered in the next chapter. Both Kikuyu taxis and KBS buses leveraged mobility to transform the social and economic arena. Kikuyu taxis were conducting oathing rituals and Nubian women were transporting gin, making the surveillance of popular transportation increasingly tempting for the state, but nearly impossible to implement, resulting in the emergence and domination of the *matatu* sector throughout the 1970s. The following chapter shows how the interior space of the *matatu* has become a moving public and mobile city center circulating popular culture, debates, and discourses over the past sixty years, facilitating meaning-making and gender and class performance in the capital city.

2

Joyriding: From Placemaking to Publics

Sometimes they kind of like, talk bad about a girl doing it [joyriding] ... it's like not doing anything, it's more like jobless, you're jobless ... they kind of take a bad picture of this. Like she should be doing something important with her life other than going round, round, round, round with the car.

Maryam, Nairobi, 2007

It was 2004, in the middle-class neighborhood of Buru Buru, a suburb of Nairobi, Kenya's capital city, where I had my first encounter with the youth transportation practice of joyriding, where young riders transform the commute itself into a destination. Jackie, a neighbor of my host family, was tasked with hanging out with me and showing me what young people did for fun. We walked through the neighborhood greeting people who were outside chatting, but instead of going to one of the "shops" where young people often hung out, we walked to a nondescript spot on the side of the main road and waited. I didn't know it then, but we were waiting for a *matatu*.

But, not any *matatu*, a *manyanga*.[1] The *matatu* vehicles that pulled up in front of Jackie and I that day in Buru Buru, were far bigger than the fourteen-seater, Nissan *matatu* minivans, ubiquitous throughout the country. These vehicles could carry at least forty people, and were equipped with flashing lights, pounding sound systems and elaborate paint jobs. There were airbrushed portraits of celebrity's faces and slogans from English football clubs in huge letters along the side of the vehicle. Some had coordinated their horns with the lights on their vehicles, so they flashed along in unison. When the first one pulled up, I instinctively moved toward the vehicle as the young man working as the conductor, gestured for me to enter. Without speaking, Jackie gently touched my arm, silently imploring me to stay where I was. She signaled to me that we would not be taking this vehicle. Soon, the large, loud, blinking *matatu* sped away without us. This happened several more times as vehicles came and went, each one seemingly louder than the last.

---

1 Some say that *manyanga* is just a play on the slang word *nganya*, meaning "new" or "good."

To communicate to the conductors that we would not be boarding a vehicle as it passed, Jackie, nearly imperceptibly, nodded her head or simply looked away from the conductors who were hanging out of the *matatu* doors. I remember being surprised that we were spending so much time choosing how to get where we were going instead of getting on the first vehicle heading our way. I was still thinking of *matatu* minibus taxis as analogous to city buses or subways where one bus or train car is the same as the next. I was also confused as to what criteria we were using to choose our ride and why none of the vehicles stopping to pick us up so far were satisfactory. Meanwhile, Jackie was waiting for a "good *matatu*," calculating her choice of vehicle using a formula based on music, graphics, and reputation that like many Kenyans, especially in the commuter hub of Buru Buru, she had built throughout her young life. Residents of Buru Buru used an array of criteria in several categories to determine which *matatu* was the coolest, safest, most popular, or played the best music.

Buru Buru's sizeable commuter population has contributed to the intense aestheticizing of the vehicles serving that neighborhood as they competed for passengers. Construction for Buru Buru estate started in May 1973, and was "initially planned to be self-contained, with all facilities – social, cultural and employment facilities … so as to eliminate the journey to work. However, it was developed eventually as a commuter neighbourhood and a dormitory town" (Bonna 1985: 88). Although it is only a few miles from the city center, commuting to and from Buru Buru can be a long and arduous journey down jam-packed Jogoo Road, which connects the estate to the city center. This trip can commonly take several hours, especially during the morning and evening rush. This long commute due to the infamous traffic congestion in Nairobi is thought to have compelled more and more comfortable vehicles to enter the market.

When we finally boarded a vehicle, climbing the two steep steps up into the bus felt like entering another world, and that world was a night club. It was dark, illuminated with multicolored lights dancing around the edges of the windows and the floorboard. The music was so loud you could feel the bass vibrate your teeth when you sat down. Perhaps the most striking feature from my perspective was the huge video screen mounted behind the driver, which faced toward the passengers and played the music video of the incredibly loud song to which we were listening. The loud music made it impossible to talk, as we rode along with the forty other passengers from the neighborhood. As we pulled away, I quickly got lost in the music videos on the massive screen and in Nairobi's streets passing outside our windows. Later I came to understand that these *manyangas*, one with pricy "graphics" and a costly sound system were indeed different than the Nissan minivans, more expensive but also an escape route out of the doldrums of daily life.

During the trip, the *matatu* conductor walked through the vehicle asking passengers their destination and collecting money. When he approached Jackie they exchanged Kenyan shillings, a few words, and smiles. When we arrived in Nairobi's city center, located just eight kilometers away from Buru Buru, it was nearly an hour later. Jackie motioned for me to stay seated. Again, I was confused, and again, I complied, staying in my seat as the vehicle emptied out except for the crew members, Jackie, and me. A few minutes later the vehicle was full of new passengers, and we were heading back toward Buru Buru. When we arrived at the nondescript part of the road where we boarded this vehicle, the young conductor hit the metal ceiling of the *matatu* twice with his fist signaling to the driver to pull over. The *manyanga* slowed to a stop just long enough for us to climb down the steps and jump on to the road before it sped away. For Nairobi's joyriders, like Jackie, the journey is the destination.

As we walked back through the neighborhood, we passed the young people still hanging out at the shops, but it was as though we had traveled distances far greater than the eight kilometers separating Buru Buru and Nairobi's city center. It was like the *matatu* had acted as Bakhtin's chronotope – where time and space had been compressed (Vokes and Pype 2018). We had passed small street vendors and large, bustling markets, we saw *manyanga* vehicles that were like works of art and we witnessed many different people coming and going, greeting one another. We consumed the newest local Kenyan and Tanzanian Swahili hip-hop sounds and images, as well as global music from Jamaica, Europe, and the US. Some scholars argue that the space-time compression present in automobility culture causes places to lose their meaning and to erode the distinction of locales. You can be anywhere or nowhere simultaneously. Geographer Edward Relph (1976) was convinced that cars eroded "a sense of place" because they destroyed intimate relationships. His conceptualization of automobility "placelessness" is similar to French anthropologist Marc Augé's understanding of transportation zones as so ephemeral and anonymous to be categorized as "non-places" (1995). But anthropologists of place and space (Low and Lawrence-Zúñiga 2003) along with mobility scholars have come to challenge these ideas about the placelessness of travel locales (Sheller and Urry 2006). Whether it be walking (Richardson 2005), cycling (Spinney 2007), driving (Thrift 2004) or "passengering", the different modes of transportation are not all "non-places" of ephemera, but are important pathways for people to access and make meaning out of the city, collectively and individually. Mobility, at many levels then, is not a non-place, but a meaningful sensory and urban placemaking experience.

From Placemaking to Publics

Placemaking refers to the practice of making a space useful and meaningful, converting a place with one use or meaning into another (Paulsen 2010: 599). Language is a fundamental tool for this meaning-making practice, as are sounds, smells, architecture, and other forms of design (Paulsen 2010: 600). As *matatu* vehicles circulate images, slogans, songs, and people along with their conversations and ideas, they become an important "place" in the city. The circulation of new *Sheng* words, identities and performances, as seen in the joyriding practice described above and in *matatu* and more specifically *manyanga* vehicles themselves, can be conceived of as more than just moving people from one place to another but as a cultural process with its own "forms of abstraction, evaluation and constraint, which are created by the interactions between specific types of circulating forms and the interpretive communities built around them" (Lee and LiPuma 2002: 192).

The circulation of "seditious music" and political speeches and sermons in *matatu* vehicles during the 1990s, as previously mentioned, acted as a type of free speech in an era of censorship due to Moi's single-party rule (Haugerud 1995), and as *matatu* design flourished in the past three decades under the influence of globalized hip-hop it has become more than simply a system of transportation but a media infrastructure. The images, sounds, and performances of *matatu* vehicles and their workers constitute a media landscape that circulates throughout the city, and, through a circulation of images, neologisms, political ideology, and religious symbolism they become an active part of making the city (Çaglar and Glick Schiller 2018). Instead of approaching infrastructures as separate from media, anthropologists have started thinking about approaching media *as* infrastructure (Schiller 2019). Joyriding and *matatu/manyanga* design and circulation expand on that concept to theorize *matatu* transportation infrastructures as media.

Understanding *matatu* vehicles as a type of infrastructure that acts as a media infrastructure as well invites potential theorization as publics and counterpublics. The category "public" can be understood as "one in a spectrum of forms of sociolinguistically-created authority" and perhaps the anonymity of public spaces and the "voice from nowhere element" of something like a transportation infrastructure may be constructed as the "most authentic of voices competing for recognition as the embodiment of a certain community" (Gal and Woolard 2001: 133–134). As thinking on publics has progressed, scholars have argued that there are multiple publics operating all the time, and that this is not simply the outcome of structural features but is a highly moveable, malleable, and borrowable idea (Gal and Woolard 2001: 136). Publics, then, are a type of social totality or people in general, although they are increasingly organized around visual and audio texts (Warner 2002). A public organizes itself independently from the state, the church, law, and frameworks of citizenship, similarly in the way that *matatu* vehicles and the savings and credit co-operatives (SACCOs) that run them operate. *Matatu* vehicles fulfill other elements important to "publics" such as being a relation among strangers, including both personal and impersonal speech, and being constituted through mere attention (Warner 2002: 55–60). The performance art that is in process on a *matatu* (Reed 2018), and the ideas presented below about how owners design their vehicles to grab the attention of potential passengers, transforms this transport system into a public.

Much of the theoretical purchase around the idea of "publics" is how it works to create political subjects through mass-mediated communication (Cody 2011) and how Habermas's concept of the "public sphere" provided a way to clarify the confusions of the political theories around progressive social movements (Fraser 1990). Anthropologists are increasingly concerned about how mass-mediated subjectivity and communicative practices shape the field of politics (Cody 2011). The concept of "counterpublics" emerges as a way to discuss the ability of subordinated groups to formulate oppositional discourses in a range of parallel spheres (Cody 2011; Fraser 1990). A counterpublic is theorized to "maintain at some level, conscious or not, an awareness of its subordinate status" as the "[f]riction against the dominant public forces the poetic-expressive character of counterpublic discourse to become salient to consciousness" (Warner 2002:86). In this way, *matatu* vehicles become places that shape dominant and subaltern political subjectivities. Joyriding, then, should be understood as far more than just a leisure activity, but as a political subject-forming practice.

Like the Nubian women in colonial Nairobi transporting their gin on the colonial buses in collaboration with Nubian drivers, access to mobility has a way of staying just out of the state's reach, and because of this *matatus* have often been a place where Kenyans collectively and somewhat freely perform urban identities. *Matatu* vehicles could be said to provide a type of "subversive mobility," which can be understood as "mobility that threatens the continued existence of a ruling political regime" (Shell 2015: 4), but I find it more constructive to consider the *matatu* as a moving urban public or even counterpublic. For example, Haugerud found that in the 1990s, under Kenya's second President Daniel arap Moi's authoritarian regime, a network of *matatu* workers passed around cassette tapes of outlawed political speeches, "seditious music" and sermons (1995: 29–30). Because *matatu* vehicles were already generally operating out of regulatory reach of the state, they were one of the few places where oppositional politics could be safely discussed and shared. These outlawed speeches worked like "hidden transcripts" – subversive messages about the dominant culture by those with less power (Scott 1998). Similarly, during this era using stickers inside *matatus* to communicate oppositional ideas became popular. The circulation of these hidden transcripts and the stickers and the ways that *Sheng* and music videos circulates during consumptive, leisurely joyrides provide a generative space among strangers where some collective subjectivities are constructed and performed. From the Nubian women in the colonial buses to the joyriders of Buru Buru, urban transportation infrastructure has always been an ideal and productive place for hidden transcripts to be read aloud. Like colonial buses, the joyriders use *matatus* as both an infrastructure of transportation, and a type of moving media public where consumption is key.

Ambivalent Aesthetics

As mentioned, not just any regular *matatu* will do for the purpose of joyriding. A joyride requires a *manyanga*, a spectacular *matatu* with beautiful graphics, the newest music and motifs that reference current local and global popular culture. As referenced in the Introduction, *matatu* vehicles can be wrapped in Burberry plaid or feature the face of Kenyan environmentalist Wangari Maathai. A more subversive example from research undertaken in 2005 and 2006 included *matatu* designs featuring the Artur brothers, Armenian investors/mercenaries who had traveled to and were living in Kenya under mysterious circumstances and who were implicated in several scandals.[2] When owners take their vehicles to be built, decorated, painted, and wired for video/audio people say that the vehicle is *iko jikoni*, "in the kitchen." The process was described to me as, "*gari imefika jikoni, halafu* it is fried and *wakati imeiva imeenda*." This sentence, "the car arrives in the kitchen, then it is fried and when it is ready, it goes," uses *imeiva*, a verb specifically used to describe food when it is ready to eat, linguistically linking the decorated *matatu* to food which is consumed.

Tony, an underemployed *matatu* worker in Nairobi described a *manyanga* in the following way: "To most people, *manyanga* is a *gooood* (stretching out the word) *matatu*. Ok, something beautiful, like this, you see," pointing to a big, colorful minibus parked near where we are having our conversation, written boldly on the front and sides of the vehicle is the *manyanga's*

---

[2] The Artur brothers – Artur Margaryan and Artur Sargsyan – were two infamous figures, Armenian mercenaries posing as investors, living in Kenya in 2005 and 2006 who were named in several scandals at the time, the most notable being their alleged involvement in the Standard Media raid rumored to be organized and carried out by John Michuki (Omulo 2022; Wrong and Williams 2009).

name – "Indomitable." In 2005, the average cost of getting a *matatu* on the road was 1.2 to 1.6 million shillings ($15,000–$20,000 USD in 2005), more if it is a bigger *manyanga*. In 2018 vehicles that cost 7.5 million shillings ($75,000 USD) were reported (Reed 2018). But as Tony explained, there is believed to be a return on your investment:

> You would call it a *manyanga* because you know, it is beautiful. You have the small Nissans and you know, you call them *manyanga* with the colorings and the music, so *manyanga* doesn't just stand for a big bus. A *manyanga* stands for something *nice*. A *nice matatu*. That is *manyanga*, yeah. The money, as in what you get in the evening after work, is ... you know 'cause most customers prefer taking *manyangas* to these other ordinary *matatus*. You know, you have many customers that would like to go watch in the DVDs, the screen, listening to music, the loud music, you have other customers that don't like the music, you know. But they are quite few, there are quite few of them. So, at the end of the day you find that the *manyanga* has more money than the ordinary.

Some *matatu* companies advertise their *manyangas* as "mobile clubs," where, in addition to playing loud music and showing music videos, they also serve drinks and will reserve the vehicle for thirty to forty of your closest friends. Instead of taking the vehicle to the club, it becomes the club. There are a variety of joyriding versions that exist in Nairobi, such as the "chew and chill," where young people chew *miraa*, or *khat* (a plant that when chewed has a mildly stimulating effect) and ride the vehicle around for hours watching music videos. Additionally, in 2010 *The Star* newspaper reported that a "porno mat" was providing a commuter experience where people were rumored to watch pornographic "skin flicks" in the privacy of public transportation vehicles. It is important to note, however, that not all these joyrides are as transgressive as the ones mentioned above. Around 2013, *matatu* vehicles started offering wireless internet in their vehicles and in the early evening hours you could find several students diligently doing homework in the vehicles. These various types of joyriders are individually and collectively making their own places of leisure inside the *matatu*, thus transforming the place symbolically but also economically by identifying the value of the space of the *matatu* as more than just transportation.

The meaning-making processes and production of identity that occurs through the mobility of public transportation shows how the multiplicity of mobile experiences deserves increased ethnographic attention. Scholars often ignore how people "dwell in cars ... how the car is an instrument of personal agency and collective identity," and how experiences of mobility can vary by age, gender, skin color, religion, and citizenship (Waitt et al. 2017: 3–6).

The aesthetics of *matatu* infrastructure expressed through joyriding, and the boundaries drawn by their routes, are productive avenues of analysis because they incorporate multiple scales – from vehicle to neighborhood to route to city to nation. Through the practice of joyriding important characteristics of place – geographic location, material form and investment with meaning and value – remain bundled reflecting how both domains (the material and interpretive) work autonomously and in a mutually dependent way (Gieryn 2000: 473–475). In other words,

> Rather than being one definite sort of thing – for example physical, spiritual, cultural, social – a given place takes on the qualities of its occupants, reflecting these qualities in its own constitution and description and expressing them in its occurrence as an event: places not only are, they happen. (Casey 1996: 27)

What it means to belong in Nairobi is, at least partially, tied up and expressed through *matatu* vehicles (Wa-Mungai 2013). Residents of Nairobi spend a lot of time in traffic, either in or out of a *matatu*. They are a big part of life in Kenya and structure discourse long after commuters have disembarked.

Ethnographic reflection on this youth transportation practice provides recognition that these vehicles are places that "are politicized, culturally relative, historically specific, local and made of multiple constructions" (Rodman 1992: 640). They are perceived as risky, dangerous death traps as well as symbols of the nation and an example of indigenous ingenuity in the face of an oppressive colonial system (Mutongi 2006, 2017). It is important to provide examples of how passengers, like the young people discussed here, use urban infrastructures in ways that are often overlooked by policy makers and scholars alike. Like cruising in lowriders, riding in a *manyanga* is a spatial practice in that the *manyanga* impacts the space it occupies (Chappell 2017: 27). This is increasingly important in the face of climate change, increasing privatization of neoliberal urban spaces and migration contributing to accelerated urban change in cities throughout the world.

Matatu vehicles ambivalent aesthetics polarize Kenyan society, often along generational lines. In the taxi from the airport upon arriving for an early research trip the driver corrected my description of *matatu* culture by saying, "Oh, so you are studying youth culture? Youth culture is *matatu* culture." Youth are important political and social actors, especially in urban African contexts, where they often make up 40–50 percent of the urban population. Their practices, therefore, are instructive. Scholar Tshikala Biaya argues that street culture throughout the continent often involves how "youth appropriate existing forms of leisure while transforming them for their own ends. Once spatialized in this manner, leisure becomes a founder of street culture; it expresses the violence of a reclamation and fabricates its own legitimacy in the public space" (2005: 216). African youth face a crisis of unemployment stemming from structural adjustment and a colonial model of education. By adopting "cultural aesthetics in sharp rupture with post-colonial logics" youth culture in urban Africa often "mingles 'globalized' images, attitudes and physical practices that sketch new popular forms of insurrection," and these practices give expression to new forms of sociability (Biaya 2005: 215).

For example, Figure 8 pictures a *manyanga* called Funkadelic which features a large mural across the side of the vehicle with an image of urban violence, where a man is aiming a shoulder mounted rocket launcher at a police helicopter while another engages in a firefight with a police vehicle. The windows show several slogans above the violent mural with the word "Run," the title "The Night City Drifter," and an image of a person with headphones holding a gaming controller, with a slogan just above saying "Eat, Sleep, Game, Repeat." Funkadelic is a good example of the layering of messages on *matatu* vehicles and the potentials for counterpublic or alternative and subversive messages to be expressed.

By exploring various ethnographic examples of *matatu* owners, workers, and passengers discussing the aesthetic dimensions of *matatu* mobility, we can see how the *manyanga* becomes a place for everyday acts of self-improvement, leisure, and pleasure and attempts to make an urban self. Circulating economic and symbolic capital, *matatu*, and particularly *manyangas*, transform an already complex transportation system into a media infrastructure of communication creating, delivering, and disseminating sounds, images, and languages, as well as passengers. The *matatu* counterpublic and the aesthetic practices embedded there are also expressions of the city and act as public statements from the street. The emotional and sensory relationships that residents have with *matatu* vehicles at multiple levels construct and shape the social geography of contemporary Nairobi.

Circulating Selves

Kenya's *matatu* vehicles are always named. Naming and decorating a *matatu* is a serious, personal endeavor for owners. Many whom I spoke with enjoyed telling me about their process regarding creating, managing, and maintaining their *matatu* vehicles' image. When I first encountered *matatu* minivans I assumed that the crew had something to do with the naming of the vehicle on which they worked because the decor seemed so youth oriented, but it is an important point to make here that it is owners make huge investments in the design of their vehicles based on what they think young people will like.

Figure 8 A matatu called Funkadelic, featuring a scene where armed men are shooting at police vehicles and helicopters, wreaking havoc in the city. Elizabeth, a key interlocutor, is featured in the image as well. (Photo courtesy of Elizabeth Njoki, 2023).

Matatu art and aesthetics are a lucrative part of the economy, and is often the way that many artists make a living, but the branding of their vehicles is more than simply economic. As mobility scholars suggest, we should explore people's feelings about cars, because by looking at how owners feel about their vehicle's aesthetic can give us insight into how the production and circulation of global images work through public transportation providers and make their way into public space. In 2006, during a meeting with several *matatu* owners in Mombasa, I asked each one how they named their vehicles. The next thing I knew we were driving through town looking for each owners' vehicles. These owners were not young or naïve about the business, but when it came to describe the process of naming their *matatu*, they were giddy with excitement.

When I asked each owner what the name of their vehicle was and what it looked like, so I could keep watch for it, Kamau told me that he had nine *matatu* vehicles, all nine of them decorated with the theme, "Resurrection." He explained that the name was meant to represent his Christian faith. Another owner, Hakim, wearing a *kanzu*, told me that he had three vehicles, and they were all named, "Habiba, a traditional Islamic name for a beautiful woman." The third owner, Robert, laughed a little as he told me the name of his three *matatu* vehicles, "because I love professional wrestling, 'The Rock.'"[3] Each of these men had deeply personal reasons for the specific name of their vehicle, which was important for understanding how transportation practices in Kenya tie so closely to identity. I found these qualities across the board for owners. It was not just these three men who used the branding of their *matatu* as a vehicle for self-esteem and expression, the women who owned *matatu* vehicles also took great pride and care making sure their private politics or religious beliefs were publicized on their vehicles, as the discussion with Joyce below shows.

Keith Basso argues that places are part of "working on the self" (1996) which aligns with Foucault's ideas about how "technologies of the self" can affect how individuals transform themselves in order to attain a state of calm, reach happiness, or perfection (quoted by Richardson 2005: 29). In urban environments especially, people shape their subjectivity through mobility.

> Mobile subjects and their real practices, based on logics of mobility and ideas of wants, needs and desires among particular people can be included in relation to the spaces they inhabit, enact, produce and move around, give meaning to and are shaped by. This shows how governmental practices of normalizing, disciplining, forming modern selves and also rationalities relating to mobility rely on particular measurements, conceptualizations, imaginaries and productions of urban spaces. Further it stresses how such – contested – ways of seeing modern selves ... mobile selves in urban spaces also possesses the potential to become part of urban subjects own shaping of their selves, under the constraint of freedom and individual autonomy. (Jensen 2009: 262)

How mobile subjectivity is expressed aesthetically and how the self is shaped through Kenya's *matatu* sector is encapsulated in the story of Joyce, a *matatu* owner, wife, mother, and sister. Joyce had joined Nairobi's route number 44 in 2006. In 2007 I had befriended her brother Chalo who was driving her vehicle, Tythes. Joyce decorated her vehicle with passages from scripture and preferred to have her brothers, who she employed, drive them. She wanted them to play only gospel music because she wanted to "take her Christianity to the street." Not only did she want to capitalize on commuters

---

[3] "The Rock" alludes to Dwayne "The Rock" Johnson, who was a major star of the WWF (World Wrestling Federation, later becoming the WWE, World Wrestling Entertainment) from the years 1996–2004 and 2011–2019.

like her who preferred this type of religious messaging, but she also wanted to feel like she had some sort of claim on urban space. The way Joyce understood the practices of visibility in the *matatu* sector was communicated clearly when she said,

> You have to come up with something unique because the customers like what they see first before they come in. So that is why we did it as a Christian bus and we tried to do something different. Nobody has done this decoration with Christian things. So, I told my designers to work on something different, like it has a lot of God information ... and they researched for some time, they had to look at scripture.

Joyce said that sometimes she sees images on *matatu* vehicles that she does not approve of and uses her vehicle, named Tythes, to combat those negative images with Christian ones. For each Tythes, there were infamous *matatu* vehicles, such as one called Global Terror, adorned with pictures of Osama Bin Laden and George W. Bush with the words "war criminals" splashed on the side (Mutongi 2017). Owners of *matatu* vehicles craft a public persona of their private interests, hobbies, or beliefs. In a city of ever-increasing privatized space that is off-limits to many Kenyans this is a way to lay claims, albeit mobile and shifting claims, on the city itself.

It is not just the faces that are painted on the outside of the vehicle that are important for the attractiveness of the *matatu*, but the one peering at you from behind the window and wheel. The "famous operator" is one of the factors that passengers contemplate while choosing which vehicle to take. In the publication *Matatu Today*, Patrick Theuri was announced as the winner of a contest called "*matatu poa*" (cool *matatu*) because he had received the most call-in votes. The magazine rewarded Patrick with a Nissan minivan and published an interview with him (April 2006). He was chosen for being well known throughout his neighborhood and polite.

Matatu operators supply an important public service and over time, they become well-known fixtures in and around their routes. Being known all over town can be an important part of being a Nairobi resident, and matatu work can provide access to this type of celebrity. Take EZ for example, a young conductor whom I met in Nairobi in 2006. I asked him what the best part of being a conductor was, and he responded matter-of-factly, "because you are known and you know people," glancing over at his friend as if the answer was obvious. He told me that "when you know people, and are known, you are safe anywhere you go." Martin, a thirty-year old *matatu* owner living in Nairobi told me that he made a habit of poaching drivers and conductors who were known on a route. He would offer them a few thousand shillings ($20 to $40 USD) to switch to his new "loaded" *matatu*.

Being known and having a following is also relayed well through Maryam's description of supporting a *matatu* worker whom she knows,

> He is a childhood friend and we grew up together but then again, more like a brother. And that *matatu*, we are used to it, we just get on it because he is working there. So, it is more like promoting him. The more people that are coming because of him the more it is like … if the owner sees that Abda is not on today, I am going to have less people.

For *matatu* operators, much of their social prestige is built on their linguistic skills and mastery over neologisms and because *matatu* operators often represent their neighborhood and route, and their linguistic patterns and mastery of the newest *Sheng* can reflect that. Linguistic research shows that *matatu* operators are important creators and disseminators of the urban slang *Sheng* (Wa-Mungai and Samper 2006; Samper 2002). The networks of *matatu* workers on a route form a type of reputation for the community, some positive, some negative. This large workforce shapes the mobility of Nairobi and its members often come from the communities they serve and as, Tarini Bedi argues, taxi drivers not only are intimately related to the material infrastructure of the city but also in the social infrastructure of "sociality, labor, migration and politics" (2016: 392). This element of the *matatu* forms a social web of infrastructure.

Mbugua wa Mungai, a Kenyan scholar who has done extensive research on the *matatu* sector, remarks that it is common practice to conflate "the crew's identity with that of the mechanical body; the man becomes the car and vice versa" (2013: 74). Crews' stories and the power of joyriding have been dramatized in local Kenyan productions, mainly theatrical and TV, and larger projects throughout the world. In 2015, Netflix released a series called *Sense8*, a science-fiction drama by the Wachowski siblings (creators and directors of *The Matrix* films), which features a *matatu* driver living in Nairobi named Capheus as one of the main characters. Capheus's *matatu* is named after his personal hero, Jean-Claude Van Damme, the Belgian martial artist, and actor. On the side of the vehicle, Van Damme is featured shirtless and kicking an invisible target while sweat flies off his headband. Jela, the conductor of Van Damme, is in charge of collecting money and corralling passengers into the vehicle while playing the role of Capheus' always encouraging best friend.

Throughout the series, Capheus, a good guy who spends all his meager earnings to buy his HIV-positive mother medicine, encounters standard *matatu*-sector trouble (street thugs, hijackers, shady politicians, corrupt police) and defeats them, often spectacularly, with the help of his psychic siblings. In the first season's finale, as the Van Damme *matatu* arrives in town and after most of the passengers departed from the bus, Capheus and Jela realize several passengers have remained seated, claiming that they are not on the *matatu* to go anywhere, they just wanted to ride on the vehicle to absorb some of Capheus' power. They were joyriding – riding the transportation for the journey, not the destination. When Capheus asks why they want to stay on the vehicle just riding around and around, they reply, "we heard the spirit of Jean Claude guided you and protected you ... and now, we're hoping the spirit of Jean Claude will do the same for us." Capheus and Jela look at one another and exchange a knowing smile. Their positive personal reputations were sealed and, therefore, riding their *manyanga* had become an avenue to attaining redemption, fortune, power, and strength, which would mean good money for the foreseeable future. In the show, the commuters were linking the driver's successes to the vehicle and the experience of just riding in the *matatu* itself meant the passengers were consuming some of Van Damme's and Capheus's bravery. As Alessandra Stanley, television reviewer for *The New York Times* observed, "[e]ach story line taps into a different cultural cliché' (2015). It is no mystery as to why the cultural cliché for Nairobi was the life of a *matatu* driver because it shows the ways that *matatu* vehicles, especially *manyangas*, capture the imagination of people in Nairobi and the way they use the *matatu* (both physically and symbolically) in transformative ways. Although *Sense8* features supernatural elements and fantastical story lines, the writers of the series do accurately capture the essence of the joyride as a cultural practice in Nairobi, especially when it comes to the idea that the message of the vehicle is something riders can consume.

Urban Soundscapes and Aural Practices

As anthropologists are being called to look at the ways that the circulation of new technology produces new emplacements for music and sound, youth are instructive for understanding and conceptualizing the aesthetics of urban infrastructure and how it links place and identity. Technologies of mobility, like these urban transportation systems, take on a life of their own, and the spaces of the vehicles can be used and transformed in productive ways. Throughout Kenya, *matatu* vehicles are synonymous with the categories of urban youth culture. For young people in Nairobi, the world of the *matatu* is often understood as their intimate domain. A *manyanga* can create what some anthropologists call a "soundscape," where the vehicle provides a space for the cultural production and consumption of dislocated sounds that accompany new forms of place in the global economy (Samuels et al. 2010; Hirschkind 2006).

Anthropologist Thomas Blom-Hansen describes how through the kombi taxi, Black residents of South Africa explored the formerly White world of beaches, parks, and shopping centers (2006). Then, with the emergence of "swanking taxis," which were kombi taxis that appeared "painted in bright colors and sporting striking and dramatic motifs, seats in matching colors, and huge sound systems," Indian residents of urban South Africa carved out spatial, cultural, and economic claims for themselves in the taxi business (Blom-Hansen 2006: 195). In urban South Africa, like Nairobi, teachers, politicians, parents, and journalists complained that the loud music and flirting that happened in the "swankers" make them like "rolling nightclubs" but their aesthetic and aural themes were also important for establishing identities.

When I asked Maryam, who lives in the neighborhood of Eastleigh, known for its Somali population and its fleet of *manyangas*, if she had any favorite vehicles, she described the one called Limousine, "the maroon one. You've seen it?" When I asked her what she liked about it she said,

> I was more like drawn to the color of it and at the same time, the calligraphy, and the pictures. And at a time, it used to play the best crunk music. Yeah, I was into the crunk. So, I was like oooh, the only *matatu* I can get on and who is going to play crunk at this time is *this matatu*. So, I can get on this. But sometimes when I'm bored ... they put on the bass ... it is *way* [thumbs up, shaking head yes]. At the same time, it is not good for the ears, but at the same time when you're bored, stressed ... it helps. Like, when your mind is dented, and I feel like relaxing, that's what you do.

Maryam loses herself in the music and is consuming the newest songs and best mixes at high volumes as an escape of everyday stress. As Maryam's remarks show, in Kenya having a name, motif, or theme, is crucial to having a successful *matatu*. She talks positively about the name, the color, and the music it plays inside. I asked her what the difference is between listening to music on a *matatu* and listening to music at home and she said,

> The difference is there, because at home you don't have the bass, and at the same time it is hard to go to the studio and say I want this type of song to follow this song. They have the nice mix. But in the *matatu* it's like, just there. It follows up, one hit after the other after the other.

In this case, joyriders like Maryam use the PSV as a therapeutic experience, where she can access not only the music itself, but specific sounds and volume that cannot be accessed on her own.

Music is an integral part of how bodies and cars are synched, and music can provide therapeutic qualities in our lives (Waitt et al. 2017: 3). The interior and exterior aesthetics of manyangas specifically include practices that build urban subjectivities and even work therapeutically, and send expressions of faith out into the world, as exemplified by Joyce and other owners who were trying set a good example by only playing gospel music, and Myriam, retreated to the *matatu* for a listening experience that will be relaxing "when her mind is dented." These mobile aesthetics, interior and exterior, individual and collective, provide a space for the construction of an urban mobile subjectivity. As Tanya Richardson found among participants of walking tours in Odessa, particular types of mobility can construct collective identification and "subvert and recreate aspects of the city as an urban space that is distinct from a national space" (2005: 13). Similarly, joyriders are making the *manyanga* an urban space that is distinct from the city itself and yet, is a way to experience the city.

Noise Pollution

As he moved through ministries, Michuki never strayed too far from the transportation sector that he had successfully "disciplined" years before. In 2008 there was a bylaw passed restricting decorations on *matatu* vehicles. The exterior of a *matatu* is one of the most important canvases for the messages they disseminate. These messages often include concepts from commodity culture, like brand names and celebrity culture ranging from Beyoncé to Obama, but it is also important to realize the way that *matatu* artwork reflects the larger concerns of society, such as the firefight with police featured on the Funkadelic *matatu* pictured earlier in this chapter. This is an important type of social media in Nairobi and an important way that messages about local culture and globalization are spread throughout the city. *Matatu* artwork is also a significant wealth generator for Nairobi artists as it props up a crucial economic sector of garages and graphic designers. *Matatu* designers can make good money and stay constantly busy if they are talented and skilled. Part of what Michuki was doing was also controlling the economic flow to artists and young people working in this industry.

Steve Langat, the driver of Frost, articulated the ability of the vehicle to act as a canvas where alternate views of current events are expressed, described earlier as a counterpublic. When I asked him how he felt about the restrictions on the designs in the sector in 2010, he replied, "*Mbya* [bad] … it's bad … 'cause when you see graffiti … you kind of see culture, Nairobi culture. Cause sometimes they are political, so … you constrain what is in society. Something like that? There is a message in all the colors." From bible quotes to illustrations of violence, *matatu* "colors" reflect the urban context that Nairobi residents live within. From peace activists to mercenaries, *matatu* graphics and the artists who render them attempt to tap into the wide range of urban identities available in Nairobi. The messages in the colors of *matatu* vehicles communicate the positive and negative aspects of urban life. Acting as moving urban publics and counterpublics, the censorship of the messages reflect the power of the vehicles to formulate political subjectivities for urban residents.

By March 2006, the fever of the 2004 Michuki Rules had died down, and John Michuki was in a new government role as Minister of Internal Security. People watching the Kenyan Television Network (KTN), a channel that was highly critical of the government, saw a grainy video of masked men in black, carrying guns, raiding the offices, and destroying the *East African Standard* newspaper's press, burning copies ready for distribution, and beating staff members (Nyabuga 2007).[4] A few days later, journalists from KTN asked Michuki about the incident live on camera. He took responsibility for being the one to shut down the TV station with guns but had no remorse and instead he responded by warning that "if you rattle a snake, you must prepare to be bitten" (Nyabuga 2007). It was later reported that Michuki was provoked by some critical comments made about the government on the station.

Aggressive actions like these continued during the lead-up to the highly anticipated and polarizing 2007 elections, between the incumbent, Mwai Kibaki, and the opposition leader, Raila Odinga. In the evening of 30 December 2007, days after a deeply flawed election, Mwai Kibaki was sworn in for a second term as Kenya's president by a handful of politically powerful elites in the back garden of Kenya's State House (Kiberenge 2022). For nearly two months after this event, violent clashes tore through urban and rural Kenya, infamously culminating in the heinous 2008 act of burning down a church in Kiambaa, with over fifty women and children inside, killing 35 people (Wrong and Williams 2009; Rice 2008). A power-sharing agreement between President Kibaki and Prime Minister Odinga was reached in February of 2008, and kept Michuki in the cabinet as a minister, close advisor, and confidant to the president (Wrong and Williams 2009). Kibaki's "rainbow coalition" that promised so much for the peaceful unity of a multiethnic Kenya, was also tainted by an authoritarianism that was supposed to have gone with Moi.

---

[4] KTN and the *East African Standard* are part of the same media company and were located at the same headquarters.

In 2009, Michuki, who was at this time in the role of Minister of Environment, used NEMA, the National Environmental Management Authority, to implement a bylaw regulating the amount of noise made in the city; if you were over seventy decibels you were liable to a 350,000 KES fine ($4,482 USD at the time) and up to eighteen months in jail (Korongo 2009). It was not only criminal for *matatu* vehicles to play loud music, but also for clubs, bars, private parties and even church services to project sounds above a particular decibel level. His disciplinary actions seemed to be spreading. For *matatu* owners and operators, it was simply another avenue for police officers and the Nairobi City Council to harass *matatu* operators and collect money from them.

Although Michuki did his best to silence dissent through television and *matatu* media forms the aesthetic tradition of *matatu* design never completely disappeared. In November 2014, Kenya's fourth president (and son of the first president Jomo Kenyatta) Uhuru Kenyatta publicly stated that the prohibition on *matatu* "graffiti" should be lifted, and acknowledged the impact on young people when he said, "I don't see anything wrong with artwork and creativity in *matatus*. We should surely support our youth to do business with their talents" (Rajab 2014). *Matatu* owners, graphic artists, crew members, and passengers all collaborate to construct an aesthetic that is sensorily affective as well as globally informed, using international music to create "global soundscapes" and celebrity culture to exhibit their cosmopolitanism, or a global gospel superstar to perform their faith in the street.

To control human movement is to control human interaction, labor, production, sexual desire, the spread of news and the exchange of language and ideas. The regulation of Nairobi's urban space, enacted by constraining the aesthetic and sonic features of *manyangas* is similar to what Ben Chappell describes with regards to lowrider cruising for Latino populations in Los Angeles: the spatio-cultural activity of joyriding, like lowriding, "provides an optic on the politics of the production of space, in tension with the effects of policies, practices and discourses of policing and other factors in the urban spatial regulation" (2010: 28). The regulations on the routes, design and music of *matatu* vehicles can be understood as a way to discipline how the *matatu* sector uses Nairobi's space, and subsequently as a way to discipline young people's use of popular transportation to experience Nairobi. As governments attempt to control urban space through the planning and development of the built environment in cities across the world, the innovative way that people move in and around city spaces changes urban landscapes in unexpected and potentially subversive ways.

Conclusion

People think about their neighborhoods through *matatu* vehicles. Some people, especially in particular middle-class neighborhoods use *matatu* vehicles to help construct their identities as urban, disruptive, creative, global, and cosmopolitan. The *matatu* sector transforms public urban space both on an individual level, among the passengers and in their interactions with other passengers, crew members, and the vehicle itself, and by shaping the landscape of the city in larger, more far-reaching ways. As Gupta and Ferguson argue, anthropologists should examine "how places achieve their identity as places, whilst including thinking about geographical and physical space along with how communities are formed through clusters of interactions" (1992: 8). Nothing better describes a "cluster of interactions" than public transportation. The mobile collective that is formed by gathering in proximity and traveling is relational, emotional, and transformative.

The practice of joyriding provides a productive and layered ethnographic example of making everyday places meaningful individually and collectively. The sensual aesthetics of the *manyanga,* music, artwork and the physical transformation of urban boundaries transforms the physical space of Nairobi at multiple scales. Placemaking also promotes shared understandings of places and the association of identities and memories with these places. *Matatu* route reputations are symbolic outcomes of thinking along these lines, while understanding a practice like joyriding as placemaking allows for deeper insights related to how commuters use and transform infrastructures into publics and counterpublics, and the potentials for those to formulate political subjectivities.

By looking at how joyriding is physically and symbolically transformative at various scales from *manyanga* to neighborhood, to route, to city, and ultimately to nation we see how mobile encounters in public space are composite and heterogeneous. Through the consumption of popular cultural media in music, videos, images, and even languages, the *matatu* is a place of leisure and a disruption of proper or normative values, through which *matatu* crews and their well-known vehicles disseminate neighborhood class, and ethnic dynamics, encoded in linguistic practices that take ideas, words, news, and gossip along with their passengers from neighborhood to urban core several times a day. These route reputations are built on the vehicles and crew members and the neighborhoods that they serve. As joyriders ride these vehicles, they are representatives and consumers of their route reputation or identity. The route identities are even often bounded by linguistic codes of deep *Sheng* as this chapter's epigraph indicates, where people look down on people just going round and round in the car. As a place of cultural production, the *manyanga* can feel like a powerful expression of one's own voice in the seemingly endless and deafening cacophony of the urban environment.

A similar practice to joyriding, called the *skwad*, which is a trip from a neighborhood to town and back will be explored in the next chapter. *Skwads* structure the economic lives of *matatu* workers and make up the units of which they base payments, including the dangerous negotiations they engage in with formal and informal authorities on the street.

3

Taking a *Skwad*: The Dangerous Negotiations of Redistribution

We are not bad people. The owners know we are stealing from them. It is not really stealing … we say, utanijenga, *you will build me. They know that they need to help us. So, it is not stealing.* – Maina, Nairobi, 2010

The workers in the *matatu* sector form part of Nairobi's eclectic hustle economy (Thieme 2018) who make do in the aftermath of the globalized spread of neoliberal policies in its various forms of economic liberalization, privatization, and deregulation (for example in the form of structural adjustment programs during 1980s and 1990s), which expanded and accelerated the scope of the "informal sector" and the local experiences of economic uncertainty (Thieme et al. 2021). Over time, these workers have provided an important foundation to the country's infrastructure and have subsequently become targets of the Kenyan state's disorganized approach to transportation service provision (Klopp 2012) as scapegoats for Kenyan citizens' bad commuting behavior (Mutongi 2006) and outlets for commuters' dissatisfaction with life in the city (Wa-Mungai and Samper 2006).

Although technically illegal under colonial law, as discussed earlier, pirate taxis provided necessary services in the late-colonial era and facilitated this by paying small bribes to Traffic Police. The police, like anyone else living or working in Nairobi, could see clearly that the city had been underserved in public transportation since the beginning of the colonial bus monopoly in 1934. As Mains and Kinfu observed in Ethiopia among motorcycle taxis, "[u]ltimately, when states fail to provide basic public services, human infrastructures intertwine with particular materials and technologies to generate conflicting moral discourses concerning the politics of infrastructure' (2017: 264). The conflicting moral discourses embedded in Nairobi's *matatu* sector today, including workers' and commuters' relationships with police and extortionist groups, provide valuable insights into the social forms of the urban economy and the way it functions daily. Understanding that what are largely seen as theft, extortion, and general illegality are also redistributive elements of the urban economy helps us to understand Maina's words, which open this chapter. Maina emphasizes that this redistribution is not trickery or deceit, but open obligation: "They know they need to help us." Therefore, forms of redistribution at work in the hustle economy can be and often are stable, circular economies, which complicate scholarly understandings of employer, employee, obligation, friendship, kinship, generational relationships, moral economies, and solidarity.

The emphasis on these practices as particularly negative has appeared to some scholars as work that reinforces anti-Black, orientalist discourse (French 2000). Recently, scholars have argued that the experiences of contemporary hustlers are much more complicated than earlier connotations imply (del Nido 2022; Thieme et al. 2021; Di Nunzio 2019). In 2005, Tony, a *matatu* conductor in Nairobi describes the precarity experienced in *matatu* work as a cycle of working, making the boss mad, getting confronted about the money that was made and getting fired, only for both to ultimately swallow their pride as they realize there is "no alternative":

> This *matatu* work, we call it a contract job. It is not permanent. Today, I'll be driving this, tomorrow I'll be driving that. Today, I'll work with this *matatu*, at the end of the day I'll go see the boss and maybe he won't be happy with what we made and he'll just tell me, straight to my face, "Hey. Listen, I'm not happy about it ... so tomorrow, find your own way, OK?" So, I mean, in the morning, I just wake up, go to the stage and you know ... just wait. Something will come up. So, we call it a contract job, but we don't hold grudges with them. 'Cause, I mean, he'll sack me today and after a week or two he'll see ... there is no alternative. He'll say, "Ok, fine. Even if he made a mistake once or twice, I mean [click, a sound made to signal annoyance or, in this case, resignation] just come to work."

The hustle economy creates a particular relationship to labor that is marked by often antithetical and contradictory activities and paradoxical experiences of competition, cooperation, selfishness, and reciprocity.

Building on conceptualizations of social infrastructure (Elyachar 2010; Simone 2004) and Janet Roitman's (2005) study of fiscal disobedience, whereby the legitimacy of regulatory authority is questioned and undermined, *matatu* workers challenge multiple levels of state and non-state regulation through a variety of practices that blend danger, violence, and control with solidarity, reciprocity, and redistribution. As much as the *matatu* sector is an example of African creativity in the face of colonial oppression, it is impossible to overlook the multiple modes of suffering that are embedded in the relationships between owners and workers as well as the extreme risks many of the participants experience while working in a sector that is both perceived as victim and victimizer. As Jacob Doherty (2017) argues regarding the motorcycle taxi drivers of Uganda, concepts such as "collaboration" which are integral to the theorization of people as infrastructure (Simone 2004) must also consider the physical and symbolic violence that is operationalized through infrastructural means (Rodgers and O'Neill 2012).

Transportation policy makers and development scholars argue that instead of a target system, owners should pay paratransit operators a weekly or monthly salary or do away with cash altogether and move to cashless transportation technology in the form of transportation cards and card reading gadgets (Behrens et al. 2017). One important reason the target system remains ingrained in the sector is that many *matatu* owners service their loan payments daily with the cash they receive from their crews, but there are additional reasons to keep cash flowing, discussed below. And, although the Government of Kenya required in 2012 that all *matatu* vehicles be put under control of management companies called Savings and Credit Co-operatives (SACCOs), which were perceived to be better at controlling the "bad behavior" of the sector in Nairobi, most SACCOs still pay their drivers using some version of a target system instead of a salary (Plano 2022; Klopp and Mitullah 2015).

In Nairobi, the "target" amount of money an owner expects to see delivered by his driver and/or conductor at the end of the day usually comes from research done by the owner before joining the route. In addition to their loan payments, owners calculate the distance of routes in their entirety to understand how many trips can be completed in one day, multiplying that by the number of seats in their vehicle – from fourteen to sixty. In 2019, the daily target payouts were around 4,000 KES for small vehicles ($40 USD) and 5,000 KES to 8,000 KES ($50 USD to $80 USD) or more for larger vehicles – what remained after filling the tank with fuel was what drivers and conductors took home, around 600 KES to 800 KES ($6 USD to $8 USD). In relative terms, this, and its equivalent today makes a good wage in Nairobi considering that *matatu* rides range from 10 to 100 shillings, and lunch can be eaten for 50 shillings. This means *matatu* operators can cover their daily expenses while having some disposable income left over. This is another reason why *matatu* operators are seen as hyper urban and modern – they always have a bit of cash on hand.

To understand the potential profit that can come from each route, owners must consider several factors common to daily commuter life in addition to loan payments, fuel costs and the number of seats. They must also understand the impacts of Nairobi's built environment, as well as the social relationships that infiltrate nearly every aspect of the sector, especially the complicated redistributive networks with which crew members engage. These include time delays of Nairobi's infamous traffic jams, and the frequent payoffs to police, as well as payouts to non-state security groups, like members of *Mungiki*, a well-documented vigilante gang with a historically violent and economically extractive relationship with the *matatu* sector (Wamue 2001, Anderson 2002, Rasmussen 2012). Additionally, as interlocutors informed me several times, members of *Kamjesh* – small, neighborhood groups consisting of mostly young men who, although seen as less violent than *Mungiki*, are still menacing to *matatu* workers – demand small payouts with each interaction. Some or all of these factors may or may not be present on each individual route.

Taking a *Skwad*: Managing Reciprocity

As owners consider the structural and social factors of each route, how do they decide who will be operating their million-shilling vehicles, especially when all potential *matatu* workers are deemed untrustworthy? Even when hiring a brother, neighbor or friend, owners know that workers will inevitably redistribute at least some of the money the vehicle makes to other young, unemployed, or underemployed people, generally in their own neighborhood. Young people (touts) fill the vehicles or fill in for drivers or conductors on single trips to town and back. These one-off trips are called *skwad* or *skwadi* and support several important functions in the social infrastructure of transportation in Nairobi. *Skwad* or *skwadi* can simply mean "to take turns" or, more specifically for *matatu* workers, refers to the loop from neighborhood to town and back. *Matatu* workers will generally refer to their trips as a *skwad*, but *skwads* are also something that can be traded, gifted, or owed.

Often the permanent driver or conductor will find someone to take a *skwad* if they want to take a break or need to run an errand. They hand over the *matatu* they have been entrusted with to another, often semi-experienced but under- or unemployed *matatu* worker. They then pay that person a small sum of money to take the trip to town. Depending on the route, one *skwad* could take several hours and earn 100 KES or more ($1–$2 USD). Although extremely important in the *matatu* sector and part of what makes the sector run so smoothly, this on-demand labor force is also another reason why this job is seen to produce immoral and untrustworthy people. Two key factors of the *skwad* play into this negative perception: one is that *skwads* are used as a type of on-the-job training, which bothers passengers who feel as though they are not in safe hands when new or inexperienced workers are behind the door or the wheel. It makes people feel anxious when they see someone playing musical chairs with their transportation vehicle. Second, when owners see their *matatu* in the street, they may not recognize the driver behind the wheel, instilling feelings of frustration and betrayal in owners who do not know who is driving their very expensive investment. Interlocutors often shared stories of a *matatu* being stopped by police only to have the driver run away, leaving the vehicle unattended and in the middle of the road, because they were merely taking a *skwad* and were not the official driver of the vehicle and lacked the proper paperwork.

The complicated labor practices embedded in the sector and the redistributive activities of *matatu* workers themselves are important issues that are often overlooked, or even derided, when it comes to policy overhauls for the transportation sector like BRT or cashless transportation technology. The calculation of Nairobi driver Jackson that that "each *matatu* employs one hundred people" includes his fellow workers, as well as the police and the gangs who depend on underlying ideas of reciprocity as operators redistribute the cash that flows through the *matatu* business to other young people. It should be noted that these redistributive networks are often fraught with distrust, jealousy, and tension around proper payments. No matter how small or insignificant the payouts may be, there are often lingering questions around the relationships in question. For example, Steve, who had worked consistently with the same conductor for nearly a year when we met, openly admitted to not fully trusting that he was always giving him an honest 50/50 cut of the daily profits in Frost. Many drivers echoed this concern and even boasted of their ability to keep track of the money from watching, counting, and calculating passenger trips through the rearview mirror.

> **Steve**: Conductor [sighing deeply and laughing] is another ... biggest ... headache [laughing]. 'Cause most of them, they get to interact with the customer more than the driver. Some of them, you might hear them speaking, arguing, with the customers and being arrogant. Plus, on top of that, whatever, he is not being transparent. You find that at the end of the day he removed, like, um ... 500, and he expects, uh, you, you share the salary you are getting in the evening so that one becomes unfair.
>
> **MF**: So you don't trust your conductor?
>
> **Steve**: Actually, I don't, I don't ... I don't. Ok, actually, I don't like changing them regularly but I'm forced to change them. There are those who are serious, but that person who is serious – a serious guy, is one who is working somewhere. So, that is it...
>
> **MF**: So this guy is kind of a thief?
>
> **Steve**: Uh, yeah ... uh, let's say it is mischief [laughing] yeah. I don't have a conductor I can really trust at the moment, but I used to have, I used to have. Uh and then, sometimes the vehicle can develop problems

and what and what. He was not faithful enough to wait for this vehicle to be fixed. He went to another vehicle.

MF: So how do you find a new conductor?

Steve: So easy, come in the morning without a conductor. There are many, let me say, idlers – those people who look for somewhere for a day. So there are many but they don't have manners [trailing off, laughing].

With the high turn-around in matatus, operators employ various techniques to build trust with their conductors.

Rasta George: Maybe you see a driver and conductor. A driver, when he going there, going to Morengo or taking people here or there and maybe he is taking 390 shillings. You can get some conductors telling the driver we have say they have 350. And the driver knows that money is 390.

Steve: So ... you are counting.

Rasta George: You are counting, you are counting and that is where the trust is coming

Steve: So you can do it like randomly, like three times, tomorrow one time ... if you are getting incorrect amounts.

So, then how are trust and solidarity built? Many people assume that it is predicated on ethnic connections. However, the following data confounds this:

MF: Does employment have to do with ethnicity?

Many: ...no, no...

George: No ... this [sector] is very accommodating.

MF: Is this the only industry that is like that?

Steve: (after a pause) ...in fact, it is.

Rasta George: 'Cause you can get someone who is Jaluo, and they are working with a Kisii, a Jaluo working with a Kikuyu, a Kikuyu working with a ... Kalenjin, *nani* [whoever].

Steve: Not even working ... cause I'm carrying you. When I am carrying passengers I don't tell them ... if you are not Kalenjin, then don't get in here ...

MF: Right, so it is an equalizer ...

Steve: Yeah, we don't ... discriminate.

MF: Why? Even I can be a *makanga* [conductor], which is crazy.

Steve: [to me] It is not crazy, but it is good. We have so many things in common, when it comes to this big nation, this society, against the government.

Wilson: We have a common set of problems ...

MF: And that overrides your ethnicity?

Many: Yeah ...

The tolerance does not end with coworkers though, which also provides further hope for the possible futures of urban environments.

In the face of massive unemployment and underemployment, the redistribution of *matatu* cash through the mechanism of taking a *skwad* is a nice example of the multifaceted nature of the hustle economy. As Abdoulique Simone points out, "African cities are characterized by incessantly flexible, mobile, and provisional intersections of residents that operate without clearly delineated notions of how the city is to be inhabited and used" (2004: 407). Reflecting a classic *matatu* "hustle" that pivots on a notion of reciprocity giving a *skwad* to younger or less supported workers builds the next generation of workers through both violating the trust of the owners while providing supportive assistance to friends and coworkers. Then "these conjunctions become an infrastructure – a platform providing for and reproducing life in the city" (Simone 2004: 408). As in the case of the *skwad*, human infrastructures depend on specific methods of organizing labor that fits the nature of the work (Mains and Kinfu 2017: 273).

Often, at the end of the day owners miss their target amount, and operators come equipped with explanations of how funds were lost to outside actors – usually police and gangs. These outside actors are like hidden toll booths around the city and not only impact the bottom line of *matatu* owners but also add to the negative reputation *matatu* operators experience. The payoffs to police and gangs vary depending on the route but can cost up to 500 KES or more ($5–$8 USD), a day, and refusing to pay can often come with severe consequences. As one driver said, "In Dandora ... the owners of the vehicles are told, 'you will pay.' Every morning you pay Ksh700. So, to work in those routes, you have to be hard-core," meaning not only that *matatu* vehicles must make a lot of trips during the day, but also that they have to protect themselves from the people who collect on those payments. In the summer of 2019, a middle-aged, executive member of one of the oldest and largest SACCOs in Nairobi commented on police payoffs by saying that he "buys the police their breakfast every morning," giving them 200 KES ($2–$3 USD) in order to avoid other issues (traffic stops, arrests, harassment) throughout the rest of the day. This SACCO manages over 200 *matatu* vehicles and they all pay 200 KES to the police daily, totaling a hefty payout to police of around 40,000 KES ($400 USD) every day. As part of their daily calculations, *matatu* operators and owners therefore often take these payouts into account. Whatever the set target is, they not only have to pay for fuel and for themselves, but also must pay police and gangs and redistribute money to other young unemployed and underemployed workers. It is important to note here that due to these payouts, vehicles that are not roadworthy and that are quite dangerous can often be kept on the road well past what is deemed to be safe for a PSV, which adds to the traffic accidents and negative perceptions of the sector.

Fiscal Disobedience

The mobile, urban spaces where *matatu* workers make their living resemble what some scholars refer to as economic edges or frontiers of capitalism (Tsing 2011; Roitman 2005). People at these economic edges are often targets of violent measures by groups and institutions aiming to poach, control, and regulate their productive economic and social practices. The relationship between groups becomes a somewhat coordinated, but tense, dance along dangerous and shifting grounds of legality. Part of what makes these edges or frontiers dangerous and shifting is that they are often subject to a variety of state and non-state regulatory actors and activities, many of which can be aggressive, intimidating, punitive, and violent. Janet Roitman describes these various actors as characteristic of the "pluralization in regulatory authority" (2005: 151). The participants in these sectors – *matatu* workers in this case, bandits in Roitman's – often resist, undermine, and ultimately negotiate with formal (police) and informal (*Mungiki* and *Kamjesh*) regulatory authorities alike.

This was also precisely the case for the pirate taxis (precursors to *matatu*) that emerged to provide services to the neglected African settlements in violation of the Kenya Bus Service (KBS) monopoly in the late 1950s. These mobile entrepreneurs were creating a new frontier of wealth creation by filling a void in service where the KBS was failing to provide (see Chapter 1). Robert Heinze argues that "*Matatu* owners, once they had become established, began efforts to self-regulate, control new market entries, and stabilize the network to ensure profits, and to this end, they cooperated with state institutions such as the police" (2018: 17). Owners could only self-regulate through cooperation with police, which often included paying them small bribes, and in some respects, owners, workers, and police were all developing regulatory practices alongside the formal reaches of the state.

Debates around transportation in the 1960s, including the requests to local government to rethink the KBS monopoly and the eventual legalization, or decriminalization, of the pirate taxi sector by Kenyatta, offer an interesting angle on the transition from colony to nation (Mutongi 2017). Throughout the 1960s, pirate taxi drivers were repeatedly reported in the newspaper for criminal activities. They were arrested, fined, beaten up, or they were wanted for beating up others and/or stealing fares without taking people to their desired destination. From its inception, the popular transportation sector in Kenya has been fiercely competitive and, although unregulated by the formal government, beholden to rules and norms of its own. As the number of vehicles and operators grew, the debates also grew louder and more polarized; each side used transport as a screen onto which to project their vision of independence and proper Kenyan behavior. Pirate taxis proliferated because they were necessary even though the colonial government wanted to maintain that they were in gross violation of the monopoly agreement.

The first official complaints of pirate taxis located in the archive were made by Mr. Chun in 1960, but the police response to his complaint said that this had come up the year prior, in 1959 (see Chapter 1). By May of 1961, a large-scale police operation was launched against the pirate taxis and "over 80 vehicles were taken to the police vehicle examination center at Wilson Airport, of which 72 were found to be unroadworthy" and one inspector described the vehicles as "death traps" (*Daily Nation* 1961). These police crackdowns, like the ones that captured over eighty vehicles were common in the years just before independence as the local government had to protect their investment in the KBS monopoly. But who were these pirates? And where were they getting all these unroadworthy vehicles anyway?

Concerning the following two years, as the crackdowns continued, some questions can be answered through newspaper reports. In March of 1962, Magistrate Thompson fined Thuo Mariga, a pirate taxi man, 800 KES for driving from Makadara Estate to Nairobi ("Taxi man fined," 1962). It was reported that the driver had stopped the vehicle at Makadara bus stop and asked two plain clothes police officers if they wanted a ride to Nairobi. Upon entering the city center, Mariga asked them each for 30 cents as fare.[1] Reports on similar police crackdowns on pirate taxi drivers revealed that many of the drivers rounded up by the police were drivers of private firms using their vehicles as taxis on the way to work. Therefore, the common "pirate" was

---

[1] Please note that thirty cents is "*mapeni matatu.*"

someone who was using their access to a private car to give fellow workers a ride to work. Most of the time, the vehicles were said to be unroadworthy, and the drivers agreed to get their vehicles in proper condition. This, *carpooling*, to use the parlance of our times, was in direct violation of the KBS monopoly agreement that had been set in 1934. The men operating the vehicles were "pirates" because they were stealing customers from the KBS, and ultimately the Nairobi City Council (NCC). As the city limits expanded and the residents of the outer Eastland suburbs became more integrated with the city center, there were no bylaws in place to govern these settlements, and the NCC and the British company United Transport were at odds with one another regarding the franchise agreement. In these outer suburbs, because of the lack of bylaws, police could not, and did not, enforce the KBS monopoly. It seems very possible that it was not only easy for the police in Nairobi to overlook the "crime" of carpooling, but that it was also necessary as the city strained under the weight of increased urbanization on the eve of independence.

As Kenyan independence came and went, the city boomed, and the pirate taxis increasingly appeared in the streets and in the daily newspapers. The titles of the articles in the *Daily Nation* newspaper archives (see References) show the harsh penalties from fines to prison sentences for pirate drivers, but also a pushback from the drivers and the leaders of the Kenya Transport and Allied Workers Union (KTAWU). In one instance in 1964, the Secretary of the union argued against the Transport Licensing Board (TLB) crackdowns saying these pirate taximen "had decided to earn a living by constitutional means" (*Daily Nation* 1964). In 1965, NCC vowed to take more direct action against the pirate taxis, threatening a fine of 50 pounds or imprisonment of up to one month or both as well as threatening passengers of pirate taxis for "aiding and abetting the offence" (*Daily Nation* 1965). In 1966, after KBS drivers stopped work as a protest to a perceived insult from President Kenyatta, "hundreds of people were left stranded without transport in the town and industrial areas and pirate taxis from near-by locations swarmed" the area (*Daily Nation* 1966). In between the summer of 1966 and the fall of 1967, the pirate taxis started to be referred to as *matatu* vehicles. In an article from September 1967, a report from Nyeri indicated that a chairman of the Nyeri City Council condemned those who threatened to join the opposition if the government went ahead with plans to withdraw *matatu* service from the district. An eyewitness account from a public hearing about the potential withdrawal said, "a woman gave birth to a child on her way to hospital owing to the scarcity of transport after the removal of the *matatu* service" (*Daily Nation* 1967).

A *Nation Magazine* feature by Martin Njoroge is an early journey into the then-little-known world of the *matatu* business. Njoroge went on several undercover *matatu* journeys in 1970 as an investigative reporter, writing that he, "[w]as left in no doubt about why they are so popular," because it took him both less money and less time to get to his destinations in Eastleigh and Kariobangi (1970). He describes the vehicles as "equipped with wooden forms that serve as seats for passengers," stating that one vehicle can seat up to thirty people and reports from interviews that, "most users were against any move to clamp down on the *matatus*" because "had it not been for their operations about half of the city workers living in the locations or in the suburbs would be late for work every day" (Njoroge 1970). Njoroge reported on the stigma already present in the sector when he states: "Many *matatu* owners did not want to talk about their businesses and some said they preferred an honest living to engaging in criminal activity" (1970). The commuters complained that the Nairobi City Council did not allow the country buses to go to the city center and that the bus station was built too far from the main city area so causing inconvenience for up-country people working in the city. Njoroge describes the relationship between the pirate taxis and the police at this point:

> It is amusing to watch the *matatus* play hide and seek with the police. When one sights a police van they speed away. Often, when the driver knows he's been spotted, he will ask all passengers to alight before the police arrive and then there is no proof that there were passengers. (1970)

A letter appearing in the *Daily Nation* newspaper in December 1970 echoed Njoroge's findings. The letter writer is against the pirate taxis, now known as *matatus*, due to their susceptibility to accidents and speed, but complains that the "sensible men and women who value their lives" use *matatu* vehicles because "those who can afford to own cars or to pay for well-maintained but expensive taxis don't fully appreciate the economic urge for the bulk of the population to travel fast and cheaply" (*Daily Nation* 1970). The letter writer goes on to say that if established transport services were sufficient, the *matatu* would go out of business. Not long after this letter was written, in 1973, Jomo Kenyatta decriminalized the *matatu* by Presidential decree and for the next decade, the *matatu* sector experienced a relatively positive status as an entrepreneurial enterprise (Mutongi 2006) that, for many, provided a path to the middle class (Mutongi 2017).

By the end of the 1980s, Moi's relationship with informal transportation workers soured in light of his increasingly authoritarian approach to opposition, marked by his banning of the Matatu Vehicle Owners Association (MVOA) (Chitere and Kibua 2004: 5). Throughout the late 1980s and early 1990s, news of slum clearances and oppressive government actions spread through the public in the form of cassette tapes containing political commentary, speeches, and popular music in support of multi-party politics (Haugerud 1995: 28). When Moi heard about this "seditious music" playing in *matatu* vehicles he banned all music in the collective taxis, but once out of the reach of the state and on the street, the vehicles continued to blast popular forms of music and political commentary (Haugerud 1995: 30). In the face of mounting pressure against the one-party state in Kenya, the reach of Moi's declarations banning people from gathering without a permit, or playing music in their cars, was limited by the collective and mobile space of the *matatu*. Activists in the political opposition would tape record political rallies, speeches and sermons and would circulate them to *matatu* drivers who would play them for their passengers. For Haugerud, *matatu* vehicles were "creative channels for expressing versions of current history that differs from official scripts" (1995: 45). Just as in the colonial era, as the KBS buses provided a unique public space where private tensions and struggles (physical and symbolic) were worked out, the *matatu* vehicles of the Moi era were also spaces to share or openly debate politics, which had no other capacity in everyday life. As Moi's authoritarian practices increased throughout the 1990s, *matatu* vehicles became one of the only spaces where people could gather somewhat freely.

As the ownership and operation of informal transportation vehicles gradually became accepted, the government increasingly debated the safety versus necessity of the vehicles. Throughout Moi's twenty-two years in office, the relationship with the informal economy was dynamic. At times, the administration would be touting the benefits of the informal economy and the "*jua-kali*fication" of Nairobi, while simultaneously clearing hawkers and demolishing markets (King 1996). In this environment, the *matatu* sector resisted any real regulations on safety or capital accumulation, and for many years operated any way they wanted, as Moi and his cronies collected the profits from his role as the head of the gatekeeper state. In 2010, an older driver, Jesse, told me a story about how things were different under Moi. He recounted a time when there was a big push to limit the number of standing passengers in the 1990s for safety reasons. Moi responded by telling all *matatu* owners to add a bar to the ceiling of their vehicles so that standing passengers could hold on. In Nairobi today, it is still common for many minibuses that carry over thirty people to have a bar on the ceiling to grab, if needed.[2] Instead of supporting safety regulations that limited passengers, Moi embraced the risky elements of the sector, further embedding and legitimating all practices of the informal economy, including the corruption that was already entangled in the sector's everyday business.

---

[2] It is helpful not only to hold on to when the vehicle is moving, but also when you are coming to a stop and you need to make your way from the back to the front of the bus.

The 1980s was a turning point whereby, in the vacuum of state power, route associations that used informal, and often secretive, coercive, and even violent means to control the popular transportation sector (Mutongi 2006: 553). Powerful players entered and took control of the sector emerged, but it is important to be precise about the variation in the owner population. It was well known that transportation was, as Roitman suggests, an economic "frontier" where unregulated wealth production blossomed for both major and minor players (2005). Even Moi started a bus company, called Nyayo Bus, and subsidized it through government funds.[3] Thinking he could improve on the sector, he employed a National Youth Service (NYS) to operate the buses and stages, trained them in driving and customer service, so that the conductors were friendly and moral (Abiero-Gariy 1989: 33). Nyayo Bus was supposed to provide cheaper, better transportation in direct competition with the *matatu* sector, which after thirty years was seen to need a makeover. It was supposed to make an enjoyable, moral, and comfortable ride for the citizenry, but eventually, as Jesse explained it to me in 2010, it went under because of "corruption and poor management."

As the pluralization of regulatory authority has become institutionalized, *matatu* operators dynamically engage those they encounter every day, whether it be owners, police, or gangs – consistently negotiating the price of payouts to police and gangs, in order to further negotiate their payout to owners and, finally, themselves. *Matatu* workers often justify their participation in bribery (with police), extortion (by gangs) and theft (from owners) through a lens of paying themselves first as young workers and others like them, in order to build the life they feel they are owed. These choices can be seen as acts of "fiscal disobedience," whereby citizens attempt to sabotage regulatory authority as a response to what is seen as a mismanagement of private wealth, through taxes and other regulatory measures, for the public good (Roitman 2005). As with the trading and selling of *skwads*, *matatu* operators are both undermining the power of the state by avoiding keeping up to date with certificates and licenses and "disobedient" employees in order to maximize their own daily wage, while also redistributing wealth to others in similarly precarious positions. It is as part of this logic that payouts and bribes are a necessary part of the job. In turn, the ways that police prey on the *matatu* sector is evidence of their own hustles and fiscal disobedience. Instead of regulating the vehicles and taking them to court where the fines are hefty, police tax *matatu* vehicles through their own logics and for their own ends. *Matatu* operators' fiscally

---

[3] *Nyayo* means footprint and was another one of Moi's political slogans. It symbolized following in his footstep and letting him lead the way. Following behind without saying anything and offering up your complete trust (Haugerud 1995: 82).

disobedient practices perpetuate their stigma of untrustworthiness and their placement at the bottom of moral hierarchies in Kenyan society. As *matatu* operators take on the work, they take on these practices and the competing moral discourses that follow.

Dangerous Negotiations of Redistributive Labor

In 2002, the now defunct trade magazine *Matatu Today* published a statistic that claimed 4 percent of *matatu* vehicles on the road were owned by police; however, it is difficult to trust these statistics, as it is illegal for police to own *matatu* vehicles according to the Public Officers and Ethics Act passed in 2006. Due to the prohibition of police ownership of *matatu* vehicles, officers tend to hide the fact that they are in the transport business. James, a senior member of the transport police with whom I was put in contact because he was known to own several *matatu* vehicles, denied owning any vehicles for several hours before finally admitting that he had been in the sector for years and owned three vehicles. Once he was comfortable, he was casual about the deeply rooted connection between police and the *matatu* sector. He explained that in the 1980s and 1990s, "[d]uring Moi, it was fine for police to line their pockets with money from the *matatu* industry, now, in 2010…" shaking his head no and waving his hand, implying that police did not make as much as they once had. Still, once he heard that I had been moonlighting as a conductor on route #48, with the 14-seater *matatu*, Frost, he assured me that I would not get in trouble if I worked on his *matatu* signaling that they still enjoyed some level of impunity.

James explained that by working on a vehicle owned by a police officer, you do not spend all day in court or a jail cell, like other operators do. He claimed that police often hide their *matatu* ownership and even their colleagues do not know if they have one. They send people in their place to get the vehicle out of jail, if they find themselves there, which many reportedly do not. When I asked him if there were still a lot of police who own *matatu* vehicles, he answered as though I had asked a ridiculous question, and explained that they indeed owned them, "but through proxies … so they never go to court." He clarified that "such *matatus* are not even arrested, by the way … because it belongs to them." By this he seemed to imply somewhat contradictorily that police know which vehicles are owned by other police and may even be positioned on routes where their own *matatus* are working, operating like an open secret. Working for a police owner has other privileges, as Tony, a Nairobi conductor pointed out to me during a discussion we had in 2005:

> Most of these *matatus* are owned by police. So, they get a phone call, they release it. Whoooosh [hand motion to show it is gone] and it's off,

you know. It's advantageous cause you ... get arrested and you say, "my boss ... is a ... is a big boss." So, I won't worry much, even if they put me in jail, he'll just come and tell them, "Hey! He's my worker, OK. So, get out! Go back to work!"

Thus, the relationship between police and *matatu* operators is deeply connected and intertwined, mutually constituted through their illicit economic relationship. This speaks not only to the lived experience of *matatu* hustles, which blurs the line of legality for workers, owners, and gang members, but attends to the fiscal disobedience that law enforcement officials practice themselves.

The list of offenses for which a police officer can arrest a *matatu* are seemingly endless. As I was told more than once, "[e]very *matatu* on this road is guilty." Given that no *matatu* vehicle is deemed truly roadworthy, according to Kenya's official road rules and regulations, in order to operate in the business, one must be willing to pay a bribe or go to jail. Steve often complained, "they can always take you in and charge you with touting. And, in a court of law, you can never prove you are not touting." Steve further articulates interactions and motivations for the constant bribery of police by *matatu* operators in the following statement:

> The issue of corruption is ripe on our roads, okay. We are compelled to be corrupt cause whenever the traffic officer come here and tell you "I'm going to charge you with the offense of obstruction and what..." In the court of law it goes for 10,000 [shillings], or 10 to 15,000 ... and this *askari* will need 1,000 or 1,500. Okay! It's not right, but what do I do? One thing, in a court of law, you lose a lot of time, you waste a lot of time. You know in a court of law ... seatbelts, uh, mostly charged from 500 to 300. It's a small amount, but uh, the time – you take the whole day. As in, you are arrested in the morning, most of them, they arrest you at 7:30 to 8:00am – sadly, yeah. You miss work. Cause in the ... you'll be released at around 3 or 4pm in the evening, [laughing] ... for a seatbelt.

Steve presented a common justification of *matatu* operators, along with non-PSV drivers on the roads of Nairobi as well when he talks about the cost in terms of revenue and lost time it may take to deal with the offense.

In addition to these concerns, another consequence facing *matatu* workers is extended jail time. While asking if *matatu* operators can end up in jail for more than six months, a route manager replied that "some that have been in there more than that, even up to eighteen months." Steve went on to explain that "When you argue with these policemen, depending on what is said, when he takes you with him, there will be like seven counts." Rasta George, the dreadlocked conductor from Nairobi, articulated how these fines and charges can quickly add up listing the offenses: "Contravening if you can't pay the 18,000 [180 USD] then three months. Obstruction ... 8,000 [$80 USD)] ... four months. No uniform ... one month ... so many." In this way, *matatu* operators only stay on the roads through developing fiscal relationships with the police, who are simultaneously a proxy for state regulation, but operate their own hustle that is both a threatening and violent element of the *matatu* ecosystem.

Along the route a *matatu* may encounter uniformed police who are also owners of vehicles, but that is only the beginning of the story. The following is an excerpt of a longer conversation I had with many members of the route Steve worked on, route #48 to Kileleshwa, while we were sitting in a *matatu* that was awaiting its turn to be filled at the Odeon stage in Nairobi's city center in 2009. Several people sitting in *matatu* vehicles chatting, napping or simply reading the paper is a common occurrence at *matatu* stages throughout the city center. It is worth quoting the conversation in this style because it shows ethnographically how *matatu* operators banter with one another and corroborate their experiences.

MF (author): Does harassment by police bother you?

Rasta George: A lot...

James: ...they bother us a lot...

George: *Askaris* are a major problem...

Wilson: City Council *askaris*.

MF: City Council *askaris* are even worse than the Traffic Police?

George: Yeah, worse...

Wilson: Then there is Rhino...

James: Yeah.

MF: Those are undercover police, right?

James: Yeah.

Rasta George: ...undercover...

MF: But they are police though?

Rasta George: Yeah.

Steve: And there are Rhino, A.P.

MF: A.P.? [never hearing of this one before, I was surprised] What do they look like?

Steve: They are also undercover but at times ... they wear a uniform.

MF: With a blue hat ... ?

Rasta George: No with a black hat ... with a jungle...

MF: Oh ... with camouflage?

Rasta George: Yeah, camouflage.

MF: So, you have to deal with all of those people every day? Which ones are the worst?

Gladys: All of them are worst [like that was a very silly question to ask].

From even this brief snippet of conversation, we see that *matatu* operators are dealing with at least four different groups that have the authority to take them to jail, or worse. It is common in Kenya to feel an undercurrent of violence when discussing the police and their affiliated groups, not least because in 2005, under government minister John Michuki, Kenyan police were given "shoot to kill" orders, especially if the young people were suspected to be *Mungiki* members, who are often working in and around *matatu* stages (Rasmussen 2012: 425). This shoot to kill order is still in effect at the time of this writing and has resulted in an alarming increase in extrajudicial killings by Kenyan police, especially among young people in informal settlements, like Mathare and Kibera.[4]

The danger, violence and corruption historically embedded in the *matatu* sector often leave the operators themselves with a deep ambivalence toward the morality of their own behavior. When we were discussing police corruption and paying out bribes, Anthony, a Nairobi conductor, described struggling with the work because of this aspect when he said, "I am Christian, and I have to go home and face my family." As people become infrastructure, the often already conflicting moral discourses around their laboring practices become

---

[4] For more information around police violence and the challenges of reform see Osse (2016) and van Stapele et al. (2019).

murky as they both form bonds and connections through the need to stay safe and manage their lives, while also operationalizing suffering and violence for themselves and others.

One may wonder how these workers, often young people, negotiate what seems to be a well-coordinated effort to control, extort and intimidate them by multiple arms of police personnel as well as vigilante gangs and individual hijackers. In addition to the payoffs along the routes, they often stay safe through verbal and non-verbal communication. There are hand signals they use as they pass one another in the streets to communicate the presence of police located further ahead on the route or at the next stage. Another important way that *matatu* operators deal with these various police groups as well as organized gangs like *Mungiki* or individual hijackers that prey on them daily is to develop hidden linguistic codes, which scholars have called "deep *Sheng*" (Samper 2002). It is well documented that *matatu* operators are among the key creators and disseminators of *Sheng* and it is an important feature of *matatu* operators' lives; it is the glue that binds relationships together, pivoting on occupational solidarity and friendship bonds to navigate a murky and dangerous landscape. As discussed at length in the Introduction, deep *Sheng* is a version of *Sheng* that can be developed and spoken between just a few people (Samper 2002) – which can be used to talk about pretty women, discuss dangerous looking customers or coordinate actions that will be taken in the presence of police. The safety in using, creating, and knowing *Sheng* for *matatu* operators is similar to what anthropologist Julia Elyachar has discussed as phatic labor, whereby the communicative networks of people become part of the social elements of infrastructure (2010).

For Simone, Elyachar, and other urbanists, African cities are characterized by flexible, mobile, and provisional intersections of residents that operate without clearly delineated notions of how the city is to be inhabited and used and "these conjunctions become an infrastructure – a platform providing for and reproducing life in the city" (Simone 2004: 408). Other scholars, however, see this formulation as overly celebratory and not attuned to the exploitation and power relationships that force the creative provisioning that characterizes the African city (Doherty 2017; Rizzo 2017). For instance, Jacob Doherty uses the phrase "disposable people as infrastructure" as a critical supplement to Simone's widely cited idea of "people as infrastructure" which, Doherty argues, "does not attend sufficiently to infrastructural violence," especially in the dangerous lives of motorcycle taxi drivers in Uganda (2017: 129). Matteo Rizzo's longitudinal study on minibus taxi operators in Dar es Salaam, Tanzania shows consistent labor exploitation at the hands of the owners, passengers, and the government alike. Building on these scholars, in this chapter I have intended to explore how the creative collaborations of urban transport operators act as important distributive networks and are simultaneously a conduit for survival, suffering and violence. As much as *matatu* operators must engage owners, police, and other operators in their hustles, the vigilante gangs present perhaps the most significant danger in *matatu* operators' lives.

When researching route #105 in Kikuyu, in 2010, my interlocutors explained to me that it was almost entirely controlled by *Mungiki*. *Mungiki*, meaning "mass" in the Kikuyu language (Wamue 2001), has been defined as an "ethnically homogenous Kikuyu group, characterized both by rural religious tenets and urban political activity," but in 2001 they were also responsible for deadly turf wars over control of large portions of Nairobi's *matatu* sector (Anderson 2002: 538). The group is said to have emerged as followers of the Tent of the Living God religious sect in 1987 (Wamue 2001: 455), but in the 1990s and for the next decade, they were a common and violent feature in Nairobi's *matatu* routes as they battled with local neighborhood groups over control over *matatu* stops (Rasmussen 2012; Anderson 2002).

Many drivers and conductors I interviewed would not even mention the name *Mungiki*; they simply referred to those individuals involved as "members" and were very afraid of their wrath. Jackson, a driver, was particularly vocal about *Mungiki*'s tactics on route #105, where he lived and worked. While slowly drawing his thumb across his neck, he warned, "if you don't pay, they will whip you and sometimes they can even burn your *matatu* or kill you." Jackson told me that each *matatu* on route #105 paid 200–300 KES ($2–$3 USD) per day, usually in the morning, and that you knew whom to pay because they had signs that marked them, like the way they wore their hats and some of the language they used.

Although not all routes had to deal with such a pervasive *Mungiki* presence as route #105, the group was well known by all *matatu* workers across routes, adding to their lore as bogeymen who haunt the sector. Rasta George describes the differences between neighborhoods:

> In Kileleshwa, there is no ... uh, in our routes we don't have those people who used to harass people. If you go to Embakasi, there is another group called *Mungiki*, and there, you have to follow their rules if you live there. But in Kileleshwa you don't have those people. So, let us compare these other places. I have worked almost a third of the routes operating *matatus*. The situation in central Kenya ... it is very, very ... because they are sort of small gods and you have to go as part of what they want. You can be threatened ... Not even threatened. You can be killed ... You can disappear.

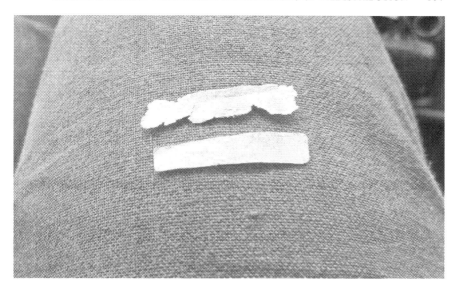

Figure 9 Two *Mungiki* receipts. One old and one more recently acquired. (Photo by author, 2009).

And, although *Mungiki* members were often implicated in violence around *matatu* vehicles and stages, scholars have noted that, like the associations before them, the *Mungiki* and cartels had "more to gain from ensuring the stable operation of *matatus* than they did from constant conflict" (Heinze 2018: 16).

Mungiki members also experimented with formalizing their role on the routes where they attempted to act as regulatory authorities. When I asked how *Mungiki* kept track of who had paid and who had not, Jackson pointed to the ashtray. I opened it and pulled out two small, colored scraps of paper (Figure 9). These receipts, however crude, were issued daily by members. They are also insightful for understanding *matatu* hustles. In the realm of unregulated sectors like the *matatu* sector, the many groups vying for a piece of the profits are using a variety of mechanisms to formulate and facilitate a more stable economic foundation. If, for example, you show this receipt to a *Mungiki* member, they will not charge you again, thus legitimizing their role in the sector through this symbolic formalization of receipts. These receipts become physical, material manifestations of legitimacy.

As I spent time talking to people about these various actors connected to the *matatu* sector (police, *Mungiki*, *Kamjesh*), I came to understand the role of reciprocity undergirding these violent interactions. Echoing Maina, who opens this chapter, Jackson offered great insight to the way that generational tensions, ethnic solidarity, and codes of urban reciprocity were formulated among *matatu* workers in the face of *Mungiki* members in 2010, as we shared fruit salad at the stage in Kikuyu. He offered this statement in response to a question about what should be done about *Mungiki*:

> For me, maybe 60 percent should continue, and 40 percent, I don't support it. For one, I support it because most of them they are members of my tribe and if I say I recommend they all get killed, there will be no generation because they are the youngest generation. I can say that they take my [money] … they demand it, so if they assess you and they write a note and they tell you, threaten you, if you have a business, "You are ancestors, so you are our blood, we have nothing, we are not working, so we need our share, you have to share the money."

This response alludes to the feeling that it is the responsibility of the older generation to provide for the younger generation, so they get their share. This is a well-known part of *Mungiki*'s justification for violent extortion (Rasmussen 2010). In Kikuyu culture, it is important for the elder generation to help the younger generation by handing down land, but during colonialism and the displacement of Kikuyu people by European settlers, it was increasingly difficult for the older generation to hand anything down, causing resentment and escalating unease over time. Part of *githaka ituika* (generational turnover of land) was to "convert personal wealth into collective peace … and was said to happen every thirty years" (Berman and Lonsdale 1992: 344–345), a built-in redistributive mechanism. When *ituika* practices ceased, in the late 1940s and 1950s, the younger generation rebelled, articulating through the demands of the Land and Freedom Army the alienation of land and rights at the hands of European colonialists and Kikuyu loyalists. This tension is especially palpable for Jackson who, as a Kikuyu, facing harassment from members of his own ethnic group, felt as though he owed them something because he is considered an elder.

Since Minister Michuki's "shoot to kill" order for *Mungiki*, they have largely disappeared from the public eye, although it is well known throughout the sector and Nairobi in general that they are still present on some routes. But there are other groups that subsist through the *matatu* sector. Many of my interviewees claim that *Mungiki* has been absorbed into another group generally known as *Kamjesh*. Unlike *Mungiki*, *Kamjesh* is much more localized and ambiguous. They are not as well documented as *Mungiki*, although they have been referenced by scholars of Nairobi's informal settlements (van Stapele 2007) and of the *matatu* sector (Wa-Mungai 2013). People understand *Kamjesh* to be anything from "a vigilante gang like *Mungiki*" to "just a group of friends in the neighborhood." When I mentioned the violence and terror of *Mungiki*, Bena, a young *matatu* conductor informed me that *Kamjesh* is not a gang like *Mungiki*, but more like a support group for unemployed *matatu* operators and described a worker pool who were in essence waiting for *skwads*. They are known, like *Mungiki*, to hang out around the *matatu* stages and extort money or *skwads* from *matatu* operators. Bena claimed their key identifying characteristic is openly smoking *bangh* (marijuana).

The legitimacy of *Kamjesh* membership differed from that of *Mungiki* in the eyes of the *matatu* operators I interviewedand pivoted on varying ideas of work ethic between the two groups. Simply, *Kamjesh* often take *skwads* whereas *Mungiki* members rarely do, which was one of the major complaints of *matatu* workers when they talked about *Mungiki* members. As the ethnographic data of the relationships between the crew members and those who prey on them exposes, there are multiple hustles happening along the same domain. The streets of Nairobi, especially with regards to the *matatu* routes that are controlled by *Mungiki* gangs and the vehicle's personnel who may or may not belong to various gangs like *Kamjesh*, witness the constant negotiations of a precarious life. The workers are each navigating their own uncertain labor, meeting seemingly impossible targets and justifying dubious economic practices through the lens of friendship and performance of complicated reciprocity.

As a *matatu* operator starts their day, they will encounter a *Kamjesh* member at the beginning of the route whom they will pay. Then, they will face a police officer and they will again produce cash for them, often with a grin. As they move throughout their day redistributing their small sums of money they will stop for lunch and give their vehicle over to a younger conductor or driver to get some experience and a small bit of change and at the end of the day as they return home, they will drop the vehicle off, along with the target payment to the owner, which may or may not leave enough cash for themselves. The system depends on code words, deep local knowledge, empathy that fuels the redistributive cycle and a thick skin as those passengers you carry yell at you or about you. Then, you may go home to your family, say your evening prayers, and break your daily bread. This is but one of the hustles that work in Nairobi, and it is both collaborative and dangerous, creative and violent, but it is the nature of the work that hundreds of thousands of young people participate in every day.

Conclusion

In Nairobi, the large *matatu* workforce engages in a variety of collaborative, competitive, violent, risky, and cooperative practices in their daily work, providing transportation for over a million people every day. Ethnographically exploring practices like trading *skwads* and the operation of informal regulatory networks like *Mungiki*, including the way they produced and distributed receipts at the same time as they threatened physical violence, provides crucial granularity to the social forms that organize informal work. In this way, *matatu* work and the long-standing institutions of organization help us further understand the complexity and dynamism of the "hustle economy." *Matatu* workers engage in a highly social and mobile environment where they consistently interact with a variety of state and non-state actors through a combination of violent threats, competitive acts, moments of solidarity and shared linguistic codes. Many of these relationships, exploitative and benevolent alike, are framed by ideas around generational distribution and economic reciprocity. In the face of uncertainty, *matatu* workers are simultaneously creatively and competitively making do, engaging in a variety of practices that are at times violent and redistributive. The risk, competition, extortion, general threats and experiences of violence force *matatu* operators, and other hustlers, to struggle with and toggle between a variety of competing moral discourses that can often challenge these workers' subjectivity, and they also find comfort and support in those same occupational networks.

The historical legacy of the *matatu* sector, being an indigenous creation in direct opposition to the colonial administration, positions the workers, owners, and even police and gang members as engaging in a type of fiscal disobedience whereby cash is being withheld from the state due to general distrust of its ability to provide the necessary urban services, in this case transportation, and to use for their own personal needs. Meanwhile the relative "obedience" to other groups (e.g., *Mungiki* and *Kamjesh*) is integral to a kind of cultural logic of generational distribution that transforms understandings of theft into that of reciprocal obligation. In Nairobi, *matatu* work provides a complex landscape where collaborative and redistributive practices exist on top of and next to violent, competitive, and risky practices, which facilitate the management and provisioning of the sector's services. A tense balance is struck between multiple coalitions of passengers, police, workers, and owners as they make their way through Nairobi's risky streets, doing their best to dodge the most violent of interactions. As multiple regulatory authorities operate through changing institutional forms that emerged from the sector itself and can channel creativity and community, as well as danger and violence, these paradoxical and ambivalent parts of the hustle economy can co-produce moral ambiguity and struggle in the lives of urban workers.

4

Grubby Bills and Mandatory Gadgets: Financializing Mobility in Kenya

Google is not giving up, and the struggle to modernize Kenya's unruly matatu trade illustrates the challenges of superimposing cutting edge technology on some of the poorest countries in the world. Across the continent, the analog Africa of old is racing, at variable speeds, toward a digital future.

(Jeffrey Gettleman 2014)

Google's little green card has incited some strong resistance with the vast majority of Kenya's matatus *still dealing with their preferred currency – grubby bills – as they zoom around Nairobi's streets stuffed with passengers flitting in and out of traffic like a bunch of fleas on methamphetamines.*

(Jeffrey Gettleman 2014)

Analog Africans and Grubby Bills

In the summer of 2014, Google Kenya had launched a cashless transportation card called the "BebaPay" card and Kenya's *matatu* sector was receiving and rejecting a high-tech overhaul from one of the most valuable tech companies in the world. *Beba* is the Swahili word for carry and *Beba! Beba Tao!* (Carrying! Carrying to town!) one of the things that conductors and touts yell at potential passengers from *matatu* vehicles when they are advertising seats to the city center. Perhaps because of Google's involvement, the launch of the BebaPay card drew the attention of the *New York Times*' correspondent in Kenya, Jeffrey Gettleman, who reported that Google was excited about making the "little green transport card that would replace cash payments and track every transaction on the minibuses" available in all 40,000 of Kenya's *matatus* (2014). It was meant to revolutionize the infamously stubborn *matatu* sector, but, according to Gettleman, the card failed to catch on because Kenya was moving at "analog speed" and would not let go of their "grubby bills" to adopt the cutting-edge technology. This was demonstrated by the way a conductor responded to a question Gettleman asked about the acceptance of the cashless card: "Kenya is a cash-based economy!"

Instead of seeing the role of "grubby bills" to sustain livelihoods, Gettleman characterized the failure of the cards as an African rejection of technology. This could not be more wrong. As explained in the last chapter, the labor of redistribution is a key part of *matatu* work and the circulation of cash sustains many thousands of people every day. The idea that Google is experiencing "challenges of superimposing cutting edge technology" on Kenya because it is somehow resistant to new technological innovation misrepresents how much of a technology hub Kenya is. In fact, Nairobi is nicknamed the "Silicon Savannah" due to the success of the mobile banking technology, M-PESA, developed in Kenya and launched with great success in 2007 (Mahoney 2017; Poggiali 2016). Ironically, M-PESA, the technology that made Nairobi a center of cutting-edge technology in the region was the creation and adoption of a mobile money application, which enabled electronic transfer of money without the "grubby bills." To suggest that the failure of the transportation card could be explained away as a resistance to technology by analog Africans is a narrative that echoes racist tropes and obscures our understanding of the practical ways people adopt and reject technological innovation, and especially financial technology or FinTech.

The paternalism that is reflected in the imperialist tone of the quote that opens this chapter implies that it is Google's responsibility to improve this "poor" country's unruly transportation sector, even if it is against the will of local interests and experts. As Daivi Rodima-Taylor argues, many platform economies in Kenya carry settler colonial legacies as "digital economies in particular present novel opportunities for extracting value through data" (2022: 17). Linking banks to everyday activities like *matatu* transport is a type of everyday financialization (van der Zwan 2014) and can be understood as a version of neoliberal reform called "reregulation." Philip Mirowski, an economic philosopher argues that scholars of neoliberalism should not just focus on the classic features of the economic doctrine, sometimes referred to as the D-L-P formula of deregulation, liberalization and privatization, but focus on the overarching philosophy of neoliberal logics whereby the market is privileged over people and because of that driving logic, sometimes, neoliberal policy will be expressed in "reregulation" – or attempts by governments to realign certain sectors with wealthy financial institutions (2013). Reregulatory policies often "gives political incumbents opportunities to expand their authority and their support bases by reregulating sectors of the economy" that were previously deregulated or unregulated, as popular transportation in Kenya has been for decades (Snyder 1999: 174).

Gettleman reported that engineers at Google Kenya came up with the idea for the BebaPay card when they were watching traffic chaos unfold below them on a rainy night, observing from a window in a warm, dry office high above street level. From that height, the "*matatu* problem" seemed clear. Engineers at Google Kenya worked with engineers in Zurich to design something that would "minimize human contact" so that conductors would not be able to use the money in their pockets to bribe the police, while the Government of Kenya would receive millions of shillings more in taxes (Gettleman 2014). The creation of the card was meant to not only minimize human contact, but to minimize contact with humans deemed to be dangerous and untrustworthy – *matatu* operators. The BebaPay card was marketed as a way for passengers to know that transportation fares were going to the *correct people*, who turned out to be the banks and the Government of Kenya before the owners even saw the deposit in their account, let alone the workers. For Google Kenya engineers, the twenty-shilling coin ($0.25 USD) or hundred-shilling note ($1–$2 USD), should not go into the conductor's hand or owner's pocket, but should be transferred from the Google card to the person or entity on the other end of the card reading gadget, with many of these cards that was most likely a bank. And according to Gettleman's writing quoted above, it is easy to avoid paying workers when you perceive them to be "fleas on methamphetamines."

Through the Ministry of Transport, the Kenyan government demanded every *matatu* commuter acquire and use the BebaPay card by July 1, 2014, but after two weeks, hardly anyone had adopted the cards. The only cost to customers to acquire Google's BebaPay card was opening a Gmail account. As one Google executive said, "all we want are users," but *matatu* owners and commuters were not compelled. Over several months in 2014, the Government of Kenya ramped up their campaign to convince people to adopt a cashless transport card system by empowering many of the banks operating in Kenya to issue their own cashless card alternatives. The banks charged a deposit for the cards, ranging from 50 to 300 shillings ($0.50–$4 USD), and if you were an existing customer, it was easy to simply debit your account and you could get the card. In December 2014, Kenya Commercial Bank (KCB) launched a cashless transport card with Kenya Bus Service (KBS) called the Abiria card as well as a commuter/debit card that required a 60-shilling deposit called the Pepea-card. *Pepea* means to float or fly in Swahili and was probably chosen to invoke the idea of being lifted lightly across distances.

Up to January 2015, the cashless transportation card campaign continued unabated as banks advertised their cards and the initial deposits required. The cheapest option was the "My 1963" card (Figure 10) supported by Safaricom (it was a cashless transport card that you could swipe in a gadget, but it was linked to M-PESA accounts). The account had to have at least 10 KES in it to get the card. The "My 1963" card, referred to the year Kenya gained independence and most likely intended to conjure the idea of "freedom." The

Figure 10 "My 1963" cashless transportation card. (Photo by author, 2017).

card has an image of downtown Nairobi and the colors of the Kenyan flag. Most people I asked about cashless transportation cards pulled this one from their wallet, even years later in 2017.

Mandatory Gadgets

In 2014, the National Transportation Safety Association (NTSA) issued Legal Notice 23 requiring all savings and credit co-operatives (SACCOs) that manage individual routes in Nairobi to adopt cashless payment systems in order to pass their annual inspection (Aruho 2021). As people rushed to get their cards to ride a *matatu* to work, SACCOs were frantically importing card reading gadgets for all their vehicles, at 10,000 KES ($100 USD) each, so they could get their inspection certificate and continue operating. Over those first weeks of July 2014, when the cashless card requirement went into effect, there was some general resistance from *matatu* workers, conductors and touts refusing to accept the cards or use the card readers. Additionally, I was told by Nairobi River of God (ROG) SACCO workers that even those who tried to cooperate were unable to read the cards due to the inoperability between the gadgets and the wide variety of cards available for use on the vehicles. As they swiped cards from different banks, some using BebaPay cards and others using "My 1963" cards, the gadgets had a difficult time processing the payments and after even a few lost seconds, conductors were simply giving up and asking for cash.

When I asked the president of the ROG SACCO about the gadgets in 2017, he assured me that there were several in a storage room outside his office. We walked across the big parking lot where several *matatu* vehicles were under various stages of repair, about 200 meters away from the main office. We entered a room that had a barrel of old engine parts in one corner, and a box covered with paper and other debris near the door. Underneath the broken-down cardboard boxes and newspapers were about forty gadgets collecting dust in the box, amounting to around 400,000 KES ($4,000 USD) (Figures 11A and 11B). I was clearly shocked after calculating the cost of the gadgets, but the ROG President just smiled and looked at me over a pile of expensive trash, later communicating that gadgets and transport policy in general was understood to be a common tactic by the government to make money.

By the end of February 2015, the cashless cards were settled quietly in people's wallets where they would stay unused for years. The Matatu Welfare Association (MWA) was in court fighting the ordinance on behalf of owners and SACCOs who had spent hundreds of thousands of shillings on gadgets when no one was using the cards. In August 2015, it seemed like the cycle was going to start over when Mastercard won the contract to partner with banks in the region to make a single, unified, cashless transportation card, but when I was in Kenya in 2016, there was no progress on cashless cards although it would come up in casual conversation at times. In May of 2016, the *Daily Nation* newspaper's daily debate question was: "Do you believe PSV owners will this time succeed in their plan to launch a cashless fare system?" Although the question is probably misleading as to who the responsible parties are for launching the initiative, the answers are telling. They were all some version of what Victor Abuka stated clearly in his answer: "This cashless fare system is a digital scam in the offing. Bigger than anything else." When I returned to Kenya in 2017, a Kenyan friend, a professional in his mid-thirties, offered this conclusion: "This was the government trying to get people to pay taxes. You have these things (the cards), and they are synchronized to some database somewhere." But, even in 2019, when I asked to see people's cards many still had them and cited their expectation that they will, at some point, be useful when the government finally does require cards for transport. Upon visiting in 2023, the cards were still not being used, although some *matatu* passengers used M-PESA to pay their fare, while many still paid their fare with cash.

Figure 11a Card-reading gadget, unused and collecting dust. (Photo by author, 2017).

Between 2013 and 2017 there were at least four major cashless card initiatives launched by multinationals such as Google, Mastercard and Visa, with the Kenyan Banks working in conjunction such as Equity Bank, Diamond Trust Bank and Kenya Commercial Bank and sometimes in collaboration with transportation or transport adjacent firms like KBS and the Matatu Owners Association (MOA) (Aruho et al. 2021: 4). To read the cards and process the payment, operators were expected to have a smart, preferably Android phone, that could run an application to read BebaPay cards, or they could use a hand-held credit card machine, referred to as a card reading gadget, to collect fares. The combination of institutions interested in launching the cashless fare cards gives an indication to the reregulatory nature of the enterprise, in that the multinational corporations work in conjunction with Kenya's financial institutions in an effort aimed at controlling the everyday transactions of millions of individual commuters. As Richard Snyder argues, "Reregulation can thus

Figure 11b A box full of card-reading gadgets in a storage shed. (Photo by author, 2017).

serve not only as a way to preserve power ... but also as a way to expand power" (1999: 178). Or as Rodima-Taylor notes, "FinTech does not simply formalize informal relations" but "creates new sociotechnical assemblages" that can blur boundaries of inclusion and exclusion (2022: 417).

The cashless transport cards are not the first-time equipment has been required for the *matatu* sector only to fall by the wayside. For instance, during the initial phase of the Michuki Rules, it was reported that some matatu owners spent 50,000-100,000 KES ($5,000–$10,000 USD) to equip their vehicles with seatbelts and speed governors, putting many out of business completely (Mitullah and Onsate 2013). Out of all the safety regulations from the 2004 Michuki Rules, the least popular one was the installation of seatbelts for each seat in the vehicle. The seatbelts frustrated owners, workers, and passengers for different reasons. Owners did not want to have to invest even more money into their already expensive vehicles, to buy and install seatbelts for every seat in their *matatu*. Workers did not want to have to check, or even try to check, if everyone had seatbelts on and this was yet another thing for which they could be bothered by police. Passengers did not use them because they would often lie on the floor of the vehicle and get dirty and when it came time to put them on it seemed like a messy and needless measure. The seatbelts quickly became twisted straps of mud-caked fabric that people avoided touching, resembling old, dried ropes hanging along the seats, dragging on the floor. The belts would get disgusting, and no one wanted to touch them, but if police officers pulled the *matatu* over everyone would groan and put the long, rope-like fabric across their laps gingerly trying to minimize the damage to their clothing.

One of the ways that anthropologists understand neoliberalism is through Foucault's (1991) concept of governmentality, techniques directed at the managing of the self through the regulation of everyday conduct. In some neoliberal reform, this looks like the transfer of responsibility from the state to the individual, or the reorientation of the self (Ganti 2014: 96), which could be seen when, in addition to *matatu* workers, passengers could be arrested and fined for not wearing seatbelts. When there were police crackdowns people were been dragged to jail on their morning commute for not having money to pay a seatbelt fine. Steve reported in 2009, "Several times … most of my customers [have gotten caught]. There are times when there are crackdowns of seatbelts. I think two times I have been caught without my … [pointing to seatbelt] my customers … taken to central police station." With a wave of his hand, he gestures to the whole *matatu*. Wide-eyed, I asked, "With all the customers inside?" He answered with a grin, "Yes, all the customers."

Seatbelts were also a point of contention during the 2004 regulations because a rumor emerged that Michuki had a relative in the seatbelt import business (Lamont 2013). Even if this is merely a rumor, rumors are an important way that public perception is shaped in Kenya. The possible scenarios that people create about powerful people are important, especially when times are cloudy and chaotic (Osborn 2008). The seatbelt rumor indexed the nepotistic practices common in Kenyan politics but also implied that this regulation was needless and must be benefiting someone in particular. By 2006 seatbelts were infrequently used in the vehicles. Seatbelt policy is one example of how efforts to improve safety were experienced by the public and industry as merely mechanisms for getting more money from the government. This perception and experience of the public highlighted the way that policy initiatives in Kenya are often looked at with suspicion (Wrong and Williams 2009).

Financializing Transportation

The attempted and potential transformation of *matatu* transportation payments from majority cash transactions to cashless, digital transactions is an example of the process of everyday financialization by which financial institutions grow and exert influence on economies. Natascha van der Zwan points out that financialization is "a convenient word for a bundle of more or less discrete structural changes in the economies of the industrialized world" and across the social sciences, financialization research falls under three general themes of study (2014): (a) theories of shareholder value (Ho 2009; Boyer 2005), (b) regimes of accumulation characterized by the switch from industrial manufacturing to outsourcing jobs to flexible labor markets and expanding credit, and leveraging debt (Krippner 2005, Arrighi 1994), and (c) the financialization of everyday life through the adoption of financial products that increase the role of banks and finance into people's daily lives (Kusimba 2018; van der Zwan 2014; Erturk et al. 2007).

Financialization is more thoroughly and commonly studied in industrialized nations generally because the cash economy is still the overwhelming transactional currency in many cities of the Global South; however, it is increasingly important to look at the ways financialization, and especially financial technology or FinTech, works throughout the world (Rodima-Taylor 2022). Often, it is less about democratizing the opportunities of investment and more about tapping into emerging markets in the interest of multinational corporations like Google and Mastercard, sometimes through infrastructural avenues. Transportation has become an important avenue to this type of financial process, partly because it is such an important part of everyday life. Additionally, infrastructure is a popular avenue for neoliberal reform because it is made to seem neutral and technical, not political (Ong 2006).

Alongside the cashless fare reform in Nairobi, there is a broader set of policy and infrastructural projects being promoted throughout cities of the Global South. These are the megaprojects of the BRT, a "bus-based public transport that delivers rapid mobility" through segregated bus lanes (Klopp et al. 2019: 3). Although popular transportation like *matatu* leave much room for improvement, they are also largely overlooked when considering these large-scale reforms. The idea that BRT systems are generically better suited to all diverse African cities, from Lagos to Nairobi, presents a good example of what anthropologists of development have called "development narratives" or "off-the-shelf" development projects, which lending institutions such as the International Monetary Fund (IMF) and the World Bank promote (McMichael 2000; Roe 1991). As Emory Roe's (1991) classic argument about "blueprint development" highlights and critiques – if it works in Colombia and China, it will work anywhere in Africa, too. Development narratives have a long history in Africa, even before the neoliberal era of structural adjustment, and this history frames the current situation for the *matatu* sector in Nairobi. In the early 1940s, British politicians attempted to restructure the colonies through failing modernization projects called colonial "development" projects, which often expropriated massive tracts of land and led to more intrusion, meddling and alienation of local populations than first intended (Parsons 2011; Edelman and Haugerud 2004; Cooper and Packard 1997; Leys 1975).

Matteo Rizzo's longitudinal work with transport operators in Dar es Salaam, shows how neoliberalism characterized by austerity in the transportation sector gave way to increasingly aggressive interventions by the state, through reforms that could be understood as reregulatory, especially considering the implementation of Tanzania's BRT system (2017: 143). Rizzo argues that instead of the state disappearing and letting people fend for themselves, it has increasingly absorbed different parts of the economy, one of which is the transportation sector. Rizzo asserts that megaprojects like BRT are the latest policy trend at the World Bank, which includes collaboration with a variety of powerful institutions including important members of the global financial sector like Goldman Sachs (2017). Expert lobbyists, including the World Bank as well as the Institute for Transportation and Development Policy (ITDP) and Latin American experts who have positive experiences with the Transmilenio BRT in Bogotá, Colombia tend to promote BRT as a one-size-fits all transportation solution that can be seen as often more in line with the priorities of the World Bank and multinational corporations than with local interests (Klopp et al. 2019; Rizzo 2017).

Across cities of the Global South, BRT projects are not simply understood as transportation projects, but as a way to "restructure" entire informal or popular transportation systems and, in African cities particularly, BRT systems are expected to be accompanied by institutional and political transformations (Klopp et al. 2019; Dewey 2016). The BRT projects are often portrayed as a way to create technical capacity that depoliticizes "a significant reorganization of power, authority and accountability" (Klopp et al. 2019: 4). In 2007 there were 40 cities with a BRT system, by 2016 there were 202 and there are expected to be nearly 300 by 2022 (Rizzo 2017). Although Nairobi's BRT is rumored to be ready to carry passengers in December 2024, as of October 2023 construction had yet to begin (Kinyanjui 2019).

Disciplining *Matatus*, Reregulating Neoliberalism

According to scholars of the *matatu* sector there have been at least four to six major campaigns to reform transportation in Kenya including the original transport monopoly agreement in 1934 and the 2004 Michuki Rules (Mutongi 2017; Mitullah and Onsate 2013). In addition to the first initiative to monopolize transport in 1934 in order to secure British investment in the colony, as well as the rise and fall of Moi's government fleet, Nyayo Bus, which went out of business in early 1990s, Mutongi (2017) includes several safety campaigns that were launched but fizzled out, or were thwarted by informal transport organizations (often called cartels but comprised of route associations, groups, gangs, companies, lobbyists, and police). The historical memory of these failed attempts was part of the reason the 2004 Michuki Rules were so groundbreaking and widely praised. Many people believed that John Michuki was the only government minister who would ever be able to get anything done in Kenya's *matatu* sector. Many years later, the memory of the Michuki Rules implementation was powerful. As one of my interviewees, Rasta George recalled in 2010,

> Me, I came here in 2000, maybe 2001. And, by that time, in the route, eh, it was hard, it was dangerous, because even more there was … people used to be beaten! You know that time? People, we are not seating … there were no fourteen-seaters. We were eighteen! In the same vehicle, eighteen, there were! We did not, we did not used to … close the door in that vehicle. Even in town, we used to hang out the door. Even in the city … hanging, hanging … you see, at the door hanging, maybe six people are hanging … the *matatu* is still … [motions to it moving along the road].

Steve added an additional comment to summarize: "That's why Michuki is regarded as a … revolution."

Although the regulatory mechanisms of the Michuki Rules are often seen as another failure (Mitullah and Onsate 2013), perhaps Michuki was most successful in the reregulation of the transportation sector that facilitated a significant transfer of wealth and power from the small-scale entrepreneurs who had largely controlled the sector up to that point toward the hands of the wealthy and politically powerful. Michuki framed transportation regulations strictly in terms of safety and efficiency, but they also exemplified government-based policies that increasingly fell along neoliberal lines (Harvey 2007) as he "cast market-based solutions to social problems in strictly technical terms" while eliding the political and ideological interests motivating the policy decisions (Ong 2006: 6). Since the Michuki Rules there have been several other policy reforms, including the (failed) 14-seater phase-out, the CBD decongestion plan, and the 2012 SACCO management requirement (Mitullah and Onsate 2013), which will be expanded on below.

14-seater phase-out

Just a few months after the Michuki Rules went into effect, there was a full-page advertisement for a Matatu Transport Business Start-Up Seminar in the *Daily Nation* (2004), proclaiming that Legal Notice 161 (Michuki Rules) "Gives Owners Total Management Control," and below that written in bold – WANTED: OVER 20,000 EXTRA MATATUS (2004). Elsewhere in the text it specifies that the ad is referring to investment in 14-seater vehicles by discussing the profit that can be expected to be made from the vehicle's thirteen passengers. Only a few years after this supplement appeared, the same newspaper featured a full-page spread (*Daily Nation* 2007) promoting the BRT system as the future of "sustainable transport" in Nairobi in a pullout-section that suggested that the city should do away completely with small, 14-seater *matatu* vehicles. In 2008, the government announced a systematic plan that would phase out every fourteen-seater *matatu* in the city and replace them with buses that had a carrying capacity of over sixty passengers by the year 2012, effectively ending the investment avenue they had promoted only a few years before (Ommeh et al. 2015). Jaqueline Klopp (2012) cogently analyzed the perplexity exemplified in this seemingly contradictory and inconsistent transportation planning approach. Klopp explains how four features contribute to these conflicts in planning: (a) the large and distorting role of external actors, (b) the fragmentation of institutions, (c) the closed and top-down planning processes, and (d) the absence of mobilization for policies and projects that serve the majority of the public, especially poor residents (2012: 3). In a sense, the political economy of transportation planning in Kenya is more "chaotic" than the matatu sector seems to be.

According to *matatu* owners, the 14-seater phase-out policy promoted unemployment and discrimination, and squeezed out the small-scale investor in favor of wealthy fleet owners who could afford large investments into bigger vehicles (Ommeh et al. 2015). Transport workers complained that the measure would cost them their jobs, and, because of the cumbersome size of the vehicles, it would actually increase congestion, not relieve it. Owners also claimed that those in charge of developing transport policy were simply serving their own privileged interests. In the years following this announcement, the rumors of a 14-seater *matatu* phase-out floated around the stages where I worked, but every year I returned to Kenya to see newly registered fourteen-seaters still traversing the city. Over time, it has become a phantom that was always looming, but never realized.

Franchising Privilege

Shortly after the Michuki Rules were put into place in 2004, the government started allowing the biggest bus companies, sometimes called transport management companies (TMCs) (Plano 2022) preferential access to areas of Nairobi's city center, including the smaller area around the Parliament buildings known as the Central Business District (CBD). The CBD is an important space in Nairobi's urban milieu, particularly in terms of aesthetic concerns because it contains the large international hotels, government buildings and national monuments. The CBD was off-limits to a majority of the *matatu* sector starting in 2005, when the Transport Licensing Board (TLB) began to require a permit for them to enter. In 2009, a manager for one of the large TMCs (KBS Ltd) explained that in order to get a CBD license the applicant must have a fleet of over forty buses, and all of the buses had to have a seating capacity of over sixty people. Additionally, to address congestion issues the government together with the Nairobi City Council identified termini away from the CBD (Muthurwa, City Bus Station, Hakati and Globe Cinema Roundabout) as termini for *matatus* (Mitullah and Onsate 2013: 3). These two requirements, along with an application and a hefty fee, would secure the fleet operators with the necessary permits needed to operate in the CBD. These allocations were done without any research and resulted in a pattern where commuters have to alight far from their destinations, while car owners drive through without restriction, reflecting "elite thinking" (Mitullah and Onsate 2013: 3).

In 2010, there were only three major transport companies that operated in the CBD – Citi Hoppa, KBS Ltd. and Double M – meaning that they had fleets of large buses.[1] Although they manage *matatu* vehicles similarly to the ways SACCOs operate, these larger companies are defined as TMCs and do not operate any small, 14-seater vehicles (Plano 2022). The TMCs operating currently in Nairobi are Express Connection (previously known as Double M), Citi Hoppa, KBS Ltd., and Citi Shuttle.[2]

In 2010, a middle-aged, Kenyan operations manager for KBS Ltd. told me that he wanted to connect this bus company's new brand with the "privilege" of working within the CBD. He claimed that by using the KBS reference to colonial exclusivity he would attract more customers, which would also help make up for the overhead that comes with owning a company. He explained that it is important to regulate competition through things like "privileged space" because larger transport companies pay more taxes: they pay advance tax, income tax and employee benefits for those on the payroll. He offered this pithy justification for the exclusivity of the CBD permit framework when he said, "to give the city shape, you have to have a company." In other words,

---

[1] Plano identified four TMCs operating in Nairobi in 2022, but during my research in 2010, there were only three operating in the CBD.
[2] KBS Management Ltd. specifically targeted the colonial nostalgia embedded in the brand of the Kenya Bus Service, dating back to the colonial monopoly in 1934 (see Chapter 1).

transportation, planning, and the aesthetic of the city must not be left to the general citizen, small-scale *matatu* owner, or urban planning and government institutions, but to a wealthy company's interests. This manager believed KBS Ltd. deserved to get special treatment because he wanted to "standardize the privilege" of working in the CBD.

These permits can be understood as "'technologies of subjection' – government policies that aim to police urban space, movement, travel because they differentially regulate groups for 'optimal production' through spatial practices that engage market forces" (Ong 2006: 6). Considering that at the time, 2005, the average *matatu* owner only owned one or two vehicles, the idea that one must have a fleet of over forty vehicles felt extremely exclusionary and helped operationalize the transfer of wealth from the small-scale entrepreneur to the large fleet investors, who included Michuki himself.

The division of urban space in Nairobi's city center is demarcated through the lines of where *matatu* vehicles are allowed and not allowed to travel. Moi Avenue is seen as the line dividing Nairobi into the haves and have-nots. It is also the boundary of where *matatu* vehicles can go. The north side of Moi Avenue is the CBD, where hotels, government buildings, and nice restaurants are located. This is also a space that is off-limits to all but some *matatu* vehicles, vehicles that are deemed more formalized and professional and often owned by government officials or other wealthy elites, which are allowed to operate north of Moi Avenue. Its south side is where the informal economy thrives with small lunch shacks, *jua kali* artisans and, of course, the majority of *matatu* stages (Macharia 2007).

SACCO Management

In 2010 there were only a few ways to own one *matatu*: as an individual, small-scale owner, or as a member of one of the larger transportation companies like KBS or Citi Hoppa. During fieldwork in Nairobi in 2010, I found that small-scale entrepreneurs were often reluctant to sign up as members to larger fleets. Take Joyce, the woman owner of the Christian *manyanga* Tythes, who described how she weighed her options of private ownership, with the franchise model as such:

> When I decided to go to *matatu* initially I didn't have this idea [the idea for the Christian messaging]. I wanted to take it to City Hoppa so they could learn for me [*sic*]. But when I decided to go to *matatu* I didn't have the idea of what I came up with. I just bought the bus and it takes several months to make. So on the finishing I realized I don't have to go to City Hoppa 'cause I have to pay 2,000 every day for management and

there is an entrance fee of about 50,000. So I calculated ... if I manage it I can pay them [her own workers] 500 a day. So why lose 1,500 a day?

Joyce's logic stated above ceased to matter when the TLB mandated all owners of *matatu* vehicles join a SACCO or a TMC by January 2011. The TLB stated that SACCO membership would be a better way of organizing the *matatu* sector that would ensure self-regulation, efficient operation of the sector and would eventually limit cartels from operating in the sector all together (Mitullah and Onsate 2013). As the requirement took place on the ground, many SACCOs were formed rapidly, without proper education in management or even a plan of how to run a successful *matatu* operation. There have also been reports that some cartels simply branded vehicles with certain colors and names and operated as usual, ultimately legitimating their operations (Mitullah and Onsate 2013).

As the institutions meant to regulate the transportation sector promoting either a self-regulating or reregulating policy, the actual groups of managers and investors who run the *matatu* sector are important to understand ethnographically. Because they are largely left to their own devices, the way they operate this infrastructural sector, that works as a media infrastructure and moving public can tell us quite a bit about the ways that Kenyans understand the workers of this sector and how these groups become institutions of supervision each attempting to effect urban change in their own unique ways.

Hybrid Institutions of Supervision

The Mwangi Rules

The Michuki Rules probably should have been called the "Mwangi Rules," named after Mary Mwangi, the mastermind behind Double M's Express Connection bus line. Double M's Express Connection was the third big bus company with a CBD permit in 2010, but it was not owned and operated like a franchise. It was a family business. The couple, Mary and John Mwangi, built their large *matatu* fleet one vehicle at a time. In 2005, Mary recounted their story to me at her office. They started their firm in 1979, as a bodybuilder – building vehicles up from the wheelbase to the final paintjobs for other *matatu* operators. Eventually, they entered the passenger transport business themselves in 1986. Their Double M enterprise grew into one of the most successful businesses in Kenya, providing a model of bus transport for the developing world.

Before the Michuki Rules, in 2001, Mary Mwangi, the managing director of Express Connections Bus Services, was focused on filling the growing demand in her middle-class neighborhood of Buru Buru.[3] Buru Buru, as noted in Chapter 2, is a commuter-dense neighborhood located in the Eastlands of Nairobi and is well known for its joyriders and *manyanga* culture. Mary wanted to emphasize "respect and comfort" in her transport services telling me in 2010, "my service is like a cross between executive transport and *manyanga*." The Mwangi's Express Connection Bus started in 2001 in Buru Buru, and, unlike its competitors, Express Connection buses were painted purple, played no music, issued tickets for each passenger, and only allowed seated passengers to ride. The Mwangis trained each of their staff to their specifications and required them to wear a uniform of blue shirts, black ties with black sweater vests for conductors and purple shirts for drivers. They hired many women and young people who had never worked in the sector before and gave their employees a salary that they could count on, daily, so that they were less tempted to steal and would instead budget their money. During the morning rush hour there were often lines for the Express Connection vehicles.

In the first few years, Express Connection's big purple buses multiplied on route #58, throughout Buru Buru and spread to other routes. Not long after, Michuki's government task force on transportation called on the Mwangis for input for the forthcoming safety regulations. Although the government met with the Mwangis and other owners and invited them in on the process as owners, they were still stunned by the disruptive impacts of the regulations. For Double M, their vehicles were ready for Legal Notice #161 when February 2004 arrived, except for the seatbelts. They were fined just like anyone else and made to spend the exorbitant amount on the thousands of belts for their large fleet of vehicles. Also, Express Connection's employees were arrested or "fined" for not wearing the correct color of uniform, although Mary Mwangi had been requiring uniforms for her work force for the previous several years. She spoke with pride about how she eventually won the uniform battle and was able to keep her preferred color combination: purple shirts for drivers and blue for conductors accented with black vests and pants.

Mary lamented that, although some of the Michuki Rules have helped the sector, she generally saw it creating a problem for her business. Her success came in identifying a group of people who wanted to have a different type of transport experience. They wanted a quiet ride to work in contrast with the young commuters from Buru Buru who preferred a *manyanga* that played loud music and videos in the relentless traffic jam. Thus, first, Michuki mined Mary Mwangi for ideas about her successful business and then worked overtime to readjust the transport industry to fit this image. He invested in

---

[3] Double M is the name of the body-building business that the Mwangi's created, fabricating vehicles for others in their workshops and garages, this part of the business was run by John Mwangi until his death in 2011.

his own transport company that was a direct rival to the Mwangi's product, Citi Hoppa, and by using government policies to stack the deck in his favor Michuki undermined the very middle-class entrepreneur that the *Vision 2030* plan and the World Bank claimed to be supporting.

By 2019 most of the Express Connection buses were sold off to other owners and were still purple but had Embassava SACCO written across the front instead of Double M. Although not put in place until almost a decade after the original Michuki Rules in 2004, the requirement to belong to a SACCO and the creation of the NTSA also mirrored much of what Mary Mwangi was doing. She had a hotline on her buses for complaints that rang to her phones in the office. As noted, she also hired mostly women or people that had not worked in transportation before, and paid them differently. SACCOs have taken much of their lead from ideas like this but each one has their own twist. They are ultimately held responsible for their workers, so they all have different ways to supervise and manage unwieldy *matatu* workers and their variety is an interesting part of the ways transportation acts as social infrastructure, despite its near-constant reforms and reregulation.

River of God SACCO

In 2016, I visited the ROG SACCO in Nairobi's Buru Buru neighborhood. The four main owners of this SACCO met in church and had all worked in the *matatu* sector for many years as drivers and conductors. The executive board of this SACCO was interested in dealing with worker concerns like wages, precarious work lives, the threats of danger and injury, and their inability to get loans. The ROG SACCO was formed in 2014, as a response to what they saw as problematic SACCOs that did nothing for the *matatu* owners or crew members and, as their Chief Finance Officer told me, they wanted to be different and "do something with a purpose, not just make money." The management of ROG SACCO had a focus on discipline, Christian values, cleanliness, and assistance for the crews. As ROG SACCO executive member Peter explains, "The drivers and conductors, we mentored them. Most of the drivers and conductors who will be employed, most of them are drunkards, they used to chew *miraa*. We disallow. We are reforming. Rehabilitation … a job and a business."[4] "You can't do that while you are working for ROG. So, it is like reforming them," Brian chimes in; "now, many of the crews, they save with us." What he means is that one of the most important ways that the SACCO manages the lives of their workforce is by setting up savings accounts for them and providing them with small loans. At the same time, the workers

---

[4] *Miraa* is a plant with leaves that, when chewed, provide a mild stimulant effect, and also goes by the name *khat*.

are still stigmatized and highly surveilled, as the above quote from Peter implies. The managers of ROG monitor the music drivers play, their driving and their behavior on the roads by fielding phone calls and spending large parts of their days jumping on and off their vehicles at various points of the route for surprise inspections. If a crew is playing music that is not Christian or Gospel music, the driver and conductor will be punished. Sometimes this means they simply take money from their account or suspend payment from that account.

ROG SACCO, Mary Mwangi, Michuki, and Google all attempted to tame the *matatu* sector, and they have indeed impacted a small part of the sector for a short amount of time, but like all the people who have kept the buses and subways of the world's cities going for decades, it is a joint effort. In Nairobi, because there has been little by way of oversight, their independent approaches to routes, regulations, and worker management are extremely telling in the days of increasingly precarious labor.

From Citizens to Customers to Users

Although the cashless transportation card failed to launch, the concerns of surveillance capitalism have extended further in Kenya, with the passage of Kenya's National Integrated Identity Management Scheme (NIIMS). Proposed in 2019, NIIMS is the biometric database of the Kenyan population that will eventually be used to give everyone a unique "*Huduma Namba*" to access services, weed out fraudulent IDs and fight terrorism (Nyakundi 2020). Just like the cashless card, the *Huduma Namba* invites more discussion on the securitization of data and the growth of surveillance capitalism with increasing collection of citizen data. The polarization over technology into binary camps of empowerment versus technocolonialism can foreclose conversation and learning around technology use and datafication (Weitzberg et al. 2021). It is therefore methodologically important to look at the "emic" perspectives on various digital technologies no matter how contradictory, ambivalent, or diverse they may be.

In the case of the transportation cards, it was also about more than simply adopting the technology, it was about what happens when the technology is not adopted, but the regulatory machinery rolls on any way. In this way the transportation card is interesting because people did not want that technology, even as the government pushed it and owners had to spend money on the mandatory gadgets of cashless transport cards that no one ever used. This promise of technology is also a goal of the projects. These types of reregulatory schemes are working on many different levels, some more successful than others.

The cashless transport cards and the gadgets that read them exemplify important insights into challenges to financialization and responses to various types of neoliberalism, as well as illustrating the uneven regulatory environment in Kenya that is operationalized through infrastructure. The Kenyan government routinely coerces citizens using regulatory language and the language of public safety to extract funds from small-scale entrepreneurs and workers alike. Advertisements and announcements in newspapers were repeated on radio and television news. Regulations on the exterior paint, the interior music volume, the uniform of the conductor and even the lights, horns, habitus, and language of the operators is meant to curtail the autonomy of urban workers and residents, their messages, and their incomes, and to provide a foundation for a system that transfers risk and responsibility from the administrative state to a vulnerable public.

Google stating clearly that they want nothing more than "users" from a massive investment in Kenya should immediately prompt some interesting questions about the value of users. It is well documented that one important aim of neoliberal economic doctrine is shifting people's perception and category in society from citizens (someone with rights and entitlements) to customers (Mirowski 2013). For Shoshana Zuboff, a similar shift is occurring in what she calls surveillance capital firms like Google and Facebook, where customers and consumers are transforming into users and their data is being harvested as raw materials and sold to companies without their knowledge (2019). This transformation into a surveillance capitalism era is well documented, but through these technologies, even the failed ones, we can see how discreet processes unfold in people's everyday lives. When the projects of financialization fail, it is important to understand why they did, and to think about ways to protect people from the increasing inequality that neoliberalism has wrought.

Conclusion

The repeated failure to successfully launch the cashless *matatu* card and gadget technology in Nairobi is a case that shows how institutions including multinational technology corporations, like Google, in cooperation with governments, invest massive amounts of time and money into developing unnecessary technologies without taking into consideration the workings of local economies. In Kenya this happens for a variety of intersecting reasons such as the desire to appear more modern and as a global urban center of Africa and the world, and this happens through neoliberal reforms that see an increase the reregulation of everyday life through a variety of interventions, many driven by wealthy individuals, groups, and institutions. From seatbelts to cashless transportation cards and card readers, this chapter wraps infrastructural ethnography together with political economic theory in a way that can help us further understand how the financialization of everyday life can lead ultimately to different levels of empowerment, risk, and surveillance through transportation technology and digital platform economies.

When owners complain that much of the transportation policy reform in Kenya has been a thinly veiled transfer of wealth from small-scale owners to more powerful politicians and business owners they are often characterized along the lines of Gettleman's "analog Africans" who do not want to change with the times. They are often seen as greedy or reckless "thugs" who would prefer things to remain the same so they can continue to operate with nefarious motivations. I, along with others (Klopp et al. 2019; Mitullah and Onsate 2013) argue that instead of these characterizations it is important to ask the questions about how these confused and contradictory policies might be implemented on the ground and who would suffer or benefit after their implementation.

By tracing a variety of regulations across the past twenty years, you can see the uneven but clearly neoliberal trajectory of the interventions into the transportation sector. Not only that, but transportation by the nature of being mobile and on the frontier of social and material life, is often on the cutting edge of exchange. For Nairobi's *matatu* sector, that means an increasing push toward financial technology and platform economies, which is what the cashless transportation card and ultimately the other biometric projects are trying to do. These products are part of the everyday financialization that pushes people more deeply into the global economic sphere and, increasingly into a relationship with surveillance capitalism. Even though many people are doubtful that transport card technology will ever be adopted widely it is an important trend for scholars to recognize and highlight the myriad ways that infrastructure operationalizes suffering, power, and inequality.

5

Paradoxes of Empowerment: Gendered Labor in the *Matatu* Sector

One evening in July 2019, I had a tense but telling interaction at a South Asian restaurant in Nairobi with a man who came in for take-out. He was a middle-aged Kenyan of South Asian origin and as he overheard my conversation while he waited for his food, he began nodding disapprovingly in my direction.[1] I was seated at the bar eating ginger chicken wings and chatting about new *Sheng* words with two bartenders in their late twenties and a younger barback, all of whom were Kenyans of African origin. After a few minutes, the man turned in my direction and asked me frankly, "What are you doing here?" He did not mean in the restaurant; he meant in Kenya.[2] When I answered that I was there to "learn about *matatu* workers," he shouted at me without smiling, "I love *matatus*! *Matatus* are great! There is nothing wrong with *matatu*!" I assumed this man was defending the *matatu* sector so virulently to me because he anticipated that I, an *mzungu* (White/foreign person), would be critical of them.[3] Although not friendly, I was happy to continue this somewhat hostile interaction because Kenyans of South Asian origin are often highly critical of the *matatu* sector and known to avoid riding *matatu* vehicles, largely due to their upper socioeconomic status and ability to afford other, usually private, and more expensive, means of transportation.[4] For an example of the off-handed way

---

[1] There is a substantial number of Kenyans of South Asian origin whose families immigrated to Kenya from Gujurat, Punjab, and Goa. The majority of the population lives in Nairobi, and they are known to be "urban, heterogenoeus and relatively wealthy" (Herzig 2006).

[2] I know this because my first response was, "eating chicken wings," an answer he found to be unacceptable.

[3] As discussed at length in the Introduction, *mzungu* generally refers to a White person or foreigner/non-African more broadly. It comes from the root *kuzunguka*, to turn around, implying that the name is less about skin color and more about the people with the ability to move around the world, originally applied to missionaries or colonial officials.

[4] As briefly mentioned in Chapter 1, Nairobi was racially segregated and had a large population of South Asian workers who came to Kenya to build the railroad and then settled in Nairobi and Mombasa and opened shops. Since then, Kenyans of Asian

matatu vehicles are generally dismissed by Kenyans of Asian origin, in 2022, a prominent Kenyan Asian businessman slightly sneered when I informed him of my research interests in *matatu* workers. He responded quickly, "We ... don't like them," pointing to his adult daughters who appeared to be embarrassed by their inclusion in their father's strong opinion. Feigning surprise, I asked, "Oh, you have ridden them?" Smiling a little, he quietly admitted that "No" he had never ridden a *matatu* in his life, and neither had his daughters, both of whom were raised in Nairobi.

This well-known aversion to *matatu* by Kenyans of South Asian origin is why I was excited to get the unique perspective of the man getting his take-out. I offered more information about the project I was investigating, "Right now, I'm working with women *matatu* workers." At this statement, he looked at me in a way that communicated displeasure and incredulity, "*Women* conductors? Impossible! No way!! I don't believe that any African man would ever let his wife work on a *matatu*!"[5] Getting louder, "*No fucking way* do women belong on *matatu*!" The bar staff and I quickly exchanged that look people exchange when they know things may get out of hand. I reminded the take-out man that moments ago he "loved *matatu*" and thought they were "great," so, I asked "why weren't they great for women?"

Without answering me, he proceeded to interrogate the two bartenders about if they would let their wives and girlfriends work in a *matatu*. The young barback looked terrified throughout the entire encounter, but, Joseph, the full-time bartender, eagerly engaged with the man while nonchalantly polishing a glass. He said that he would support his wife in whatever job she wanted to pursue, and that *matatu* workers made decent money, which would also be nice for their household. The man waiting for take-out shouted, "*Mwongo*! Liar! Are you saying this so that this *mzungu* will give you a better tip?" gesturing in my direction. Joseph laughed it off and assured him that he really felt fine with his partner working on a *matatu* if she wanted, and the man continued to call him a liar. The man's food arrived shortly after this exchange, and he left. When processing the interaction afterward, Joseph assured me that the man was a regular and that there would be no backlash

---

descent have been a crucial part of Nairobi's economic and social life, numbering about 100,000 people and making up about 2 percent of Kenya's population (Oonk 2013). In 2017, President Uhuru Kenyatta named Kenyan Asians of Indian descent the 44th tribe of Kenya (Ombuor 2017).

5   Although the speaker was probably born and raised in Nairobi, he was specifically referring to Kenyans of African descent when he says "African man" in this sentence. And, although we were in a South Asian restaurant, apart from the management and some kitchen staff, all front of the house, servers, and bartenders, were Kenyans of African descent.

for what I perceived as potentially causing a hostile interaction at the bar of my favorite restaurant. It turns out, Joseph was correct and on a recent visit to the restaurant in 2022, he was still behind the restaurant bar and even nonchalantly polishing a glass when I arrived. I ordered some wings, and we discussed how angry the take-out man might be now, three years later, when the number of women who work in *matatu* had only grown.[6]

Women and Mobility

Women do not need to be employed in the transportation sector to be stigmatized for their mobility. Studies have found that in rural settings in the Global South, women who travel frequently are stigmatized, where men's travel is rarely restricted (Fernando and Porter 2002: 5). This is even more troublesome because women often carry heavier transportation burdens than men and although they make shorter trips, they travel more frequently (Williams et al. 2020; Porter 2008; Khosa 1997). As will be reflected in this chapter, the tensions women in the *matatu* sector face between work and household structures often compound women's mobility and transportation burdens, even when the woman is seen to be empowered (Porter 2011).

Negative perceptions of women on the move can inform the fact that women make up only 22 percent of the world's transportation workforce (Wright 2016: 1). Transportation is one of the most male-dominated fields in the world, second only to the construction sector and in professions from aviation to long-distance truck driving, women are barely represented (Wright 2016). In an informal survey among researchers of minibus transportation in African cities, in October of 2022, researchers reported that in their field sites in Ibadan, Lagos, Dakar, and Accra, there were no women whom they had observed working in transport.[7] Women have, however, been working in the minibus taxi sectors in both Durban and Gauteng, South Africa since 1990, making up 7 to 10 percent of taxi operators in those places (Khosa 1997). The employment of women in Nairobi's *matatu* sector, even at low levels is yet another unique feature of popular transportation in Kenya, in addition to it surviving as one of the only indigenous African minibus and midibus taxis (MBT) sectors that was never fully, or even partially, controlled by the government and its role as a moving urban public and type of media infrastructure.

Public transportation is one of the most dangerous places for women in the world, especially in urban environments where women are at increased risk

---

[6] It is difficult to know how many women are currently working in the sector.
[7] Personal communication with transportation scholars Daniel Agbiboa, Godwin Boateng, Sidy Cissokho, and Jaqueline Klopp, New York City, October 2022.

of gender-based violence (GBV). The numbers of women who have experienced sexual harassment on public transportation or waiting for transportation is staggering: 50 percent of women in Delhi reported sexual harassment on public transportation, 89 percent in Santiago, Chile and 78 percent in Karachi, Pakistan (Williams et al. 2020: 4). In Kenya, 2014, several women were stripped and assaulted by male *matatu* workers and passengers for allegedly wearing inappropriate clothing, and an assault of a young girl in a *matatu* that year was captured on the perpetrator's phones, which was subsequently released to the public and went viral identifying the *matatu* and offenders, one of whom turned out to be a police officer (Nyabola 2018: 127).

There are places where women do provide transportation services, and even dominate some of the modes (Grossman-Thompson 2020), but they still face the multilayered contradictions of this type of labor. In Kathmandu, Nepal, for example, women make up the majority of *tuk tuk* (*tempo*) drivers, the workers numbering around 700 (Grossman-Thompson 2020). Women entered this workforce in the 1990s and have, in the past decade, overtaken it. *Tempos* are ubiquitous in Kathmandu and the women are publicly celebrated for their work, but the lived reality for women *tempo* drivers is very different indeed. Through the lens of gender as social structure the opportunities and challenges that women in male-dominated work experience are felt as individuals in their homes and among their family. Women experienced these challenges and opportunities during public interactions with other people or groups, like police officers as well as feeling the contradictions at the macro level, among institutional domains (Grossman-Thompson 2020: 877). Just as the Nepalese *tempo* drivers experience the multilayered ambivalence of their intersectional stigma, so do women in transportation in Kenya experience the dynamic vicissitudes of their work in their home lives, in the streets and on increasingly bigger stages.

Gendered Work in Nairobi

Women in Nairobi have a long history of accessing and controlling urban spaces and using them to their own ends, as shown by the settlement and renting of property in early Nairobi (White 1990) and the brewing, transportation, and selling of gin by Nubian women (De Smedt 2009). Louise White describes the sex workers who built Nairobi as pioneers who had "always been beyond official regulation," not because they were impossible to control, but because "control was already being exerted in the spaces Africans established, negotiated and controlled, with their own ideas about property, family and loyalty" (1990: 228). In these spaces they exerted their own power and constrained colonial control.

Transportation is one of the most ephemeral spaces in urban life and that Nubian women took advantage of it during in the 1950s to smuggle gin throughout Emergency era Nairobi, challenges these assumptions about women's roles in colonial Kenya (see Chapter 1). The ephemeral space of city life (the informal settlements built and destroyed, the migration and movement of workers through the city, the displacement of people from their families) allowed for spaces to open in Nairobi where women could thrive. Even in the highly controlled era of Operation Anvil, African women and men were exerting power in spaces like the colonial bus that straddled public and private domains to build their own businesses and tend to their own communities in the face of extremely violent measures previously not experienced in Nairobi. The Kenya Bus Service (KBS) vehicles provided an important space in late-colonial Nairobi where African women were challenging European settlers and their claims over urban public space.

African women continued to challenge claims over urban space in postcolonial Nairobi as well. Not only through markets and hawkers and *jua kali* sector workers but through the activism of women like Wangari Maathai, 2004 Nobel Peace Prize winner and first woman to obtain a PhD in Kenya (Florence 2014). In 1989, Maathai organized women to stage protests and sit-ins in Uhuru Park when President Moi was planning on building a skyscraper there called Times Tower. On behalf of the Kenyan public and generations of Kenyans to come, Maathai protested the building of Times Tower in Uhuru Park and organized women to save one of the only green spaces in Nairobi, which they did. Uhuru Park was never developed by Moi. A decade later in 1999, she and Kenyan women demonstrated to save Karura Forest, an urban forest in Nairobi and was injured by police in the protest (Florence 2014; Maathai 2007).

In 2010 Kenya adopted a new constitution that is one of the most progressive in the world regarding gender equality in political representation. Kenya ranks 48 out of 145 on the Global Gender Index, but there are still significant gaps in gender equality and a high rate of GBV (Mitullah 2020: 171). When the incidents of public stripping and assault of women increased in 2014, with the especially heinous assault that was captured on video and went viral, it prompted Nairobi feminists to spontaneously come together on the internet and in real life building the #mydressmychoice movement (Nyabola 2018). Naomi Mwaura was one of those young feminists online who was also deeply tied to the *matatu* sector by way of a long family history of ownership in the sector. These assaults by *matatu* operators impacted her profoundly and drove her to start to reimagine what safe transportation for women might look like in

Nairobi. A few months later she was not only organizing on behalf of female passengers in Nairobi, but also on behalf of the growing number of women working in *matatu* vehicles as well. In 2015 she founded Flone Initiative to organize for safer transportation for women (https://floneinitiative.org).[8]

When Flone Initiative started, Naomi concentrated on the passengers being harassed, but she quickly realized that the women working in the sector were all facing near-constant harassment and were also keys to making women passengers feel safer. The more women working on public transportation the safer women passengers feel. As mentioned throughout this book, the *matatu* itself is perceived as a masculinized place in Kenya, but through Flone Initiative and the cultural materials they have produced the *matatu* has at times become a feminist counterpublic. Flone Initiative has produced songs, music videos, plays, and posters in addition to holding workshops and other types of programming for women in transport to gain skills and learn about their rights (https://floneinitiative.org/). One important avenue of organization that Flone Initiative has developed is the Women in Transportation (WIT) chapters that bring together women working in various forms of transport (*matatu*, private taxis, and motorcycle taxi) to discuss their successes and struggles and to learn more about their rights and strategies to stay safe and thrive. There are WIT chapters in Nairobi, Mombasa, Nakuru, Machakos, and Naivasha. These WIT chapters and the ability of Flone Initiatives are a direct challenge to the masculinized tradition of *matatu* work.

The *Matatu* as Gendered Space

Women and men experience the *matatu* sector in different but overlapping ways. It is a gendered space where they perform masculinity and femininity. As discussed in previous chapters, *matatu* workers create social and economic safety nets for themselves by redistributing cash and trading *skwads* as part of everyday life and work. Through this stigmatized and dangerous work identity they form solidarities, although fragile at times. Women also experience the *matatu* as a gendered space and practice reciprocity and redistribution along with the solidarity of work, but they deploy different strategies to succeed in the male-dominated space. Women experience a double stigma as the minority group in an already stigmatized sector of dirty work (Webber and Giuffre 2019). Their minority status provides the conditions for paradoxes of empowerment where they simultaneously experience success in their professional

---

[8] For more on Naomi Mwaura's background and Flone Initiative's mission see her 2021 TED talk (https://www.ted.com/talks/naomi_mwaura_a_feminist_reimagining_of_kenya_s_public_transport).

lives, which can cause increasing strife in their domestic or personal lives. Anthropologists' and feminist scholars' work on women and empowerment highlights the centrality of social relationships in the context of power and the process through which those who are denied decision-making power acquire the ability to make strategic life choices (Kabeer 1999 quoted in Antoniello 2020: 157). In Elizabeth's remarkable story, discussed in depth throughout this chapter, she found herself on a billboard, larger than life, while being diminished at home.

In Mbugua wa Mungai's 2013 ethnography, *Nairobi's Matatu Men*, he argues that *matatu* workers use the space and recklessness of the *matatu* to exert their masculinity in the face of women's encroachment in the public sphere. Wa-Mungai theorizes that *matatu* men are marginal men angry at, and even a little afraid of, women in the professional world, which includes working in a *matatu* or even driving their own cars in a roundabout, so they make *matatu* spaces into spaces of danger and transgression allowing them to "revel in breaking the rules" and to find a place in the world (2013: 21). Other scholars have similarly argued that this masculine public space serves as a transgressive space for young men who are experiencing increasing precarity in cities with popular transportation sectors, such as Lagos (Agbiboa 2022) and Dar es Salaam (Rizzo 2017). These spaces are seen as "embedded with an idea of violence" and the idea that women should stay out of public spaces, like the street or public transportation, is enacted through the "intolerable conditions" of the male space of the *matatu* (Wa-Mungai 2013: 19).

Some of the "intolerable conditions" meant to turn people off from the *matatu* can turn them on, such as the youth who practice joyriding (see Chapter 2). The ways *matatu* operators use the urban linguistic register, *Sheng*, to create privacy or negotiate bribes with police or pay off gangsters reveals how they use their mannerisms, attire, and musical tastes to convey their cultural and linguistic capital and make transactions in the "hustle economy" (Thieme 2018) (see Chapter 3). These mannerisms, language practices, clothing, and movement choices that build one's neighborhood and route reputations to attract riders and appeal to women, are what Wa-Mungai calls "*Matatuism* – the supreme trope for improvisational transactions" (2013: 24). Doing dangerous things like hanging off the vehicle on the highway to show how fearless one is or running to *dondoa* (jump on) or *dandoka* (jump off) the moving vehicle to make a memorable entrance at the *matatu* waiting area, appropriately called a stage (Chapter 2) is another way *matatu* workers show off their bravery and masculinity in public.

Alternatively, a few savings and credit co-operatives (SACCOs) have embraced hiring women. Like the individual, small-scale entrepreneurs who came before them, these groups also take their own nuanced approaches to *matatu* management. For instance, executive members of the River of God (ROG) SACCO, discussed in the last chapter, identify as born-again Christians, and openly see their *matatu* worker employees as "lost souls" to be saved and rehabilitated (Chapter 4). While the Embassava SACCO, the self-proclaimed oldest transportation SACCO in Nairobi, was one of the first groups to hire women and still tends to employ an above average number of women in their workforce.

This idiosyncratic approach to *matatu* management can work for and against women because even when the owner and crew of a specific vehicle want to employ someone, the SACCO can overrule the owner and suspend or expel their preferred worker. Take for example, Lucia, the lone *mlami* conductor in the WIT group, and the only White person I am aware of to work steadily in the *matatu* sector. Lucia was born in Italy but raised in Kenya. Lucia's parents, a nurse and physical therapist, run a medical clinic on the outskirts of Nairobi. Lucia grew up, like many young Kenyans, wanting to work on a *matatu*. Having lived in Kenya for most of her life, she speaks fluent Swahili and *Sheng* and worked on the same *matatu* as her high-school friend Joseph, who was the driver. When I met with Lucia in 2019, she was not working on the *matatu* because she had been suspended from her regular vehicle by SACCO management. It was rumored that she had pushed a pregnant woman off the bus. She told me that the woman had come into the SACCO office to complain but would never meet up with her so that Lucia could apologize. Lucia was skeptical that the woman actually existed, saying, "I love women! Why would I push a pregnant lady?" While she was waiting to be reinstated to her vehicle by the SACCO, she was working at her parents' medical clinic, which made her parents happier than when she was working in the *matatu*. She had been suspended for ten months and was slowly coming to terms with the fact that she would probably not get to go back to the work that she loved any time soon.

Many of the women I have spoken with would like to do more *matatu* work, but there are some stereotypical beliefs that seem to be holding them back. Take for example the following cross-sectional research Elizabeth and I conducted in Nairobi, on 4 April 2023. I had spent the previous several weeks in Nairobi with Elizabeth walking through the various *matatu* stages. We visited many women who were working in and around *matatu* vehicles, often stopping just to say hello and chat. I usually introduced myself and told them about my research and then we asked a few questions. On this specific day, we started with Mary and Joshua who both managed a corner where several *manyanga* vehicles picked up customers. At some point I suggested that eventually Mary might become a conductor on one of the *manyanga* vehicles she was managing. Everyone laughed at this, even Elizabeth, as though it was a ridiculous suggestion. Joshua explained quickly, stating matter-of-factly that women do not work on *manyanga* vehicles because they "are not fast, and cannot meet daily targets." As discussed at length in Chapter 2, *manyanga* vehicles are usually equipped with expensive sound systems and decorated with quality graphics in a way that sets them apart from plain *matatu* vehicles. Because of this they are often more popular and make more money because they fill up with people faster and more often than undecorated *matatu* vehicles. As Joseph explained why women were not able to work on *manyanga*, Mary, was nodding her head yes, and seemed to instinctively agree with her co-worker. Elizabeth, perhaps sensing my suspicion around this explanation hurriedly described how "women work on *punda* (donkey) vehicles, not *manyanga*." Joshua and Mary nodded in agreement, but it took me a moment to piece together the double meaning of a donkey vehicle. Elizabeth explained that *punda* vehicles were unattractive vehicles but hard working like donkeys and boring because they all looked the same.

Although Elizabeth, Mary, and Joshua took this *punda/manyanga* distinction at face value, I convinced Elizabeth to ask our local contacts a question throughout the day and see what we might learn. We developed this question: Why do women work on *punda* vehicles and not on *manyanga* vehicles? Starting around 10:00am and finishing around 5:00pm that day, we asked seventeen women and five men a version of this question. We already knew most interlocutors, so there was some rapport built already but the question itself attracted some new participants who were interested in answering. Each of our discussions lasted between five and thirty minutes but were not audio recorded. We rarely interviewed one person at a time because most people were sitting in groups talking.

The first group of people we talked to after Mary and Joshua was a group of *matatu* men and they said that women "are not fast" and they "cannot jump on and off the vehicle while its moving" like men can. One of these men explained that women have a hard time hitting the target of 14,000 KES ($140 USD) explaining, "the *punda* target is only 7,000 KES [$70 USD] so it is easy, but to get 14,000 KES means that you have to be kind of pushy and rude ... women can't do that." Elizabeth and I laughed very hard at this statement, as did the group of men realizing that it sounded a bit naïve. The last reason the man gave was because "they can't shout." Elizabeth responded that "shouting is one of my main qualifications!" Elizabeth and I walked to where one of our favorite female conductors named Rhea often worked. When we told her what we had been hearing about women working on *manyanga* vehicles, Rhea responded that "she could shout" and that it would "not be hard" to meet the 14,000 KES target. Laughing and confident, she told us to "bring a *manyanga* and I will work on it." This conversation was cut short because her 14-seat *punda* vehicle was filled and ready to go.

Next, we ran into the Chairman of the Embassava SACCO, Mwai, who was with the SACCO Secretary Lucas and an owner and former Chairman, Zachary. We exchanged greetings and discussed the upcoming SACCO elections before asking our question about women in *manyanga*. Lucas and Mwai offered a new set of reasons saying, "the music was too loud for women's ears." Mwai attempted to elaborate, explaining that "women's ears cannot listen to music that loudly for that long … because of … " his speaking description trailed off, but he continued through gesticulation, taking both of his hands and making them like he was holding a ball, and smiling at us as though this gesture was self-explanatory. I asked what his "holding a ball" motion meant, and he said it means a "mess." I understood this to communicate that women's ears could not handle the messy loudness of the music played in *manyanga* vehicles. Soon after, Lucas took his turn to clarify the explanation by saying, "women are like … " and while he trailed off, he held his hands out like he was catching water from a faucet. Upon asking what that movement meant, he explained that it was to convey that women were "fragile and in need of protecting."

We talked with several more groups of women who argued that they would work for a *manyanga* at any time because you make more money. Several did agree with some of what had been said about politeness and loud music, but most women disagreed with the idea that women would not be able to meet the daily targets of the manyanga. We were nearly done asking questions for the day when Elizabeth cut in between several buildings which opened to an internal courtyard were a few *manyanga* vehicles were parked and where a man with a pen behind is ear, who we both immediately knew was the manager, was pointing at people and writing notes. We approached him and he was a bit skeptical, probably accustomed to being left alone in this inner urban sanctum, but as we asked our *punda/mayanga* question he said something we had not heard before, laying bare a flawed assumption under which we had been operating. He looked at us and simply said "there are women working on *manyanga*, one is expected here in a few minutes." He assured us that "she can do it all … run, jump, meet targets and yell." Sure enough, within the next few minutes a *manyanga* pulled into the space and a short woman in her mid-twenties jumped out. The manager explained briefly who we were, and she was polite enough to chat for a few minutes, but it was apparent she was in a hurry. We did not have well-developed questions for her because we had not expected her to be working on a *manyanga*. As we had her attention, we stumbled through a few basic questions about how long she had been working on her vehicle and whether she liked the work, which she answered politely before she ran off quickly to eat something before her next *skwad*.

Although Joseph, the bartender who is still probably nonchalantly polishing glasses at the Open House restaurant, was most likely telling the truth about supporting his partner if they worked in the *matatu* sector, the man getting his take-out was also correct when he said that many men in Kenya would not be supportive of that career choice. Many people in Kenya believe that a *matatu* is no place for a woman. It is seen as dirty and dangerous. Even those who employ and work with women *matatu* workers daily believe that certain vehicles should still be off-limits to women, like the *manyanga* which are "too loud for women's ears." These vehicles are still seen as a place for men, but that has not stopped women in Kenya from pouring into the sector, expanding their numbers, and breaking new ground with no sign of stopping.

Post-structuralist feminist thinkers have cogently discussed how we are constantly in the process of being made as gendered beings (Ortner 1997; Butler 1990; Collier and Yanagisako 1987). The category of being a man or being a woman is not static or always coherent but is something that we are always doing, and that doing is the production of our gender through word and deed and appearance and other people's understanding of you and your behaviors. The *matatu* provides a place where men and women not only perform various types of gendered identities but also challenge them. A *matatu* is a place where these identities can be displayed and toyed with. There is a safety in between the seats of the *matatu* vehicle where women can be vulnerable and a place that can be dangerous.

Matatu work is a gendered performance and the *matatu* is the stage, a place that is perceived as a masculine space. What is often overlooked in these performances are the variety in both the masculine and feminine performances of *matatu* work. Some women enjoy the ability to be loud and big, while some accentuate more stereotypically feminine qualities. For some men, they see the *matatu* as a space that is a masculine rite of passage, but the urban environment is not monolithic. The ethnographic data presented below shows how *matatu* workers debate and differ on their understandings of their own femininity and masculinity and the way their work and how the *matatu* vehicle itself shapes and is shaped by it.

Gendered Regimes of Labor in *Matatu* Work

The gendered aspects of *matatu* labor regimes that women and men experience and enact, and the practices they use to cope and thrive take place in a sector that is often risky, and sometimes violent. *Matatu* men's performances of urban masculinity, while carrying both a stigma and an air of admiration, are built into the *matatu* labor regime, the assemblages that "set the conditions of work [which] include materials, spaces, schedules, tools, food, conditions of social reproduction, and the rules and rewards of punishment" (Itwstu 2017, paraphrasing Murray-Li 2017). These labor regimes are integral to producing workers and include labor processes, wage relations, forms of control and domination and mechanisms of worker representation. They are also gendered in many intersecting and crosscutting ways.

The ethnographic material presented here will show how *matatu* men interpret the impact of their work on their masculinity, as well as how women experience the precarity of their labor and build both formal and informal means of solidarity to deal with the multilayered and dynamic impacts of their unique work on their personal lives at individual, interpersonal, and structural levels. *Matatu* men construct, socially reproduce, and perform urban masculinity through their work in the *matatu* vehicle and through their interactions with women passengers, explained in more detail below. Women working in the *matatu* sector attempt to carve out their own unique spaces in the absence of institutional support and in the face of intersectional stigma. As discussed earlier (Chapter 2), young men use their *matatu* worker personas, or "route reputations," to feel empowered, confident, and even famous, while *matatu* women's labor practices and personal relationships are intertwined in ways that are simultaneously rewarding and punishing, crosscutting differing domains of the household, the street, and the state. The way these layers intersect for women in Nairobi's *matatu* sector can answer important questions about the support women need as they enter this and other male-dominated occupations, about how women secure dignified labor conditions, and about how to understand the ways urban transportation is shifting beneath our feet.

As Erving Goffman observed, in addition to the disdain stigmatized people experience, there is also an awe that can take hold and produce people who are groupies or fans based on their attraction to the outcast positionality (1963). The subcultural awe that *matatu* workers can elicit impact both men and women. In fact, several upper-middle-class Kenyan men I knew in Nairobi, told me stories of working on a *matatu* as a "rite of passage." In classic anthropological terms, a rite of passage is a ritual that helps to usher people into different stages of their lives. For young men in Nairobi, and in the rural areas, *matatu* work transformed boys to men, or what were shy, demure, polite young men into the confident, capable, transgressive rebels of the *matatu* workforce. Day in and day out operators participate in the unspoken rules of the *matatu* sector which includes how to speak *Sheng*, deal with police, and negotiate with gangsters, along with traveling all over Nairobi and encountering hundreds of people a day, building the skills and traits they need to make it in the world.

The topic of urban expertise was commonly discussed in my fieldwork, as *matatu* operators saw themselves as extremely capable urban actors, who knew nearly everything about getting around the city and getting around in life. The interview data in this section comes from a several-hours-long conversation I had in 2009 over tea with six *matatu* workers from the route I worked on in Nairobi, route #48. This was one of several recorded interviews that I held with this group of *matatu* operators.[9] It is obvious from the conversation below that they feel that the *matatu* sector is a place where they gain confidence, and that the *matatu* sector helps them to grow and mature, like a journey of self-discovery.

> **Rasta George**: When people used to come into the *matatu* industry they used to be very shy, and when they come into *matatus* they come out of that shy, and that shy goes, See?
>
> **MF**: So, it gives people ... confidence?
>
> **Rasta George**: Yeah, confidence. Most of us ... when we come in the *matatu* industry, eh, you know most of them they don't know many parts of the country ... but when they get in *matatu* industry ... 'Cause you can get a job and get out of Nairobi and you can have someone hire you and go someplace like Eldoret [a mid-sized town in Western Kenya] and see parts of the city ... you have not seen.
>
> **MF**: So, you became like a tourist?
>
> **Rasta George**: Yeah, you see things you would never see if you are not into *matatu* industry.

---

[9] The people around the table (some of whom have been introduced earlier in this ethnography), are Steve, my dear friend, driver of Frost who was killed in a *matatu* accident not long after we had this conversation; Rasta George, a dreadlocked conductor who was also the treasurer of the #48 route association; George, not to be confused with Rasta George, who was bald and the oldest of the group, in his mid-40s; Gladys, a woman conductor in her 30s; and Wilson, a conductor in his mid-20s. It should be noted that the reason that we could sit and have this little tea break in the middle of a workday is because all the interviewees had given away *skwads* (round trips) to part-time workers who waited around the *matatu* stage in efforts to pick up a trip or two for some cash each day.

According to these workers, *matatu* operators grow and transform from seeing different parts of the country and meeting different people. They lose their shyness, which is seen as a weakness and gain the ability to talk to anyone because of the interactions they have in public transport.

In *Matatu Men*, Wa-Mungai discusses the ways that men treat women in the streets and in the *matatu* through a lens of transgression and misogyny, but some women perceive the bravado that *matatu* operators display as attractive. It is a common trope in Kenyan media (TV, newspaper comics, jokes), that fathers of teenage girls are constantly chasing their daughters away from *matatu* men, because they are known to seduce young women with their urban language, handfuls of cash and free rides. Here, the group discusses why they think women like *matatu* operators and then proceed to disagree on the reasons. Mutongi casts this experience as an outcome of the historical processes in Kenyans neoliberal and political past by bringing about a "Generation *Matatu*" who, born between the 1980s and 2000s had high-school diplomas and high expectations, but, disillusioned throughout the 1990s, they turned to the popular economy and used *matatu* vehicles to "announce their presence and assert their identity" (2017: 216). This 2009 conversation takes place, long after these first forays of educated and capable people entered the sector, and the interactions recorded here give a sense of variation in the perspectives of "*matatu* men," who are often lumped together as "thugs" and not differentiated as individuals.

Presenting the conversation in the format below is productive for the way it shows the constant communication, corroborating or fine-tuning arguments and understandings about the world that *matatu* workers engage with in their informal work interactions. This conversation meanders through the topic of *matatu* and masculinity, indicating that a key to *matatu* masculinity is confidence, when speaking, and especially when speaking to women.

> **Steve**: [laughing] You know the conductors ... mostly they [women] like conductors. Maybe somebody might be cute. But in the conductor, the masculinity becomes dominant. [laughing] ... uh ... like talking straight. Like, "I like you."
>
> **MF**: No beating around the bush ...
>
> **Steve**: Haha [laughing loudly] ... yeah, no beating [assuming I just made a sexual joke, which I was unaware of at the time, and then regaining composure and continuing after realizing it was accidental] ... um, and then you are a lady, you feel weak inside and I don't know what, what [trying to think of some clever line to say] ... "Today, what you are wearing looks smart" and ...

Rasta George: "It looks smart ... " [repeating the compliment in his own flirtatious way]

MF: So just giving compliments?

Rasta George: Yeah

Matatu workers built this confidence and their skills in talking to women into something valuable that working in the sector gives them, in addition to cash money every day, which they also cite for the reason they can confidently talk to women.

MF: Are other Kenyan men shy? Or would they just not say *that*?

Rasta George: Yeah ... [others at the table are humming in agreement] ... yeah, most people, I tell you, get out of the shy when they came to be in the *matatu* industry...

George: When they get out of the industry, they are very, very confident. People even tell you, in this industry, that they are God-fearing and that they go to church every Sunday. But when they enter in...

Rasta George ... they forget about the church.

George: ... they forget all about the church. They start talking nasty things. At least some that I knew back in the day ... [laughing and trailing off]

Although this last comment is made as a joke, a conductor I met in 2004 named Anthony often struggled with his Christian faith and the business practices of the *matatu* sector. In Anthony's case, it was the police corruption, not the sexualized interactions between conductors and passengers that triggered his guilt. By 2010, he was working as a security guard at a luxury hotel and no longer struggling with his morality.

The idea of access to daily cash is mentioned as one of the reasons people change in good (building confidence) and bad (losing their faith) ways in the *matatu* sector, but as "Generation *Matatu*" found as they ditched formalized labor for the "hustle economy", making money every day was often better than getting a salary and waiting for a monthly paycheck. "Daily bread" was a major benefit to working in the *matatu* sector. Having money every day allows you options.

Rasta George: It's because you have money. Money makes us to change. Money ... cause if you have money, you can buy what you want you can even buy *wasichana* [young women].

> **Gladys**: [the only woman at the table besides myself laughs loudly at this and adds] ... ha, you can even buy *watoto* [children].
>
> **George**: And sometimes, when they are riding on your vehicle, see sometimes, they just ... don't ... *waenda sare* – when they go for free. [frustrated at how to translate into English].[10]
>
> **MF**: When you give young girls rides for free?
>
> **Rasta George**: Yeah ... *sare* ... if you have a lady somewhere, you tell the conductor, that lady there, don't ask money from that lady. When the lady comes out and sees ... eh, the driver told me not pay ... [Wilson laughs loudly at this in a mischievous way].
>
> **MF**: So, you can do things for them?
>
> **Rasta George**: Yeah.

At this point, Steve jumps back in to disagree with both Georges about the reason women like *matatu* operators, and what they think women really want from men in general. The Georges see the free rides and daily cash money as the motivation for women to like *matatu* workers, but Steve clings to the fact that it is a type of masculine performance that women love and the *matatu* men have mastered, which is much different than the aggressive and transgressive attitudes generally applied to *matatu* men.

> **Steve**: Ok, most of the ... uh, the guys who are working this white-collar job, uh ... it's not like you can find a man, telling you ... "you know what, I like that lady" ... and you, you [looking at me as a woman] kind of connect to that.
>
> **MF**: Yeah, 'cause they're [the white-collar workers] a little afraid?
>
> **Steve**: Yeah ... 'cause they are a little afraid. And to some extent ... they can even pay you to go and talk for them...

---

[10] *Sare* directly translates into "uniform" but, throughout the years, the *Sheng* meaning when referring to *sare* has come to mean "free." The connection is that young school girls and boys in uniforms used to ride for free under Moi in the 1980s. However, because the *matatu* sector was unregulated and rougher at that time, *sare* came to have a sexual connotation with free rides for schoolgirls. If you are in a uniform and you expect to ride for free, you would often have to give a sexual favor in return.

MF: We call that being a wingman...

Rasta George: Yeah ... wingman

Steve: [asking me sarcastically in reference to earlier discussions we had about anthropology] is that a human universal?

MF: Most women like it when you talk to them.

Steve: Yeah, they do. They do. When they think you are interested ... they feel good.

MF: Yes, *matatu* people can make you feel good ... or bad...

Rasta George: ... or bad...

MF: If someone is abusing you ...

As we continue talking, there is a bit of a disagreement among the ways that some actions can be taken. George, who is the oldest of the group and in an administrative position in the route association, seems to understand why a woman might be feel afraid around *matatu* operators, even when the operators have no ill will in mind. He comments on how some women feel and behave around the *matatu* stage, while the other men see the interactions very differently. They all seem like they agree, touching women and ushering them into your vehicle is common, but they disagree on the motivations behind it.

Rasta George: Even touching ... you can, in a *matatu* you can see a lady and then touch his [*sic*] back...

George: You know when you are entering a *matatu* and I touch your back, I feel very confident when I touch your back, you are just getting in the *matatu*, you have seen that ... ?

MF: Yeah, they are always like ... get in! [I am referring to how matatu operators gather people in to their vehicles and sometimes put their hand on people's backs, gently and sometimes not so gently, pushing you in to the vehicle].

Wilson: ... yeah, get in ... [laughing while feigning to push someone]

George: So the ladies feel [he scrunches up his shoulders and pulls his hands to his solar plexus while pulling a shocked face] ... they hold their purses very tight.

Wilson: If you are fighting for a passenger that is the best technique you can use [sensing my confusion] ... not *fighting* for a passenger ... but

MF: Oh, so you touch a passenger and then you know ... they know ... you like them?

Wilson: Yeah...

Steve: Yeah, you [the female passenger] know the guy is ... tender. You know? This guy is kind of tender, friendly.

I asked them if they could understand how some women might see their touching as a bit aggressive. Only George and Gladys agreed, while the others assured me that they were not aggressive and that most women liked their tender touching tactics. One of them mentioning how women feel afraid and the other seemingly oblivious to how "tender touching" may be perceived.

"Commanding Our Space": Women in *Matatus*

Transnational feminist political economists have highlighted examples of transcultural anxiety around women's proletarianization as they move from domestic work to wage labor (Grossman-Thompson 2020). When women enter a stigmatized occupation that is male-dominated they can be doubly stigmatized, which is the case in *matatu* work, and in transportation work throughout the globe more broadly (Grossman-Thompson 2020; Wright 2016). This intersectional stigma comes from the occupational hazard of *matatu* work, combined with the stigma of being a woman in a male-dominated occupation. Like many women working in the neoliberal economy, their economic lives are riddled with contradictions, like the way their work often allows for more autonomy through increased access to cash, but also enables more surveillance at many nodes of their daily activities (Siddiqi 2020). Women *matatu* workers have a variety of coping mechanisms to deal with their contradictory positions on individual, household, and public levels, and at the hands of the state.

The conversation above shows that many male *matatu* workers do not understand how their gendered performances of chivalry may be interpreted as anything but charming, not understanding the ways that public space feels to women passengers. It may be difficult to render the energy of busy *matatu* stages and crowded vehicles where women might feel uncomfortable, so I turn to excerpts from a poem that I received in July 2007, through a long line of email forwards entitled, *I Call It Culture (Matatu).*[11] The author is

---

[11] I have edited some of this poem for clarity and attempted to explain a bit of the context in the footnotes.

unknown, but the message in the email to which this poem was attached said, "This one is a long poem from a true Kenyan lady fed up with the hustle & bustle of the city." Although the gender of the author is not actually known (the current author and that of the email assume a Kenyan woman) the poem provides insight into some of the multiple, and often contradictory, binds women encounter in *matatu* and in the city itself.[12]

> Some funny guy breathing down my neck
> Breath stinking like the Korogosho dumpsite
> The harassed look on my face
> The guy is violating me
> I can practically feel his!!!!Thing
> Swelling, pushing on my butt!!!!
>
> The coming look on his face
> Is enough to make me feel like I have been raped in broad day light
> I warn him as I move in front
> Ah! *Unanisikuma!*[13]
> The guy smiles
> I shift my hips, as if dancing a jog
>
> I call it a way of life
> I call it a culture
> A mad, *mathree*, menace culture[14]
> Tell me
> How many of your friends spin or drive
> Whatever jisty name you want to call it
>
> I call it a culture, with its own language
> *Beba, Kwachu, dondoa muthii*[15]
> They may not have conceived it, but they carried it
> In their mind, wombs, tongues
> *Manze, Jo! Skia hii story!*[16]
> Unto us, a sheng was born
> Our language, our way of life, our culture

This poem captures a female passenger's perspective of dynamics found in *matatu* experiences. It starts with menace, imagery of violent sexual assault,

---

[12] The *Sheng* in this poem has been translated with help from Elizabeth Njoki.
[13] "Ah! You pushed me!"
[14] *Mathree* is the *Sheng* word for *matatu*
[15] *"Carry, Catch, Jump Passenger."*
[16] "Man, Bro! Listen to this story!"

"a rape." It moves through these violent descriptions of the *matatu* sector, but most of the villains are other commuters. The man pushing against her, the woman who pushes her in the vehicle, they are both descriptions of the Kenyan public. But, by the end, it seems as though she is proud of the language and the culture claiming it as "our own" and, interestingly, invokes the femininity of the conductors as caring mothers, bringing *Sheng*, this unique language that seems to capture so perfectly the urban experience of Nairobi, to fruition.

The mix of awe and disgust, attraction and repulsion are common themes around the *matatu*, often spoken of as a "necessary evil." As the female passenger perspective is poetically portrayed, the even more precarious perspective of the women working in these vehicles is rendered in their reflections and lived experiences. Together, the poem and the lives of workers in this sector reveal just how much of an empty canvas the *matatu* can be – an inclusive, mobile party or a wildly decorated moving cage.

Some women emphasize the masculine performances of *matatu* work by using *Sheng* and maybe even lowering the pitch of their voices, while diminishing any differences written on their bodies by hiding their hair, faces and figures, especially their breasts and hips, underneath hats and scarves and baggy clothes. Some women emphasized femininized performances of *matatu* practices, speaking less *Sheng* and more proper Swahili (*Kiswahili sanifu*), or by smiling and chatting with customers while wearing makeup and snug-fitting uniforms that show off their figures. Often women operators will take extra time to assist older passengers and citizens with disabilties, something male *matatu* crew members often fail to do, and specifically avoid. In fact, assisting elderly passengers and passengers with disabilities is quickly becoming one of the signature characteristics of women working on *matatu*.

There are several studies that show how women have pushed back against unfair, hostile, and sexist working conditions, and at capitalism itself through acts of spirit possession (Ong 2010) or work stoppages (Mills 1999). *Matatu* women get angry, and sometimes it passes through to their interactions on the vehicle. Take this excerpt from Elizabeth about how she feels around men and how her anger sometimes comes to the surface during work.

> **E**: Now, I've just come somehow now to just come to hate men. It's in me. In fact, when I talk to them, yes, I'm romantic, but when I see even a man, ahead of me ... I feel, I'm in fact, Meg, I'm somehow evil ... you are laughing [smiling and then breaking into laughter].
>
> **MF**: I'm sorry, I shouldn't be laughing [still laughing].
>
> **E**: In fact, when I am at work I overreact towards men so much, when I go and ask for the, maybe when I ask money from them. If somebody

laughs at me or try to smile back to me, I'll abuse him like something else ... until one man told me, "you are depressed. You must go and visit a doctor."

Elizabeth's anger bleeds through in the bus sometimes and even follows her home. She often feels the grip of her work life on her interactions within her household.

But women *matatu* workers, like the *tempo* drivers of Nepal, also experience gendered stigmas at the micro, or household level, as they navigate the ways their own family might stigmatize their job (Grossman-Thompson 2020). Take for example the comments from Sonya, about the way her parents see her work in the *matatu* sector. This is her response to a question about the challenges of working in the sector in 2019.

> When I came into the *matatu* industry, my mother said I'm mad. They have always known I'm mad [other women laughing]. They have known. So, I think everyone is facing that. How can we make these parents accept us now? So, those who are aggressive, maybe like me, *mpaka huko* [since way back] this is an industry, it is for big women, people know we are good drivers. We are good managers. We command our space, but now how can we fight? We have so many women now in the *matatu* industry. Me, I'm so proud.

Here Sonya embraces her personal sense of being a woman, talking about how the *matatu* sector is a good place for "big women" who are "commanding their space," but also wondering how to get their families to see that they are important and empowered by being good at a difficult job.

Rachel and Ruth were the first women *matatu* workers I met during my research. Rachel, whom I met in 2007, was twenty-seven and a single mother of two, who needed to survive and make her own money, and who specifically stated that she was not going to resort to sex work. She had been in the *matatu* sector for three years, since entering around the time of the Michuki Rules of 2004 (Chapter 3). She was in a maroon uniform, wearing long blonde braids. She spoke very proper Swahili with a shy demeanor, but a strong voice.

MF: Why did you choose *matatu* work?

Rachel: The way I see it, work is work. It's not bad work, it's good work. I get a seat, and I get everything I need. *Kila kitu yote* [Every single thing] *Na penda customers. Sana.* [I really love the customers.] And these [looking out of the matatu where we were sitting at the hustle and bustle going on in the stage around us] are *kama* brothers *yangu.* [And these ... are like my brothers.]

> **MF**: do you get harassed? [It is clear to hear in my voice that I am a bit surprised that she was so happy with her work and reflected on the job so positively. Her answer is somewhat defensive in tone because of this.]
>
> **Rachel**: No! *Nimezoeza. Ninajitetea. Skia, ni kazi mzuri ... inapiga kuwa malaiya. Napenda kwangu. Nafundisha kuendesha, kidogo kidogo.* (No! I am used to it. I can defend myself. Listen, this is good work. It beats being a prostitute [laughing] and I love my people. I am learning to drive, little by little).

Rachel, like other women in male-dominated sectors reported, due to the abundance of men in their daily work lives, seems to have supportive relationships with her male colleagues and feels proud of the work she is doing (see Wright 2016).

I met Ruth in 2009, at the Globe Cinema *matatu* stage. She always had a pleasant smile and was constantly asking me about my love life and about having children. Ruth had good relationships with her male colleagues, but also used her womanhood as an advantage in a male-dominated system by capitalizing on the negative reputation of *matatu* men.

> **MF**: Do you find it difficult to yell at customers?
>
> **Ruth**: Sometimes it is easier for men to call passengers, but then they see me and they say, "Madame." [When she says this, she stands back and kind of bows, like a gentleman would do to a lady in Regency-era England, and then we laugh]. They just see that I will not make mistakes by causing problems.
>
> **MF**: Do you think they trust you more?
>
> **Ruth**: Yes, they trust me more because young men ... they will bring problems.

Here, Ruth engages the stigma that is hurled at the occupation as a reason she is successful and enjoys her job. She described to me how she would appeal to women passengers and especially older women by speaking proper Swahili and smiling at them. Although Ruth, and many of the women I spoke with, had not ever been arrested or at least not as frequently as their male counterparts, they were not at all spared from the police brutality, which is a common feature of Kenyan life, especially for *matatu* workers (see Chapter 3). The following is the recounting of an experience one woman conductor presented at the Women in Transport conference sponsored by Flone Initiative, held in Nairobi (and virtually) in 2022.

When she was laid off from her full-time office job in March 2020 because of the COVID-19 pandemic, this woman was able to go back to the *matatu* sector where she had worked years earlier. As mentioned in the previous chapters, the *matatu* sector offers many opportunities for part-time work on rotating and flexible basis. She described encountering police at the end of her shift:

> A friend wanted to take the day off, so I relieved him. At the end of the day, during the 7:00pm curfew, I was making sure the windows were closed, when out of nowhere four policemen pounced on me. They had pipes, those water pipes and they started beating me, and I pleaded but they couldn't hear my pleas. But the more beatings I got. For the fear of being put on quarantine and for my son back home alone, I gave them what I had, because they had asked me, "what do you have?" I had 1,200 shillings, I had made. I pleaded for 200 shillings back so I could take something back to my son. But I got more beatings. Though they finally left me, they asked questions related to where I worked, which vehicle I worked, and that they were familiar with the SACCO where I worked. I knew that I should not mention anything to anyone. I was badly hurt from the beatings. I had even soiled on myself.

As she recounted this experience to a roomful of people (and live on Zoom) it became very quiet, which was palpable through the computer screen. She continued to discuss this very harrowing encounter that is all too common for *matatu* operators and women all over the world.

> I remember it took me time [voice cracks] to fully open up to anybody. I didn't talk to my son for a while. I was so shocked. I was quiet! I switched my phone off. I remember my colleagues tried to reach me, but I was off. The officers had hit my jaw with a hard rod, so there was no way I could totally open my mouth. I felt pain. Like if I wanted to eat something, opening my mouth wide was a problem. It took time. And my hand was swollen because I used my hand to cover my head and my hand was swollen and it was numb. When they released me, I ran to my house like a mad woman, afraid of meeting other officers on the way. At home I was shocked, and I was in pain and I slipped into depression without even knowing.

She finished her terrible story on an uplifting note as she recounted how she had made it back to the working world.

> It was only when a colleague of mine from Flone Initiative contacted me with no knowledge of my ordeal, just to check on me. She was

courageous enough to encourage me and invited me to mingle with other women. That one call from her changed everything.

Like women in male-dominated sectors in other parts of the world, informal interactions have the power to deeply impact women's sense of well-being in highly imbalanced work environments. It is both the formal and informal networks that women build that provide them the outlet and risk management strategies that they need, covered more in the next chapter.

The Paradox of Empowerment

Elizabeth is an unusual individual not only because she is a woman conductor on a *matatu*, but because she was also a co-owner of the vehicle with her husband who drove it. She is a mother of three sons, the youngest was ten when we met in 2019. Elizabeth started her career in transportation in 2012, as a stage manager for Embassava SACCO. She found that she could make good money managing the *matatu* stages because almost every vehicle would give her 10 or 20 shillings each time they passed. She used the money to send her children to school and she rented a little house in Kayole, one of Nairobi's poorer neighborhoods. Soon she was contacted by a woman who was buying a *matatu* and wanted Elizabeth to be the conductor. While working as a conductor for the woman, she was pursued by her current husband, who was driving a different *matatu* on her route. Once the woman owner had paid back the loan on her bus, which was several years, Elizabeth and her husband decided to buy and operate a bus of their own, which they did in 2018. When I met Elizabeth in 2019, she was extremely proud. She had worked her way up in a man's world and found her niche until she had enough saved to buy her own bus. She was seemingly living the dream as she and her partner could keep all the profits of their bus and spend time together.

When Elizabeth and I first spoke in 2019 she talked at length about what she felt was her calling – to help people with disabilities – but like everywhere else in the world, she recognized it was hard to make a living that way. To honor this part of herself, she and her husband operated a disability friendly vehicle, meaning they took extra time to help people with disabilities on and off the vehicle, and if Elizabeth saw someone making their way to the vehicle who was blind or immobile in any way, she would wait for them. In general, she was known to cater to passengers with disabilities and elderly passengers. As this book has covered in depth, the *matatu* sector is known for their speed and competitiveness. The extra time Elizabeth allowed for her passengers with disabilities was endearing to some, but frustrating to others. She continued to do it anyway as a small protest and something that gave her joy. As a member of the WIT group that met through Flone Initiative, she talked about and began to frame this aspect of her work through a lens of equity, social justice, and activism, working toward bringing about better transportation for all people. When I met her at a WIT meeting in 2019, she was already talking about how women, elderly people, and passengers with disabilities should be recognized as stakeholders of urban transportation as much as SACCO leaders or lobbyists.

One day in June of 2022, Elizabeth was taking some extra time to let a blind person off her bus when she was ticketed by the *Kanjo* (*Sheng* for a Nairobi City Council (NCC) *askari* or guard). A NCC *askari* is a person who is in between a security guard and a police officer. The *Kanjo* are often the people who enforce city rules and give fines to badly behaved *matatu* vehicles. Not content to simply pay the fine, Elizabeth went to the NCC office and informed them of what she was doing when she was ticketed, assisting a disabled passenger. In a surprising move, one of the committee members ripped up the ticket and told her to come back if she ever gets another ticket for this offense and they will do the same. They told her to keep doing what she was doing in assisting disabled passengers and even took her contact information. She was shocked that they had taken her seriously but felt good that her fine was forgiven. A few weeks later she was notified that they wanted her to come to a meeting with the members of the NCC to give her perspective on how better to serve passengers with disabilities with *matatu* service. A few weeks later, in August of 2022, she appeared in a billboard advertising a new road initiative for people with disabilities in partnership with Flone Initiative (Figure 12). Elizabeth sent me this photo through WhatsApp with the following message: "Meg!!I had to cry seeing myself on a billboard. Am so happy dear."

This billboard was just one of the instances of publicity that Elizabeth has received ever since. She has been interviewed on podcasts, and webcasts about her experience as a woman in the *matatu* sector. She was featured on the radio and on TV. She was nominated for best female conductor in 2022 and won the prize in 2023. In 2023, she was hired as the coordinator for Flone Initiative's WIT chapters and in this capacity is often contacted when well-known people want to visit Kenya and experience the *matatu* sector's creative elements. For instance, on the afternoon of 24 May 2023, she sent me several pictures of *manyanga* vehicles and wanted me to choose one on behalf of a visitor coming to Kenya. She collected several and was hoping the guests would like her choices, which they did.

A few weeks later, in June, we chatted on the phone, and she mentioned that she had spent some time with the musician who had requested the *manyanga* and she was thrilled by the experience. She mentioned his name quickly, yoyoma (pronouncing it yoYOma) and assured me that I knew who he was. She said his name a few more times before it dawned on me that she was referring to the one and only superstar cellist, Yo-Yo Ma, who had visited

Figure 12 Elizabeth (circled) featured on a billboard in Nairobi, as an advocate for disability rights. (Photo courtesy of Elizabeth Njoki, 2022).

Kenya in connection with his five-year, six-continent-spanning Bach Tour, where he spoke a few *Sheng* words and "arrived at the market in a *matatu*" (Kimeu 2023). Before his concert in Nairobi, he met with the women of Flone Initiative and took his wife and team on a ride in a *matatu*. He visited with local artists and posed for pictures, even playing his cello inside the *manyanga* for a few minutes (Figures 13A and 13B). Just as with Netflix's *Sense8* series, *matatu* culture is one of the key features of Nairobi, evidenced by Yo-Yo Ma's team's arrangement of this event. Although many Kenyans may feel like they want to erase the vehicles and the people that seem to go with it, for those on the outside it is an important aesthetic and cultural element of what makes Nairobi a hub of creative innovation that attracts global celebrities.

But, just as Elizabeth's face was floating overhead, her smile beaming across Kenya reflecting a successful mission toward realizing her calling, she was simultaneously being diminished at home. The relationship between Elizabeth and her husband had deteriorated and the money from the bus was being controlled by him. Additionally, when her husband was not driving,

Figure 13a Yo-Yo Ma in a matatu with his cello on his Bach tour. (Photo courtesy of Elizabeth Njoki, 2023).

Elizabeth had a difficult time collecting the money from the workers, who were instructed by her husband not to give it to her. By the end of 2023, Elizabeth had largely given up her share of the bus and was no longer close with her husband.

It is hard to say to what degree her success in the *matatu* sector soured their relationship, but the bus and the funds around it (the loans, the daily payouts, the daily earnings, and investments to the SACCO) were all impacting their rapport. Just as many couples realize that sharing work and home life can be too much, in this case we can see how the paradoxes of women

Figure 13b Yo-Yo Ma kneeling next to and pointing to artwork on a *manyanga* in Nairobi. (Photo Courtesy of Elizabeth Njoki, 2023).

in male-dominated sectors are even more pronounced. Not only is she a successful woman, and not only is it in a male-dominated sector, it is the same sector that her male partner is also working in with less success. This small group of women *matatu* workers are getting an outsized portion of media attention when it comes to feel-good *matatu* stories, and these women know that. It just happens that this moment they are funding darlings, and they are using that to their advantage to try and make a difference in their lives and the lives of passengers.

As Elizabeth's life shifts, it is remarkably the same. In her view, she is no better off than she was when she was a stage manager. She is still in a vulnerable position but sees some potential in the *matatu* sector for women. She often considers the plight of her colleagues and herself as she ages. Although often associated with youth, the workers of the *matatu* sector are getting older. Elizabeth likes to make plans and wants to start a WIT SACCO so that women can build wealth and have something to retire on or pass down to their children. Below, Elizabeth sketches out her idea for the future in a 2020 video call.

> Well, my suggestion was, at least, as we are getting older, we could have a SACCO. I think you get it? A SACCO of Women in Transport. We will be saving a little by a little, Meg. Then after some time, like the NGO for now, would save for us. We take buses, we own buses, each woman would own a bus. So that as you get older, you'll be now a boss, you see, having that *matatu*. So even if you are not working in the industry, you wouldn't be the conductor, but you'll be having your *matatu* in the industry. So, you can bring even your kids to work in the industry and we'll still be moving on. Some women are fifty years, fifty [eyes wide, holding up a fist to indicate five] you get it, now they need, they need something that they can see and have ... my Nissan. And at least you see it coming for that money.

Generation X, millennials and Mutongi's "Generation *Matatu*" are all hitting middle-age, as they embraced the hustle economy in their youth when they could run and jump on and off the vehicles with abandon, workers like Elizabeth are attempting to leverage their nascent institutional support and intersectional solidarity among Women in Transport and their allies to build a safety net for themselves. Elizabeth sees the potential politics in the *matatu* as a public service and she has been changing it one bus at a time. Studies show that women in male-dominated sectors struggle often with problems at home stemming from their work lives (Wright 2016). More women in male-dominated space, especially when organized, can provide an important network for women that can improve their quality of life. Elizabeth's story is unique, and all too familiar. She brings to the fore an instinctual understanding of community power and the power of unity across difference and brings this to life through her inclusion of passengers with disabilities on her buses. There is a possibility of providing a new model of transportation in a way that uses the vehicle as a feminist counterpublic, as a protest space, and as sociopolitical action.

The *matatu* sector is one that blurs the boundaries of public and private space, inhabiting a frontier of unregulated economic activity both in the transitional spaces of the city and of economic practices and sociability. Due to the open and public nature of the sector, which is ironically fueled by coded linguistic practices meant to create private spaces of interaction between young urban Kenyans, it facilitates other structural changes in providing new opportunities for women in the sector.

Conclusion

In Kenya, where women are making inroads into the transportation sector at unprecedented rates, they still make up only a small portion of the working population. For men and many women, "women's incursion into the transportation sector" can cause a moral panic and is seen as "threatening the values, interests and well-being of society" (Porter and Omwega 2022: 58). As more women enter these fields they struggle with working conditions, retention, and retirement. Women who work in the sector experience stigmatization from both men and women alike, and are often perceived to be untrustworthy, promiscuous people (Porter 2011). The ethnographic data gathered from women in the *matatu* sector highlights the intersectional and layered ways that gender and labor stigma shape women's lives. The social landscape of gender in Kenya is shifting, producing important and effective collaborations and networks between marginalized communities, in this case women transportation workers and passengers with disabilities. The next chapter looks at the multiple ways that women build and network informal and formal relationships of support and solidarity through representational practices and material culture.

The following chapter looks more closely at Flone Initiative, an organization that supports both women workers and women passengers by using *matatu* and *manyanga* aesthetics and the media infrastructure of the transportation system as a site of feminist activism. As popular transportation becomes a site of neoliberal reproduction it also becomes a potential feminist counterpublic for the women of Nairobi as they attempt to realign urban space in a more equitable way. By grouping together their marginalized positions with passengers with disabilities they build networks of support. Future research questions include looking at the limits and possibilities of these networks of support. As women like Mary Mwangi and Elizabeth exemplify, the sector is not only changing *for* women, but being changed *by* women.

6

Feminist Counterpublics: Digital Platforms and Fragile Networks of Solidarity

When a young woman was publicly stripped and assaulted by several *matatu* workers who filmed it and then released it to the public in 2014 – it went viral (Cummings 2014; Warner 2014). The audacity of the men releasing the footage themselves triggered an intense response from women in Nairobi who called for their arrests and organized themselves through Facebook under the hashtag #mydressmychoice. Kenyan scholar Nanjala Nyabola argued that the event pulled women together and gave voice to the sizeable number of radical feminist activists in Kenya (2018: 127). The women of the #mydressmychoice movement organized a massive march in Nairobi in November 2014, and lobbied for legislative reforms which would include a law against public stripping punishable by ten years in prison and they also pushed for implementing a different driving school curriculum through the National Transport and Safety Authority (NTSA). Several years later, in 2017, the perpetrators were sentenced to death for the crime (Kiplagat 2017).

Through social media and other digital spaces, Kenyan women have been making themselves increasingly visible and building solidarity networks. Throughout this book, I have argued that the *matatu* sector, in addition to being a transportation infrastructure, is a media infrastructure as well and that over time *matatu* vehicles act as publics (collective political identities shaped through the circulation of images and the collective consumption of those images) and consequently, counterpublics (alternative and often marginalized identities that are sociopolitical and created through similar collective means as publics) (Cody 2011; Warner 2002; Asen 2000; Fraser 1990). In Kenya, both feminist activists and women working in the *matatu* sector, use the *matatu* as counterpublic, a place to circulate non-dominant messages and build individual and collective political subjectivities.

Flone Initiative, whose logo is a silhouette of the African continent with a heart where Nairobi is located, was originally aimed at protecting female passengers from male *matatu* workers and male passengers to prevent sexual harassment and assault, as discussed in the previous chapter. The leaders of the organization quickly realized that women *matatu* workers were experiencing gender-based violence regularly in vehicles but were also key in stopping it. As noted in the last chapter, sexual harassment of women on public transportation is widespread, but it is not universal. For instance, only 6 percent of women in Botswana experienced sexual harassment in public transportation (Williams et al. 2020: 4). Studies show that when there are more women working in transportation vehicles fewer women experience harassment there (Grossman-Thompson 2020: 878). By 2017, Flone Initiative had launched the WIT groups, which brought women transport workers together from all different forms of transportation in Nairobi, from *matatu* to *bodaboda* (motorcycle taxis) to Uber for arguably the first time.[1]

Over the past several years, Flone Initiative, in collaboration with women in the *matatu* sector, have been developing and producing cultural materials like posters, plays, songs, and videos in addition to holding workshops, conferences and trainings. Some of Flone Initiative's trainings operate like "consciousness raising" or CR sessions as the facilitators of the workshops spend time reframing women's shared experiences of their doubly stigmatized roles as women in a male-dominated sector to reflect on other forms of oppression. Like the CRs made popular by second-wave feminists in the West during the 1960s and 1970s, Flone Initiative's trainings and production of feminist materials provides potential for more women to become sociopolitical actors who can transform the urban space of Nairobi. Their case is an opportunity to reflect on ways that providing equal rights to transportation spaces can improve life for women and other marginalized groups throughout the world. In other words, this work reflects the potential for public transportation to be as a space for the creation of feminist counterpublics that build spaces of inclusion. This chapter also brings into view the tensions between the ways "Western feminism" and "African feminism" construct categories of gender differently (Mohanty 2003).[2] For instance, Oyèrónke Oyěwùmí argues that the category of "woman" is socially constructed and not a universal concept (1997).

Since 2015, Flone Initiative has grown into a multipronged organization, having trained over 700 operators from the transportation sector, including nineteen savings and credit co-operatives (SACCOs) along with organizing

---

[1] There have been other important women's labor groups and development groups, most notable *Maendeleo wa Wanawake* (Women for Development) in the 1960s and 1970s, but they eventually came to be viewed as weak and in cahoots with the Moi administration (Wipper 1975).

[2] Following Mohanty (2003) I am not attempting to imply the "Western Feminists" are a monolith, but to draw distinctions between the ways women's lives in the Global North and Global South are constructed.

the annual international Women in Transport conference, held each year in Nairobi (https://floneinitiative.org).³ By creating plays, songs, posters, music videos, and stickers in the aesthetic of *matatu* art, Flone Initiative has used a masculine space to spread feminist messages promoting gender equality. In their yearly conferences they take over the development and academic spheres to showcase women in transportation through both practical and academic lenses. Feminists in Nairobi, and across African nations, are making themselves more visible. The real life and digital ways women are developing and participating in Kenyan public life and advocacy, and the performative ways African feminists are expressing themselves speak to a shift in the media and political landscape (Nyabola 2018; Travers 2003). Due to actions like these, Flone Initiative's cultural materials provide an important look into the different ways organizations and marginalized communities build solidarity and the limits therein. Although the *matatu* women of Nairobi are fortunate to have Flone Initiative working on their behalf, Flone Initiative is not a SACCO nor do they own any vehicles, which, from some of their members' perspectives, can limit their impact.

Throughout this ethnography, I have argued that the space of a *matatu* vehicle is a particularly important urban form that can prompt protest and political action. The infrastructure itself then forms an urban public and, subsequently counterpublics, with the ability to mediate messages of marginalized or mainstream perspectives. An important aspect of creating a counterpublic is the production of political solidarities, actions, subjectivities, and sociopolitical practices.

By framing transportation work as an avenue for feminist counterpublics, this chapter explores how both physical urban spaces and digital spaces have to the potential to shape the gendered landscape of Kenya in important ways for both workers and passengers. This chapter explores the use of the *matatu* as a feminist medium that gives voice to complexities of gendered violence and urban space, as well as *matatu* work to build networks of solidarity. It also explores how the digital space of platform economies like Uber have enabled women to enter the private taxi business in Nairobi. These women would not have been able to drive a private taxi in Nairobi before platforms like Uber and Taxify because taxis were tightly controlled by an exclusive group of older men who are known to intensely harass newcomers. Even young men hoping to enter the world of private taxi driving have been met with threats

---

3   This information comes from the Flone Annual Reports over the past four years; conferences in 2020, 2021 and 2022 were held remotely due to the COVID-19 pandemic. I presented a paper at the 2021 Conference about risk and security for women transport operators.

of physical violence. Before 2015, private taxi services were a difficult and competitive business to enter, but now with the proliferation of the Uber and Taxify platforms, taxi, and motorcycle taxis (*bodaboda*) services have greatly expanded, with a significant portion being supplied by women. With the emergence of digital transportation platforms, women are simultaneously more and less visible behind the app.

Fragile Networks of Solidarity

Although the concept of solidarity was originally developed in nineteenth-century Europe as workers confronted the social fragmentation generated by capitalism, it is a modern subjectivity and an important, yet understudied, set of social relations (Gill and Kasmir 2008). As anthropologists look more closely at the concept of solidarity, they are encountering important ambiguities and complexities around what alliance building looks like, begging the question: what are the limits of solidarity as a concept and a lived experience (Kaplan 2018; Mamoulaki 2017; Gill 2009)? Solidarity has received less scholarly attention than other related concepts like "hegemony," but, as anthropologists continue to explore it in action, they have presented its limits, ambiguities, and fragilities (Appadurai and Anderson 2023). Solidarity, or "horizontal collective attachments" are "constructed and negotiated through concrete embodied interpersonal interactions" (Kaplan 2018: 82), interactions that are abundant in *matatu* vehicles and stages. As discussed earlier in this book (see Chapter 3), daily work in a *matatu* means negotiating and interacting with dangerous characters including police and criminals alike, which builds relationships of trust between workers and can lead to solidarity and political action.

Feminist political economists have shown that, where collective action fails, women make space for themselves by using informal support networks and creative workspaces to make their lives more dignified (Grossman-Thompson 2020: 874). Women working in male-dominated sectors fare much better when they have strong networks of support, but often face resistance from men and women in the workplace when trying to build collective alliances and forming relationships of solidarity. Women working in male-dominated sectors build networks of solidarity differently than women in women-dominated networks (Wright 2016). For instance, women in women-dominated work (teaching, nursing) often build solidarity through group get-togethers, which may work to form community and advance careers, whereas women in male-dominated workplaces do not use gatherings with other women for career advancement and can even be punished for joining in gender-segregated meetings (Webber and Giuffre 2019).

One of the most productive relationships of solidarity that women working in the *matatu* sector have built on their own over the past several years is with passengers with disabilities and elderly passengers. The relationship between the *matatu* women and the groups of marginalized passengers is one of the creative and informal ways that *matatu* women build solidarity and manage their risk in the male-dominated world of *matatu* work. Women's relationships to other women in male-dominated spaces, especially the measure of what some may call solidarity, take on elements that are not present in women-dominated sectors (Wright 2016). In addition to the closeness that comes from being one of the very few women working in a space, the relationships at work can be charged and suffer from tokenism, stereotyping, and gender devaluing (Webber and Giuffre 2019).

Women working in male-dominated sectors are often isolated from one another because they are primarily working with men (Grossman-Thompson 2020). This can complicate their solidarity-building activities as they lack contact with other women. Some women in male-dominated work environments mobilize performances of masculinity through identifying with masculine interests and avoiding women colleagues. This works against women's ability to collectively act in their own interests (Grossman-Thompson 2020: 358). This push and pull toward and away from women plagues many of the women operators I met in Nairobi. Some women *matatu* operators in Nairobi will say that they are happy to have their "sisters" around to only moments later mention that women are untrustworthy and that they prefer working with men. I have witnessed many female friendships tested and broken, especially when there are precious jobs or publicity opportunities available, and a growing community or network of activists. For instance, when women conductors receive media attention, they are expected to share the spotlight and the perceived benefits they are enjoying.

Informal interactions at work make a significant difference in women's lives, but in male-dominated sectors like *matatu* work many of women's most supportive relationships at work are with men. Even though scholars found that men in male-dominated sectors will often dismiss women-centered organizations or events, women can adopt this perspective as well, not wanting to attend any women-centered events or join feminist organizations because they don't want to be identified as someone who would cause problems (Wright 2018: 171). In April 2023, this trend also appeared among women in the *matatu* sector, where some women's efforts to organize were thwarted by men in positions of power who dissuaded women from meeting together or joining pro-women organizations. Even in the "progressive" SACCO of Embassava, which hires more women than the average SACCO, there is a resistance to women's solidarity groups. The following is an example of the challenges for women organizing in Nairobi's transportation sector:

MF: when they have all these women in these different SACCOs do you think that they're treated well in the SACCO? Do they talk about that? Is that what you talk about at your Flone meetings?

Elizabeth: We are never treated well! [laughing loudly]

MF: Yeah? No one is treated well? No one reports ... a good experience? [Elizabeth still laughing]

Elizabeth: No one reports, Meg. The SACCO that is having a lot of women in *matatu*, is my SACCO, Embassava. And you see, like, we try to reach for other ladies from other SACCOS. They won't be attending the trainings effectively [she is speaking of the Flone trainings and meetings where women get together and talk about their issues] because they are warned by their SACCOS. If you attend that training the next day, you're slashed and the badge is removed from the system. You get it? Now looking for another SACCO, they'll call the previous SACCO and ask him, "What did Elizabeth do in your SACCO?" and they'll say, "leave him alone, that lady, she said blah, blah, blah, blah." And you won't get job.

MF: Okay. So you can't talk about Flone?

E: No ... In fact, you see, in Nairobi ... *unaitwa chini ya maji.*

MF: you call it underwater?

E: Yeah, we do it ... under the water. You know with water, it doesn't vibrate. You just see water shaking. But you don't know what is happening under the water ... [laughing and moving her hand like a wave].

MF: So you hide it ...

E: Yeah, you hide it, *kabisa kabisa* [totally].

Just as some SACCOs like Embassava have provided an avenue for women to feel empowered when they enter the *matatu* sector, they can also restrict women's solidarity building by curtailing their meetings, at times suspending them without due process or withholding their funds, as exemplified by Elizabeth's experience covered in the last chapter.

For any worker, solidarity, collective intimacy, and other work relationships have been shown to be key to work–life satisfaction and improving working conditions. A lack of recognition of gender inequality and the devaluation of women working relationships, through formal and informal channels, undermines alliances (Wright 2016). In Kenya, women sometimes struggle to join Flone Initiative due to its connection to women's issues. The leaders of the organization have even avoided using the word "feminist" in their own public relations material because they believed it was turning people off.

Just as women workers can develop politically active identities through sharing stories and spending time together, they can also develop identities that Tessa Wright characterizes as "counter" (2016:22) due to punitive actions they have received from women in these sectors. When women adopt a "counter" identity, they feel the pressure to disidentify with associations of womanhood, especially in particular contexts where the gender identity can work against them (Wright 2016: 167). In another example from the *matatu* sector, when one of the only women in the SACCO asked for permission to do a fellowship for women in transport the solitary female executive was the only one who would not sign the permission paper.

Even more extreme examples of the ways women in male-dominated sectors have faced challenges to alliance building includes the ways that women become tokenized in those sectors, and, in one example, token women were given loyalty tests where being "one of the boys" meant turning against other women (Webber and Giuffre 2019). These various challenges become a deterrent to women participating in solidarity-building events and networks. Some of these very issues made their way into Flone Initiative's materials, discussed below, in the hopes that these messages can be conveyed in ways that challenge some of the behaviors that weaken women's solidarity networks.

Feminist Counterpublics

Various forms of popular urban transportation have been politically powerful in Kenya and repeatedly used by marginalized groups to transform society collectively throughout its history – from the Kikuyu taxi drivers in the 1940s (Furedi 1973) and the Nubian women on the KBS buses in late-colonial Nairobi (Chapter 1) to the *matatu* operators responsible for playing cassette tapes of political opposition during Moi's one-party rule (Haugerud 1995). Throughout the 1990s and early 2000s, *matatu* workers were using *manyanga* style and Hip-Hop sounds to usher in multi-party politics in Nairobi and through their protests they developed an important community perspective (Mutongi 2017: 198–199). The young, urban, disaffected Nairobi residents, what Mutongi calls "Generation *matatu*," started to make themselves seen and heard, and "[t]he combination of the music with the Sheng dialect allowed a matatu operator to transform his or her vehicle into a political space unlike almost any other public space in Kenya" (Mutongi 2017: 198–199). The parking lots and vehicles became places where "debates were waged about what was legal and who had the right to earn a living" from *matatu* (Mutongi 2017: 178). This mirrored the debates over the meaning and morality of "pirate taxis" in the 1960s (Heinze 2018), which became a proxy for debating what a Kenyan citizen, not a colonial subject, would be in the newfound nation.

In this way *matatu* vehicles have historically been a "public" and "counterpublic" communicated through circulating media images, which involves strangers sharing the consumption of these images (Warner 2002). Stickers with messages aimed at behavior change have been shown to work in Nairobi's *matatu* sector before. In 2014, there was a sticker campaign about arriving alive at one's destination and slowing down to save lives.[4] The researchers showed that there was a marked change of behavior in the vehicles with stickers or that were involved in the sticker campaign (Habyarimana and Jack 2015). Continuing in this tradition, feminist activists and women workers are using the *matatu* and other classically masculine spaces for their own messages (Nyabola 2018).

The idea of a "public" originally stemmed from Habermas' discussion of coffee houses in Europe where people, largely wealthy men, gathered and discussed the issues of the day building a collective political subjectivity (Fraser 1990). Cody draws on Latour and others to expand our understanding of publics as mediation "by material infrastructures of communication" that extends "beyond printed texts" to include parliament buildings, political rallies, literary salons, movie theatres and virtual worlds" (2011: 46–47). In other words, a public refers to texts and their circulation as well as the space of discourse, mediated by cultural forms, that unites strangers through participation and an awareness of the intimacy shared between them (Warner 2002: 49–62). The *matatu* has a style and language of its own in both visual and audio fields, as well as a history of bringing people together through the consumption of this media. Publics are personal and impersonal, ongoing spaces for the encounter of discourse and poetic world making, including speech genres, idioms, style markers, lexicon (Warner 2002: 68).

For the most part the two meanings of public have been separated and held at opposite ontological ends. The first meaning of a public is as a discursive space produced by practice, and the second meaning of a public is a physical space accessible to many people. There is a connection between publics

---

[4] For a discussion about how sticker campaigns have cast transportation safety as a health concern see Lamont and Lee (2015).

and protest because sociopolitical practices and representational practices both attend to body, place, and social relations and publics can shape how violence contours expression and how social actors respond (Bishara 2023: 437). Some recent work that contributes to thinking about the potential for a *matatu* public and counterpublic is the intimate conversations of *flânerie* in the Georgian genre of Feuilleton, where embodied and disembodied publics come together through the description of night life from the perspective of someone wandering through the urban milieu in an aimless but creatively intuitive way (Manning 2022). In this way we can start to understand what it means to have a public that is both the message and the embodiment of that message. Like the joyriders of Nairobi have already discovered, the *matatu* sector can be a ride to the club as well as a ride that *is* the club.

The following images are cultural materials created in the style of art that may appear on the side of a *manyanga*. They are colorful and expressive, like images pulled from a graphic novel. The posters discussed below were developed by Flone Initiative in collaboration with the WIT group in 2019 for a campaign called "Report It Stop It." The women transport workers were instrumental in crafting each of the messages that appear in the posters and in each image a particular type of masculine and feminine performance is sketched out alongside a public service announcement about behavior on popular transportation, or in the city itself.

The first image (Figure 14) shows two people in a *matatu* sharing a bench seat, just two commuters and zero *matatu* operators. The man is looking at his phone and engaged in the practice of "manspreading," a practice commonly defined as one where men, especially in shared spaces, "spread out" and take more than their fair share of public space, while the woman stares at him with irritation and shock on her face. He is seemingly oblivious. This image is communicating to men, that at times they may not recognize how they are "invading" other people's spaces while innocently looking at their phones. The message on the poster explains that this can be understood as harassment because is it an "invasion of personal space." Because this poster is set inside the vehicle without reference to a *matatu* worker, it highlights that the broad audience Flone Initiative is attempting to reach with these materials includes commuters, workers, and passers-by. The male passenger who sees this poster may just be made aware of this phenomenon by the poster and might think twice before innocently spreading out.

Figure 15 sets a scene that calls to mind one of the lines of poetry featured in the last chapter. The author of the poem writes that "she can feel his thing pressing into my back … it feels like a violation." In this image, the male *matatu* conductor (marked by his maroon vest) is not so innocently crowding the woman who is boarding the bus by stepping into the vehicle with her and imposing himself onto the back of her body by holding onto the sidebars

Figure 14 Flone Initiative Poster for the "Report It Stop It" campaign showing a passenger "manspreading" while oblivious to the woman sharing the seat with him. (Courtesy of Flone Initiative 2019).

Figure 15 Flone Initiative Poster for the "Report It Stop It" campaign showing a woman entering a matatu with a matatu conductor (wearing the red uniform of a conductor) crowding her space and seemingly pushing himself into the vehicle closely behind her. (Courtesy of Flone Initiative 2019).

of the vehicles. As they both step on the same step, she looks back, eyes wide and mouth agape, her face seemingly a bit angry and a bit frightened. Additionally, there is a claustrophobic feeling to this image as the woman has already boarded and this interaction does not indicate that she will be safer inside the bus as the conductor follows her inside.

The other two posters sketch interactions that take place outside the *matatu*. One of the most salient themes from the ethnographic data collected from women working in the *matatu* sector is presented in the next poster (Figure 16), which speaks to the issues discussed above regarding the complexities of solidarity in male-dominated spaces. One woman in casual, modern dress is demanding her change from a woman *matatu* operator whom she is holding off the ground. The passenger is demanding her change, and the conductor seems scared. When I spoke with the one of the facilitators of the poster project, she made sure to tell me that representing this type of interaction in the posters was extremely important to the WIT group because they wanted to show how women can be even more aggressive, rude, and abusive than some of the male passengers. Again, the poster is showing an interaction that may make a female passenger reflect more deeply about how her actions could be considered "physical assault" and harassment, as the poster makes clear.

Finally, the next image (Figure 17) sets a scene even further removed from the *matatu* vehicles themselves, showing a vehicle in the distance and only one of the men in the scene in a uniform. In this poster, three young men are calling after a young woman and commenting on her body while one of them appears to be whistling. The message describes this activity as "catcalling," another form of harassment. This image speaks to the larger message and reach of Flone Initiative. They are not just concerned with transportation, they are interested in changing gendered interactions in urban space broadly by using the *matatu* as a way into a larger discussion about gender in Kenya.[5]

All four posters presented here portray Kenyan women in a particular way when it comes to their physical appearance. They all have natural hair, feature a variety of body shapes and are wearing a range of clothing presenting looks that can be both urban and rural. Their clothing and hairstyles are important parts of the feminist message they are trying to project, especially considering that this is built by some of the women behind #mydressmychoice. These posters reflect the gendered performances discussed in the last chapter and throughout the book more generally. They give the viewer a feeling of the *matatu* space as an extension of the street and the public sphere at large, which

---

[5] Although, "catcalling" is an experience women in Kenya have, it is a good example of how Western feminism exerts influence in these materials through the naming of the behavior.

Figure 16 Flone Initiative Poster for the "Report It Stop It" campaign showing a woman aggressively asking a female conductor for her change. She has picked up the woman worker off the ground by her shirt, while the worker seems shocked and frightened. (Courtesy of Flone Initiative 2019).

Figure 17 Flone Initiative Poster for the "Report It Stop It" campaign where a young woman is walking away from a group of men who are calling after her and making comments about her body. The woman has her arms crossed and looks defiant and irritated. (Courtesy of Flone Initiative 2019).

is an extension of male space in Kenya: a place where women are trespassing or at best being allowed to pass by unharmed. As with the incidents of public stripping, some men want to punish women for being too provocative or dressing in a way they don't like.

These cultural materials created by Flone Initiative and disseminated throughout *matatu* vehicles and stages in Nairobi in 2019, reflect the way that feminists in Kenya are speaking to *matatu* men and commuters in their own aesthetic language and spreading messages about gender and urban space. But this is not the only way. They also used music and music videos to tell a story. The following are the lyrics of a song written by the WIT chapters in collaboration with an artist called Turning Tables. The song is called "Msupa Wa Nganya" (Beautiful *Manyanga* Girl). As mentioned at length in Chapter 2, *matatu* vehicles have inspired many popular cultural materials like songs and television shows. The following song is created by feminists and women workers speaking in the language of *matatus* to present an alternate view.

Code's 1st Verse
Matatu girl, just look at your swag, but this [*matatu*] is not work,
Come stay at my house, I'll take care of you, feed you, I can,
Don't worry [repeat x2]

Acey Verse 1
I'm the best that I can be, such a pity you can't see,
I'm at work from early morning,
Monday through Sunday,
Hustling to make my way,
Why you want to pull my strings?
I'm independent can't you see?
I don't tire, I know myself, have no time for this …
Code's Hook
Matatu girl, just look at your swag, but this [*matatu*] is not work,
Come stay at my house, I'll take care of you, feed you, I can,
Don't worry [repeat x2]

Acey Verse 2
Look at me, what do you see? You think I do not fit?
Those are expectations of society,
That I'm a woman I need to be cat-called needlessly?
Hands grope me aimlessly they don't want me to complain
    because "it's the industry",
But I hang on because I chose this *matatu* job,
Call me "konda" [tout] not "baby",
I'm uptown, downtown, my usual hustle,
Get home and put food on the table!

Code's Hook
Matatu girl, just look at your swag, but this [*matatu*] is not work,
Come stay at my house, I'll take care of you, feed you, I can,
Don't worry [repeat x2]

Acey Verse 3
I'm the best that I can be, such a pity you can't see,
I'm at work from early morning,
Monday through Sunday,
Hustling to make my way,
Why you want to pull my strings?
I'm independent can't you see?
I don't tire, I know myself, have no time for this …

Much like the poem in the last chapter, this song reflects the experiences of women in *matatu* vehicles. The song is from the perspective of a *matatu* worker who is pulled between her job and her home life and other caretaking abilities. In the music video, a woman *matatu* conductor is shown working on her vehicle which includes kicking a drunk man off the bus and getting roughed up by some female passengers. Later in the video, the *matatu* operator who has previously been shown scowling or being annoyed is gently smiling down at an older woman who is in bed. She is clearly performing a caretaking role with this woman and there is a small moment of reflection before she is back on the street in the *matatu* dealing with more of the same. The song lyrics seem to cover the same themes as the posters, and the music video tells the story of the double lives many *matatu* women experience, and expressed in their interviews. The song lyrics reveal the paradoxes many women feel as they are pushing against the expectations of society as *matatu* operators while trying to take care of their families and themselves. They offer to "take care of you, feed you" but also highlight that they are "independent" busy people, always hustling.

Matatu publics and counterpublics produce economic and political outcomes, through interlocking modes of interaction while functioning as a democratic discursive space, where people can debate the politics of their daily lives. *Matatu* vehicles bring people together in space and circulate creative work, images of global celebrity, local politics, religious symbolism, and pornography, functioning as an alternative public, where the circulating images are of a subversive nature and resist the dominant paradigm (Cody 2011: 41; Fraser 1990) The ways that publics and counterpublics, or alternative publics, are defined and delineated is less useful for this analysis than understanding the political importance of multiple subaltern counterpublics among subordinate groups who formulate oppositional discourse. Counterpublics show how "those who can't speak in the public sphere still speak publicly" (Fraser 1990).

Questions remain around whether counterpublics should be defined by the content of the discourse, the social status of those who articulate their opposition to a dominant public by the spaces of articulation or by marked cultural style (Bishara 2023; Warner 2002). Because the *matatu* is seen as a masculine space, in this way, the images and messages that Flone Initiative have circulated and continue to circulate, are of a subversive nature even in the subversive space of the *matatu*. Similarly, working on the subaltern levels of discourse, like social media and digital platforms, has allowed feminists in Kenya, women in the *matatu* sector, and in the changing transportation sector more broadly, to create an important collective place for urban women to become further empowered and politicized.

Consciousness Raising in Nairobi

In July 2019, in a small hotel in Nairobi, south of River Road where the streets are filled with people, peddlers, and potholes, I turned into the dark hallway, climbed several flights of stairs and arrived breathlessly at a bright restaurant nestled on the fourth floor of the six-floor structure. There were several tables where people were having their morning *chai* and reading the newspaper or chatting. A group of women were huddled over tea and a computer. They were Flone Initiative moderators, there to meet and prepare for Flone Initiative's WIT meeting where they would discuss their latest digital advocacy campaign and how to change the *matatu* sector for the better through "influencing behavior change and creating safer spaces for women, and all passengers" (floneinitiative.org). The main facilitator was a Kenyan woman in her thirties named Mary, assisted by Susan and Sarah, both of whom were White women working with Flone Initiative in short-term research or capacity-building roles. Soon a few of the participants of the focus group started arriving and we moved into a large room with a small table in the center. Until more women arrived, nine women workers in total, there seemed to be nearly equal numbers of Kenyan transportation workers to facilitators/researchers (myself included).

As more Kenyan women came into the room, our workshop group came into view, and it was quickly obvious that this was a jovial bunch. They chatted and smiled and caught up with one another over tea and donuts and they passed around the four-month-old baby of one of the women. When it was time to begin the session, Mary, the only Kenyan facilitator, gathered us together, away from the table and we went through a fun icebreaker to learn each other's names. After that, Mary went around the room and each of the women introduced themselves and talked about their mode of transportation work. There were several *matatu* workers present, as well as Uber and taxi drivers and one *bodaboda* (motorcycle taxi) driver. As they shared their own experiences, they listened attentively to one another's stories. Winnie, the *bodaboda* driver was not new to male-dominated work, had previously been working as an electrician in Nairobi, but when digital platforms made it easy to organize rides, she transferred her business to *bodaboda* for hire. Winnie, a tall, broad-chested woman with short-cropped natural hair said that the *bodaboda* helmet and heavy, motorcycle jacket helped her gender stay undetected, but when she spoke her clients realized she was a woman. Usually, it was not a problem with her customers, and sometimes, especially for her repeat women customers, it was even preferred.

Mary's first substantial question to the group was: What do you want people to know about your experience, as a woman, in the *matatu* industry? As the women took turns answering in a mix of Swahili, English and *Sheng*, they discussed common issues of the sector. They complained how the "customer is always right, but the boss is also always right" and the common tension *matatu* workers feel when they are attempting to serve the customer and hit their daily targets. They were annoyed the passengers were always walking in front of the vehicle instead of behind when crossing the road. The women went on for several minutes each before Mary interrupted in Swahili:

> *Kukumbuka, gender ni wamama, wewe ni mama ya mathree, ama wewe ni taxi ... driver?* [Remember, gender is mothers, you are mothers of a *matatu* or are you taxi ... drivers?] *Toa ijumbe kama a woman in transport* [So you want to bring up things about a woman in transport] ... [*silence*] ... *Tuko sawa?* [Are we together?] ... [*some murmurs among the women*]. [Mary switches to English]. We want to have a very specific campaign message ... it's not any transportation messaging but it's a messaging from women ... working in [pausing for effect to bring everyone along] ... transport [they all say together].

A few moments passed, then Mina, a *matatu* conductor in her early twenties stood up and asked in Swahili about whose responsibility it was to get her out of jail when she is arrested. The SACCO or herself? Mary, a bit defeated answered patiently, translating a little to Susan, the American outreach coordinator at Flone Initiative who was still learning Swahili.

After a little while, Susan cleared her throat and asked slowly, "What misconceptions do you feel your riders have when they see you are a woman?" Again, a long pause until Carol, another conductor in her late twenties, offered her perspective and seemed to finally articulate the themes that Susan and Mary had been trying to draw out. She introduced herself and said, "when women work in the *matatu*, they don't think you can manage, so most of the time *wanakuunderestimate* [people underestimate you] ... so you use double the effort." This comment seemed to unlock the concept for the other women who soon offered up their own stories of common misconceptions they heard at work, and countered with statements like, "women are good managers," "women are not weak," "women support women," and "women are not your enemy!" With these statements it was clear the facilitators were happy to have the women tapping into their own gendered experiences and developing a shared vocabulary across different but connected fields.

As these women worked through what it meant to be women in the *matatu* sector with their Flone Initiative mentors and workshop facilitators, it was reminiscent of the consciousness-raising sessions common among feminists in the 1960s and 1970s, that fostered conversation about women's shared struggles (Firth and Robinson 2016: 8). Just as in the CRs held by second-wave feminists, the WIT group was considered more than just a self-help, therapy, or venting session, it was also a form of political transformation.

Through formal and informal coping and solidarity-building strategies, women find ways to impact their labor and change their working conditions, as they create and protect spaces of dignified work and worker solidarity (Grossman-Thompson 2020).

In the Flone Initiative training discussed above, one can see a feminist encounter in real time, there was a mix of feminist perspectives where the women transport workers understood themselves first as *matatu* workers and had to be coaxed into seeing their work struggles through a gendered lens, which nods to the biological determinism in Western feminist thought that has been critiqued by African feminists and others (Mahmood 2004; Mohanty 2003; Oyěwùmí 1997).[6] Some feminists from the Global South argue that the categories Western feminists use to organize against are either (a) different in non-Western communities, or (b) simply non-existent (Oyěwùmí 1997). But as one could see in the same example, by using the idea that these women were mothers of the *matatu*, women workers could give shape to the gendered critique they were being asked to comment on by the facilitators. In this way, it was reflective of the empowering status that motherhood has for many African women and African feminist scholars (Kilimo 2022). In the exchange above, Mary uses motherhood to help clarify the category of gender for women on *matatus*.

As women enter the male-dominated workspace of transportation, their gendered status comes into play in important and contradictory ways. As shown in the last two chapters, their identities as women can both advantage them and disadvantage them. For both African feminist activists as well as African women workers, the digital realm is an important site of activity that has allowed for them to seize on opportunities previously out of reach. For African feminists, social media became a collective organizing space that provided them access to very real political outcomes, from the massive #mydressmychoice march in Nairobi to the legislation they were able to shape around public transportation training. For women workers, evidence from the WIT group shows that they are accessing economic opportunities from ride-sharing platforms like Uber, Bolt, and Taxify for car and motorcycle taxi services. As the digital economy has had mixed outcomes for workers throughout the world, with some workers praising their increased "flexibility" and others lamenting their increased exploitation, women in this sector, while not free from some of the drawbacks of the gig economy, are also experiencing new opportunities in sectors previously off-limits to them.

---

[6] I am not arguing here that all feminists in the West find motherhood limiting, but just that the emphasis on women "having it all" (often meaning career and motherhood) points to what scholars frame as "antagonistic" discourses (Mahmood 2004).

Platforms of Power

When Uber first emerged in 2010–2011, they positioned themselves as a company that would facilitate flexibility among workers who were underutilizing their automotive resources (Isaac 2019), but along the way the company's leadership made destroying urban public transportation part of their business model. The company referred to this approach as "disruption," but it can be seen as a dismantling of the public transportation sector of cities and towns across the world. In a cache of leaked documents known as the Uber Files, communications of executives showed that the company would often ignore city laws and ordinances regarding taxi services, knowingly operate illegally while, at times urging their drivers to stage protests or counter-protests with knowledge of the danger that their workers would likely encounter, the CEO Kalanick once telling executives that "violence guarantees success" (Davies et al. 2022). Uber used a business model that intended to subsidize rides for a period until the urban transportation system was so neglected that the amount of money needed to fix it was off-putting. Huge changes in the ways cities are structured happen through transportation projects. Many of these projects have been violent in nature – exemplified by the classic case of Robert Moses in New York City and the way he constructed roads to make it more difficult for poor people on buses to access the beautiful amenities of the city, like the beaches and hiking trails north of Manhattan (Caro 2015). It is not only about Uber and the "uberization" of the economy, but devaluing public transportation is also about limiting the ways that transportation mobility and movement capture imaginations, can prompt radical acts and can make urban struggles plain to see.

Uber started as an elitist fantasy. In 2008, Garrett Camp, a Canadian billionaire, was frustrated by his experience of being unable to get a taxi in San Francisco in under a half-hour and this frustration with urban transportation options prompted Kalanick to tell his young employees that he wanted to provide a world where "transportation was as reliable as running water" (Isaac 2019: 83), although perhaps not realizing that in the US, depending on where you live, running water is not always reliable. And, interestingly, for as much as popular transportation in Kenya is criticized, research has found that *matatu* service reaches over 95 percent of households across the country (Salon and Gulyani 2019).

In the early days of Uber in Kenya, in 2015, the company used incentives to sign up drivers and riders. Incentives for the company translated to free money given to drivers and riders and was meant to get people hooked on Uber. In 2015, Uber spent $2 billion USD worldwide to incentivize people to use the service (Isaac 2019: 136). It took 20–30 percent of the fare, and the driver got the rest. Additionally, in the USA, the driver got a phone and tons of perks and bonuses like hundreds of dollars extra for hitting a minimum of rides (Isaac 2019:40). The riders, too, got perks like free rides and credit card offers as Uber subsidized rides every month. With every ride free and subsidized, that is a ride not taken with public transport or a taxi. In Kenya, in 2015, people embraced Uber's arrival.

> People needed jobs, and the taxi industry was privatized ... At the outset, Uber drivers were making 60 shillings per kilometer – about 97 cents a mile. The company took a 25 percent commission and established requirements for cars it would sign up: They had to be relatively new and about sedan size, and they had to have large engines, four doors and four seats. (Sperber 2020)

In May 2016, Uber launched its first loan program with Sidian Bank, a commercial bank in Kenya where loans were given for cars belonging to Zohari Leasing, a company that was established just a month before the loan partnership was announced (Sperber 2020). The hammer blow for many drivers came two months later, in July 2016. After other digital taxi apps launched in Nairobi, Uber cut its prices by about 35 percent. Drivers who had taken out loans predicated on making 60 shillings an hour were especially upset. They were earning one-third less than they had expected. Protests broke out, and hundreds went on strike, refusing to turn on the app (Sperber 2020). In March 2017, following driver strikes, Uber raised rates by about 20 percent, upon which drivers were making about 40 shillings per kilometer. But at that point, there were many more Uber cars on the road. And the worst was yet to come.

In 2018, Uber launched a new category of cars. The *ChapChap* (*Sheng* for fast) is a Suzuki Alto, a smaller, two-door vehicle, which costs less than the cars that thousands of drivers had previously leased, rented or bought to meet the Uber standard. *ChapChap* rides were priced accordingly, starting at just 16 shillings per kilometer. Kenyans would pool together to take a *ChapChap* and say it was nearly as cheap as a *matatu* (Sperber 2020). Uber rolled out a *ChapChap* promotion for drivers: after they completed fifteen rides each week, the Uber commission would change from 25 percent to 3 percent. That has helped some drivers pay off their loans. A female driver called the promotion "awesome," but national media outlets in Kenya reported high rates of repossessions on the *ChapChap* model, and when the COVID-19 pandemic hit, Uber ended the promotion.

The journalist covering Uber's story in Kenya describes Nairobi in pre-Uber times: "Before Uber, a taxi rider could be charged almost as much in Nairobi as in New York. Most people got around on crowded 'matatus' – unreliable buses that charged less than 50 shillings a ride, or about 50 cents" (Sperber 2020). Although Sperber is critiquing Uber and the way that workers are struggling, she falls into the familiar trap previously explored in this book where many journalists, experts and even scholars negatively frame popular transportation in Nairobi, and Africa more broadly. By comparing taxi prices in Nairobi to New York City, the author reveals an ethnocentric perspective on African cities. Nairobi is a city of 4 million people and serves as the central economic and political hub of the East African region. The idea that it would be shocking that a taxi could be expensive in Nairobi, is what some might call an orientalist perspective on urban transportation in urban Africa.

Uber has transformed work and the hustle throughout the world, but there is value in looking at the different ways people experience this digital transformation. For women in Kenya, the emergence of Uber has provided some surprising and lucrative opportunities. Notably, some of Uber's issues in the US, for example California's 2020 Proposition 22 legislation which exempted transportation and delivery-app-based companies from providing employee benefits by claiming they are independent contractors is not necessarily as salient an issue to Kenyans. Due to the low rate of formal employment among the Kenyan population, many people run their own small businesses where they are independent contractors. When Uber came to Kenya, then, it made some interesting and important impacts, some of which are visible through the transport work history of an Uber driver in Nairobi named Eunice.

Eunice

Eunice is a Kenyan woman in her early sixties. When a friend and I exited a restaurant in Nairobi in July 2019, the *askari* at the front door asked if we needed a taxi, when we responded yes, he waved to a car sitting in the dark. The tiny car flashed the lights and pulled up very slowly. The windows were tinted and hard to see into, so we were surprised when we opened the door and there was Eunice with a big smile. She was sitting impossibly close to the steering wheel and told me to sit in back because I was "a little bit fatter" than my friend. My friend and I happily climbed in. Although my colleague and I had both called Ubers in Nairobi and gotten female drivers, for both of us, Eunice was the first Kenyan woman "taxi" driver we had ever had. The relationship that Eunice had with the *askari* at the restaurant facilitated her individual taxi business beyond working for Uber, although she also drove for Uber, which is how she got into the taxi business in the first place.

When we first got into Eunice's cab, she immediately started telling a story about how her husband was a somewhat well-known politician who worked with Kibaki and how she had been his mistress, or, more accurately, his second wife. She was also raising a young adult son, who was still living with her. She talked at length about how to handle men and mentioned that her politician partner had passed away a few years before, which is when she started driving for Uber. She worked her way to buying a new car and then losing that car. By the time I arrived at my apartment, I knew I would try and use only Eunice's taxi for transportation the rest of the trip, and I was lucky because as I started to climb out, she handed me her card.

For the past five years, I have kept up with Eunice and used her as my taxi driver during research trips. Much like with Steve and Elizabeth and the many other *matatu* workers I have become close to over time, our relationship is largely built through riding around and chatting. Eunice has lots of stories about driving for Uber, one is particularly harrowing. She describes picking up a Kenyan of South Asian origin, who wanted to be taken to Parklands, a historically South Asian neighborhood in Nairobi. Eunice thought nothing of it, except for the fact that she thought the man was handsome and she was a little surprised that he did not have his own car. As she drove him home, he directed her to go down an alley where his gate was located. As she did, several gunmen appeared and made her get out and exit the vehicle. The man with her got out of the car, at first acting afraid and begging her to comply so they would not be hurt. But when the thieves seized her car, she realized he was colluding with them and perhaps even the mastermind of the crime. He got in another vehicle and left the scene, while two young African men put her in her own vehicle and drove to a wooded area. She described being in the woods with these two young men who were holding her at gunpoint as they discussed what to do with her. She told me she convinced them that she did not blame them for carjacking her, but instead blamed the structural conditions they faced like the lack of jobs and support from the government. She claimed that one wanted to let her go and one wanted to kill her, but she ultimately got away through the woods and ended up at a church. Her car was never recovered, so she bought a very small one, which she was driving in 2019 when she told me this story.

A few weeks after Eunice and I met the first time, I called her again and she came to pick me up filled with stories of her driving adventures. One of them, which she talked about for several days, involved picking up a passenger who ended up being a man in nothing but a woman's robe, and bare feet. She speculated that he was having an affair with a married woman, and the woman's spouse came home unannounced. Another story she told me was about picking up a man who was visiting Nairobi for a week, who paid her to take him to all his meetings for the whole week. At some point he helped her avoid getting arrested by the police by forcefully coming to her aid when they were stopped by police. They became friends and he paid her well. Eunice does not exhibit much solidarity with other transport operators, women or otherwise. When there was an Uber strike in July of 2019 in Nairobi, Eunice made me sit in the front seat as to avoid detection by the activists in the street.

She said that if they see you working, they will beat on your car and try to break your windows. When I asked her if she should just stay home that day, she exclaimed that "No way! There is money to made!"

Before 2015, there would be no way for a woman to work as a taxi driver. A woman *matatu* conductor who worked their way up to a driver is even rare. What sets this group of women apart from the other transportation providers discussed in this book is their class. To be an Uber driver, you need to know how to drive relatively well, and have access to a car. This is middle-class knowledge. The enrollment of women in driving schools has skyrocketed in Kenya in the past few years, perhaps connected to Uber or just because Nairobi is getting richer and there are more professional women in the market for cars. In fact, I met an aid worker from Singapore who came to Nairobi ten years ago, and who just learned how to drive and bought her first vehicle in in 2018. As women enter more public spaces, and build solidarity online and offline, they can start to harness collective political power through urban publics and counterpublics.

This preliminary research of women in transportation regarding Uber specifically would suggest that, although ultimately Uber is not a great place for workers, it helps us reflect on the different ways companies like this work in different places and what that means for the people involved. Gig economy workers, contract workers and the tension around worker benefits and Uber do not have the same impact in Kenya where there are no substantial worker protections. The idea that Uber would provide workers with health care or benefits does not really cross the mind of Kenyan workers in the same way it may for workers in California. But it does seem to allow for women to enter the transportation space in a new way. Even though SACCOs have been shown to facilitate entry to *matatu* work for women, the entrance to taxi driving in Kenya is much different. It is very territorial and even more exclusive. Not only is it male-dominated, but it is also skewed toward older men, and largely Kikuyu men in Nairobi. Eunice is an older Kikuyu woman, but before platform economies came, she would not have been able to work successfully as a private taxi driver.

Conclusion

The potential for urban workers to transform society is the focus of research on infrastructures, including this project. Urban workers are constantly changing and adapting to the ferocious capitalistic competition within which we are all entrenched. To build and maintain solidarity networks in the face of workplace violence, sexual harassment, and structural disappointments is a challenge, and the women working in transportation are masters at finding ways to reframe their lives and put themselves at the center of new transportation economies. Just as *matatu* routes have defined and demarcated Nairobi for decades, new transportation technologies have and will continue to emerge and be adopted and absorbed, and Nairobi will adjust. Some statistics put *matatu* use at 70 percent of the Nairobi population of 4.4 million, so odds are that these moving urban public spaces will continue to be a site for creative expression and political community in the coming decades (Salon and Gulyani 2019). Exploring institutions like Flone Initiative and SACCOs, as well as platform economies like Uber, provides opportunities to understand the current approach to popular transportation reform, which has consolidated wealth but not solved some fundamental problems of the sector (like police corruption). Digital spaces provide potentials for counterpublics to politicize and empower women working in transportation. While the ethnographic data from working with the women of Flone Initiative provides a glimpse into possible futures and is positioned at the intersections of gender, labor, and mobility in Nairobi.

In the fragile solidarity *matatu* men and women construct through stigma, and the social cohesion that results from being excluded, new rules of circulation are being negotiated. As dramatic shifts in Nairobi's urban landscape are made and remade under the neoliberal vision of a global city one can only hope that the multifaceted and rich urban life that is facilitated through this form of popular transportation continues. People are often quick to assume if something is old, it needs to be replaced instead of understanding that longevity can also be a marker of sustainability.

Conclusion
Roundabouts: Kenya's Transportation Futures

The featured image on the home page of Kenya's Vision 2030 website is a multicolored train, blurry in motion, floating atop grey concrete pylons over a vast savannah landscape dotted with Acacia trees (vision2030.go.ke). This image speaks in the vocabulary of global infrastructure, in which a major portion is concerned with "sustainable urban transportation." The future planning of Nairobi, sometimes referred to as the Silicon Savannah, is made legible through very expensive and voluminous master planning documents, called Vision 2030, which have been criticized as "superficial, highly business oriented, unrealistic documents embedded with destructive modernist ideas, which relies heavily on the language of neoliberal globalization" (Myers 2015: 339). The phrase "sustainable urban transportation" is used dozens of times, but the Standard Gauge Railway (SGR), the featured train whizzing over the savannah on the website's homepage, rips through both the Tsavo National Park and Nairobi National Park disrupting the landscape and disturbing the wildlife. Additionally, throughout all the planning materials, there is not a single mention of the current popular transportation sector which carries a majority of Kenyan citizens daily – the *matatu*.

There are reasons why Vision 2030 does not "see" *matatu* vehicles, even though they are designed for hypervisibility. This glaring omission exposes the massive gulf separating the technoscientific future imaginaries of Vision 2030 with life as it is lived on the ground in Nairobi. As transportation infrastructure is increasingly a target for neoliberal expansion, this book has traced how local transportation infrastructures can be key sites of economic and political life and urban meaning-making but are often deemed problematic and then slated for improvement, overlooking how they contribute to the culture of Nairobi. Although the aesthetic elements of the *matatu* are often dismissed, they are not unnoticed by the world at large. When Yo-Yo Ma made a visit to Nairobi in 2023, he and his team made sure he was able to ride in a *matatu* and even play his cello inside. As a world-famous musician, his recognition of matatu culture in Nairobi should be an indicator that this *matatu*, and the media it circulates, are important parts of making the city.

Transportation infrastructure in the twenty-first century is a branded spectacle through which city managers advertise and imagine themselves to attract international investors and young professionals. Public transportation services are one of the metrics of modernization used to rank cities along urban hierarchies (Robinson 2013) and improving "sustainable urban transportation" is an important funding avenue, leveraging the language of climate change to attract global finance (Smith 2019; Myers 2015). Vision 2030 is the aspirational plan for Kenya's future. It is filled with smart cities and smart transportation (Smith 2019: 21).

Transportation scholars, urban planners and policy makers overwhelmingly suggest large-scale urban infrastructural upgrades to improve troubled sectors through the adoption of urban megaprojects like BRT systems and expensive planning documents like Vision 2030 (Klopp et al. 2019). These expert lobbyists tend to promote one-size-fits-all transportation solutions that are more in line with the priorities of the organizations like the World Bank and multinational corporations, than with local interests (Rizzo 2017). The trend has been to use paratransit problems to justify urban interventions, which increasingly diverts transportation profits from the traditional small-scale owners into the hands of wealthier investors and powerful interests, undoing one of the most dependable avenues to the middle class for Kenyans for the past sixty years (Mutongi 2017).

Transportation technology, and the "development" narratives around transportation spectacles, are used to sell smart cities to investors and gloss over real infrastructural problems. Infrastructure-led Vision 2030 is an urban plan to "reinvent Nairobi as world class African metropolis" and was to be included as a "spectacular node in a network of global cities" (Smith 2019: 1). Futuristic images and illustrations circulated on billboards obscure complex economic transformations ranging from from the roll-back neoliberalism of austerity that drove the emergence and dominance of paratransit systems throughout African cities to the roll-out neoliberalism of reregulation and urban megaprojects while new technologies introduce various financialization schemes and elements of surveillance capitalism, "[c]irculating plans, global vocabularies and imagined futures of Vision 2030 create new entanglements' (Smith 2019: 23).

This book has focused on the conditions and potentialities of political subjectivities of transportation work in Nairobi, Kenya. How workers build and maintain solidarity networks is crucial to understanding how they survive the many risks they face. As women make their way in the transportation sector by building unlikely and sometimes fragile collaborations, what does the future hold for transportation in Nairobi in the face of "sustainable urban transportation" goals, or as platform economies come speeding toward Kenya's popular transportation sector changing the landscape for everyone? The women of Flone Initiative are attempting to make their claim on parts of the *matatu* sector as a marginalized group of people; they are coming together with other marginalized riders to make themselves stronger. This solidarity has resulted in potential policy changes, but how far the promises go remains to be seen.

Mobility is important to the economic, social, and political lives of most people and can be an important site of resistance for marginalized people throughout the cities in both the Global North and Global South (Feliciano 2024). Popular transportation in Kenya, especially Nairobi, has been key to the political life of Kenyans for the past eighty years and throughout their entire decolonial history. From the Kikuyu taxis of the 1940s to the colonial bus during Kenya's "Emergency" in the 1950s and throughout Kenya's embrace of *jua kali* and all things *matatu* in the 1970s and 1980s, popular transportation has had a major impact on the political, social, globalized identities of its growing urban population. In the 1960s and throughout the *jua kali* era, the onus was on citizens of Kenya to fill in the gaps left by the state and build the social infrastructure of the city (King 1996). The idea that they could self-regulate and fabricate their own mass transportation sector reflected first in debates around the rights of newly formed Kenyan citizens to road safety, and later the grit and resilience of Kenyans to build the nation and move the people, without help from foreign donors and even the Kenyan government (Mutongi 2017). It wasn't until the 1980s and 1990s, with the introduction of powerful audio-visual technology and systems, that some popular transportation transformed into places of consumption and globalization. This transformation from citizen to customer, is a classic and well-noted function of neoliberalism as it shifts the weight of responsibility from the "state" to the "individual." As Mirowski sums up the power of reregulation, "one way to exert power in restraint of democracy is to bend the state to a market logic, pretending one can replace 'citizens' with 'customers'" (2013: 79). This pivot was completed through the Michuki Rules where neoliberal reregulation promoted the idea that when passengers purchase one seat with a seatbelt it is then their responsibility to make and follow their own rules regarding safety.

Commuter status shifting from citizen to consumer is again a version of transforming customer to user. Take for example the huge impact Uber has had on transportation since 2015 when it entered the market like a bomb. In what she calls "extraction infrastructure," Shoshana Zuboff describes the familiar process where "profound technologies weave themselves into the fabric of everyday life" and argues that ultimately trying to withdraw from these utilities is difficult due to the "involuntary merger of personal necessity and economic extraction are the same channels we rely on for daily logistics, social interaction, work, education, health care and access to products and services" (2019: 16–25). In this way, we can be even more specific in the ways that transportation infrastructure is being used as an avenue for neoliberalism, and as a case study to understand the broader implications of regulation and reregulation.

Urban transportation, one of the most important elements of any functioning city is more complicated than it seems, no matter where in the world you are.

The problems around issues of transportation and mobility and the labor that supplies it all are not ones that can be solved with off-the-shelf solutions and one-size-fits-all approaches, but there are things that work better than others and there are spaces that our research can expand upon.

The Future (of Transport) is Female?[1]

At the 2019 WIT meeting with Flone Initiative organizers, described in the last chapter, one of the women conductors was wearing a bright red T-shirt with crisp white lettering splashed across the front: "Better BRT needs WOMEN" (Figure 18). I learned later that Flone was lobbying for BRT to hire women because they make better transportation operators, and they make transportation safer for women. Since at least 2019, representatives from Flone Initiative have been invited to meetings with the Institute for Transportation & Development Policy (ITDP), the body that is the driving force behind the BRT project in Nairobi, even when *matatu* owners and savings and credit co-operative (SACCO) leaders were not.

After the violence that shook Kenya in 2007 and 2008, Kenyan leaders and politicians attempted to "plan their way out" of the mess they were in (Klopp 2012: 12), which included a plan to transform the transportation sector in Kenya. The Vision 2030 plan invites both foreign and private investment to the transport sector by supplying and managing larger buses to form a BRT system, or light rail, like the ones operating in, Bogotá, Colombia and Guangzhou, China (Wood 2015).[2] Both of these cities have a BRT system that runs on a well-maintained portion of highway, which is exclusively for big buses carrying commuters. This system works well and has eased congestion in these two cities. When BRT is combined with other policies such as shared bicycles, more bike lanes and lit pedestrian walkways, it can heavily reduce the congestion in even the most populated urban environments (Wood 2015).

But just because the BRT works in these cities does not necessarily mean it will work everywhere. Take for example, South Africa where, similarly to Kenya, the minibus taxi sector represents a subversive sector that is also

---

[1] "The Future is Female" was a saying that was popularized during Hillary Clinton's 2016 presidential campaign, but originally appeared in 1972, in a photo spread by artist Liz Cowan titled, "What a Well-Dressed Dyke Would Wear," which appeared in the lesbian feminist magazine COWRIE, published out of New York City.

[2] The 2011 film *Urbanized,* by Gary Hustwit shows how BRT in both Bogotá and Guangzhou function to relieve the city of congestion. In a lengthy interview with the Mayor of Bogotá, he makes a fundamentally important assertion when he says, "when you build more roads, you don't reduce congestion, you get more cars, and more congestion."

Figure 18 A member of Flone Initiative's Women in Transportation Group, with "Better BRT needs women" T-shirt, received earlier that year during an Independent Technical Review Panel (ITRP) workshop to which WIT were invited. (Photo by author, 2019).

a point of pride for the African population. In Johannesburg, South Africa, the owners of the informal taxi system protested the introduction of the BRT system (Graeff 2008). The informal transportation sector, in Johannesburg especially where they are still referred to as, "black taxis", enjoys a historical legacy as a particularly African enterprise, operating for the African population during apartheid (Blom-Hansen 2006; Khosa 1992). The BRT was seen as a revival of oppressive colonial policies surrounding the question of who is allowed to provide transportation for which populations.

In 2016, DART, the BRT in Dar es Salaam, Tanzania, funded by the World Bank through the Prime Minister's Office started running after years of delay (Rizzo 2017). Rizzo argues that the BRT is the latest expression of neoliberalism for the World Bank. These huge megaprojects are ways that the state can realign with capital. Rizzo (2017) and others (Dewey 2016) argue that urban megaprojects are simply a process of "reregulation" where government regulations, generally seen as a check on neoliberal tendencies, are used as a way to realign local institutions with global capital accumulation (Mirowski 2013). Scholars argue that with each new BRT system constructed in African cities there is a transfer of wealth and a neocolonial urban planning schema underpinning many of the recommendations (Diallo 2022). In Tanzania, as the BRT came in and displaced some transportation operators, it was decided by the directors of the project that no Tanzanian transport owner already established in the local business would be able to fill the position of the BRT head because he had never been the head of a BRT system (Rizzo 2017).

In Kenya, the BRT lobby was happy to promise to reserve some positions for the WIT group that Flone Initiative had organized, but during a recent update with the BRT planning group in 2023, it was decided best to restrict employment for people above 35 years old. Many of the women in WIT are older than that, so they will not be employable in this promising new sector.BRT is often seen not as an additional transportation solution but as transportation reform (Klopp et al. 2019). It is understood as not simply a bus upgrade but a wider transformation of the sectors of the economy and society that are informal. BRT needs to be understood as a political project as much as a technocratic infrastructural solution (Klopp et al. 2019: 3). Is the BRT for Nairobi full of broken promises like it was for transportation operators in Tanzania? What ways will women find success in the coming era of transportation technology in Kenya's future? If Uber is any indication, they will be at the forefront of the sector.

Roundabouts

In thinking about the space of the *matatu*, I am left with a question about the future which is, what does feminist transportation look like? Is it men behaving better, or is it a radical departure from the status quo that provides a safe space for women and other marginalized groups (including people with disabilities and LGBTQ+ passengers) as well as young men and women alike? As much

CONCLUSION

Figure 19 Basi Go Electric bus in depot charging station. (Photo by author, 2023).

as a *manyanga* may seem like a masculine space, could the electric vehicles appearing in the market be the feminist space of transportation?

In April 2023, I met with Jit Battacharya, founder of Basi Go, an electric bus company that builds and imports electric buses that it leases and sells to the SACCOs of the *matatu* sector (Figure 19). It does not sell the battery, but instead leases it to the customer and collects a small fee for charging it. Basi Go is limited by their charging network but there is already some interest in expansion, especially by women. Basi Go buses with their quiet, orderly exteriors seem perfectly positioned to be a type of space that can be associated with women. Just as women were not seen as able to work on a *manyanga* because of their dislike of noise and their adherence to rules and polite manners, they are easily associated with electric vehicles. Only a few months after that meeting with Jit, Elizabeth contacted me to give me the news that Sofia, a woman in her late forties, who had been stuck driving as a *karmagera* (someone who drives *matatu* vehicles from the back of the line to the front of the line before handing them over to the driver who will embark on their route) for several years, was chosen as the driver of one of the first Basi Go buses leased by the Embassava SACCO.

The odds for a radical feminist transportation revolution in Nairobi may be low, but the instructive nature of *matatu* counterpublics helps us see potential avenues for change. Women are not going to stop working in the sector and this has already transformed several aspects of transportation throughout the city. Women are poised at the edge of these sectors in important ways that were sketched out in the last two chapters, but the future has yet to be written and we must wait and see the transformative potential for Kenya's transportation sector. It has already undergone great shifts and much flux in the past twenty years, and the next ten will see more and more climate events and increased movement to cities. I think the symbolic, economic, and social roles of different types of transportation will only become more important in the face of climate crisis and urban transition. This book aims to be part of the conversation around the ways that cities work – not only in East Africa, but throughout the world.

From the Nubian women transporting their baskets of bottles in the middle of the locked-down colonial landscape of Kenya's Emergency to Yo-Yo Ma playing his cello on a *manyanga* and to the public service posters created by the women of the Flone Initiative, urban transportation vehicles are a media infrastructure that circulates images, gives meaning to place, and gives voice to multiple marginalized and alternative identities. It is a place where political subjectivities are built, and solidarity is formed and expressed. It is an urban space that is not the private home, or the public street, but a small, mobile space of public intimacy that impacts the behaviors and interactions of the city. Extrapolating from this, the workers who create and shape this space are key to the making of the city and have built their own social institutions to protect themselves and each other from the risk under which they are operating.

Matatu Work

Transportation itself, from subway cars to dollar vans to colonial buses to airplanes will always be important *places.* This lived infrastructure is often overlooked or taken for granted. In this work, I am adding to the literature on the anthropology of infrastructures and to the large field of mobility studies, but I am also contributing to the discussion of places for protest, practices of politics and circulation in urban life. Anthropologists and urban ethnographers often look at street vendors and sidewalks, but we need to also look at the ways that urban life moves, and that requires a flexible and agile ethnography. The Kenya Bus Service (KBS) bus and the *matatu*, and countless other places, have been in have been important places to make social struggles visible in the past and will be in the future.

Social history demands that we incorporate people's memories and personal lives to understand change over time as it impacted various members of the community from elites to the most marginalized. Although not in strictly chronological order, *Matatu Work* can be read as a historical ethnography, where the social history of Nairobi can be read through the lens of transportation. The simple fact that Kenya, and Nairobi especially, was an afterthought beholden to building a railway shows how the policies that impact transportation reflect and shape larger issues in the world.

The first chapter of this book traces one of these transportation policies – the one-class, one-fare policy – floated by KBS to the Nairobi public. Although it meant raising the prices, the policy produced an outcry from a group of European women settlers and, from their complaint letters, they sketch the outline of everyday life for some of the most invisible people in the historical record.

The book has illustrated the importance of considering popular transportation in Nairobi as a form of public and counterpublic, and how these shape sociopolitical subjects in the city. Throughout the history of transportation in Kenya, it is not that *matatu* vehicles themselves are unique (although they are) but rather that public transportation itself is a very important urban space that largely goes unrecognized. This is changing, as noted throughout this book, but the imaginaries of future public transportation often do not consider the lived practices of ordinary commuters and workers. Here a historical and anthropological analysis is vital, alongside the work of urban planners and tech investors because the framing of the popular transportation sector as a place for alternative expressions and political identity is crucial to deepen what other scholars have called the "*matatu* generation," or the "hidden transcripts" of the *matatu* in the 1980s. The historicization and anthropological reading of the *matatu* includes the Muslim women of Kibera transporting home-brewed gin in colonial Nairobi in the colonial buses that African men were driving and includes the settler housewives. It also includes the significance of the joyride and the ways in which *matatu* vehicles reflect and shape popular culture across the city.

The story of African movement is a wider one than just these minibuses, but they are a good microcosm of the postcolonial lived realties in Nairobi. *Matatu* minibuses are not the whole story, but an important story that reflects the nuanced lives of urban Kenyans. They are targets to be scapegoated, upgraded, improved, renewed, disciplined, and regulated. They are a representation of Nairobi in moving text. As noted earlier in this book, being inside of a *matatu* is like riding inside of a newspaper. It is media *and* transportation, and it creates perspectives. As this book illustrates, *matatu* are also reflections of other systems: sexism, the climate crisis, the history of informality and development, the risk, death, and suffering at the hands of lack of basic care. There are so many elements of the story that matter but cannot necessarily be fully expanded on, which is why the potential of this newest turn in the *matatu* tale: That is, the influence of women and the transformation that their work is creating or has the potential to create.

The women and men of this sector are important actors in the social world of Kenya. The *matatu* sector has always been a bit of an outlier in the urban transportation of the Global South, with its independence and its wild style, but with women now entering the scene it is once again ahead of the curve. It has been surprising to see just how far the women operators can and will go, and what it takes to get there. It is already a very tough sector, and to be successful means to be extremely adept at navigating complex social relationships. They are the news anchors of the *matatu*, the faces you see daily who circulate the dynamic energy of Nairobi, and through their creativity and hustle, they make the *matatu* work.

REFERENCES

Primary Sources

Kenya National Archives (KNA)

AA/35/44/12, Letter to Transport Licensing Boards regarding the cases of Kiorie Kinyanjui and Samuel Githu. 19 June 1961.

K380.5 No. 81–97, Report of a Committee to investigate considering the desirability of coordinating and regulating all forms of transport in the colony. 1936.

MNR/94601/10. Proposal of Kenya Bus Company to make all buses of one class and one fare. July 1956.

POL/128/60, Letter to the Traffic Police from C. E. Chun, Traffic Manager for Kenya Bus Services. 4 April 1960.

94601/158, Letter from "The Housewives," to Mayor of Nairobi. 7 June 1956.

94601/161, Memo from the Mayor of Nairobi. 20 June 1956.

Street Accidents Inquiry, Letter from Reginald Mombasa, President and L. O. Johnes, Secretary, Kenya Welfare Association to Town Clerk, Nairobi. 14 April 1938.

Bus Operating Account – Traffic – Salaries & Wages. Kenya Bus Services Limited. 3 November 1949.

Public Records Office (PRO)

The British National Archive, London (PRO), CO822/796, Colonial Office, Report of the Emergency in Kenya – Operation Anvil and Resulting conditions in Nairobi, 1954–1956.

The Daily Nation Newspaper Archives

Daily Nation (1961) "80 'pirate taxis' arrested", 25 May.
———. (1964). "Pirate taximen", 30 July (p.5).
———. (1965). "Crackdown on pirate taxis", 10 March (p.3).
———. (1966). "Busmen strike after 'insult'", 11 June (p.20).
———. (1967). "Nyeri crisis after transport ban", 25 September (p.24).
———. (1970). "The road pirates", 5 December (p.6).
———. (2004). Advertisement: "Make money from matatu", 21 March.
———. (2007). Supplement on sustainable transportation, 5 July.

Secondary Sources

Abdulaziz, M. H. and K. Osinde. (1997) "*Sheng* and *Engsh*: development of mixed codes among the urban youth in Kenya", *International Journal of the Sociology of Language* 125(1): 43–64.

Agbiboa, Daniel. (2022). *They eat our sweat: transport labor, corruption and everyday survival in urban Nigeria.* Oxford: Oxford University Press.

Anand, N. (2017). *Hydraulic city: water and the infrastructures of citizenship in Mumbai.* Durham, NC: Duke University Press.

Anand, N., A. Gupta and H. Appel (2018). "Temporality, politics, and the promise of infrastructure," in N. Anand, A. Gupta and H. Appel (eds.), *The Promise of Infrastructure.* Durham, NC: Duke University Press.

Andae, G. (2021). "UK retains Kenya travel ban." *The East African*, 19 July.

Anderson, D. M. (2000). Master and servant in colonial Kenya, 1895–1939. *The Journal of African History* 41(3): 459–485.

———. (2002). "Vigilantes, violence and the politics of public order in Kenya." *African Affairs* 101(405): 531–555.

———. (2005). *Histories of the hanged: the dirty war in Kenya and the end of empire.* New York: W.W. Norton.

Antoniello, P. (2020). *For the public good: women, health and equity in rural India.* Nashville: Vanderbilt University Press.

Appadurai, A. and E. Robles-Anderson (2023). "Solidarity's Fragilities." *Public Culture* 35(1): 1–6..

Arrighi, G. (1994). The *long twentieth century: money, power and the origins of our times*. New York: Verso.

Aruho, A. T., R. Behrens, W. Mitullah, and A. Kamau (2021). A case study of matatu cashless fare collection initiatives in Nairobi. Southern African Transport Conference 2021.

Asen, R. (2000). "Seeking the 'counter' in counterpublics". *Communication Theory* 10(4): 424–446.

Augé, M. (1995). *Non-places: an introduction to supermodernity*, trans. John Howe. London and New York: Verso.

Balaton-Chrimes, S. (2013). "Indigeneity and Kenya's Nubians: seeking equality in difference or sameness?" *The Journal of Modern African Studies* 51(2): 331–354.

———. (2016). *Ethnicity, democracy and citizenship in Africa: Political marginalisation of Kenya's Nubians.* Abingdon: Routledge.

Basso, K. (1996). *Wisdom sits in places: landscape and language among the Western Apache.* Albuquerque: University of New Mexico Press.

Beck, K., G. Klaeger and M. Stasik (2017). "An introduction to the African road," in K. Beck, G. Klaeger and M. Stasik (eds.), *The making of the African road.* Leiden: Brill.

Bedi, T. (2016). "Taxi drivers, infrastructures, and urban change in globalizing Mumbai." *City and Society* 28(3): 387–410.

Behrens, R., D. McCormick and D. Mfinanga (2015). "An introduction to paratransit in sub-Saharan African cities," in R. Behrens, D. McCormick and D. Mfinanga (eds.), *Paratransit in African cities: operations, regulation and reform.* Abingdon: Routledge.

Behrens, R., D. McCormick, R. Orero and M. Ommeh (2017). "Improving paratransit service: lessons from inter-city *matatu* cooperatives in Kenya." *Transport Policy* 53: 79–88.
Berman, B. and J. Lonsdale (1992). *Unhappy valley: conflict in Kenya and Africa* (Vol. 1). Athens: Ohio University Press.
Biaya, T. (2005). "Youth and street culture in urban Africa: Addis Ababa, Dakar and Kinshasa," in A. Honwana and F. DeBoeck (eds.), *Makers and breakers: children and youth in postcolonial Africa*. Oxford: James Currey.
Bishara, A. A. (2023). Publics, polls, protest: public representation as sociopolitical practice. *Annual Review of Anthropology* 52: 437–453.
Blixen, K. (1937). *Out of Africa*. London: Putnam Press.
Blom-Hansen, T. (2006). "Sounds of freedom: music, taxis and racial imagination in urban South Africa." *Public Culture* 18(1): 185–208.
Boyer, R. (2005) "From shareholder value to CEO power: the paradox of the 1990s." *Competition and Change* 9: 7–47.
Branch, D. (2009). *Defeating Mau Mau, creating Kenya: counterinsurgency, civil war and decolonization*. Cambridge: Cambridge University Press.
———. (2011) *Kenya: between hope and despair, 1963–2011*. New Haven, CT and London: Yale University Press.
Bravman, B. (1998). *Making ethnic ways: communities and their tranformations in Taita, Kenya, 1800–1950*. Oxford: James Currey.
Bujra, J.M. (1975). "Women 'entrepreneurs' of early Nairobi." *Canadian Journal of African Studies* 9(2): 213–234.
Butler, J. (1990). *Gender trouble: feminism and the subversion of identity*. New York: Routledge.
Çaglar, A. and N. Glick Schiller (2018). *Migrants and city-making: dispossession, displacement, and urban regeneration*. Durham: Duke University Press.
Caro, R. (1975). *The power broker: Robert Moses and the fall of New York*. New York: Vintage.
Carpiano, R. M. (2009). "Come take a walk with me: The 'Go-Along' interview as a novel method for studying the implications of place for health and well-being." *Health & Place* 15(1): 263–272.
Casey, E. S. (1996). "How to get from space to place in a fairly short stretch of time: phenomenological prolegomena." *Senses of Slace* 27: 14–51.
Chappell, B. (2010). "Custom contestations: Lowriders and urban space." *City & Society* 22(1): 25–47.
———. (2017). "Custom contestations: lowriders and urban space." *City & Society* 22(1): 25–47.
Cheeseman, N., K. Kanyinga, and G. Lynch (eds.) (2020). *The Oxford handbook of Kenyan politics*. Oxford University Press.
Chege, M. (2020). "The political economy of foreign aid to Kenya," in N. Cheeseman, K. Kanyinga, and G. Lynch (eds.), *The Oxford handbook of Kenyan politics*. Oxford University Press.
Chitere, P. O. and T. N. Kibua (2004). Efforts to improve road safety in Kenya. Report for Institute of Policy Analysis and Research (IPAR). Nairobi, Kenya.
Collier, J. F. and S. J. Yanagisako (1987). *Gender and kinship: essays toward a unified analysis*. Redwood City: Stanford University Press.

Cody, F. (2011). "Politics and Publics." *Annual Review of Anthropology* 40: 37–52.

Cooper, F. (1980). *From slaves to squatters: plantation labour and agriculture in Zanzibar and Coastal Kenya, 1890–1925*. New Haven, CT: Yale University Press.

Cooper, F. (ed.) (1983). *Struggle for the city: migrant labor, capital and the state in urban Africa*. Beverly Hills: Sage.

Cooper, F. and R. Packard (eds.) (1997). *International development and the social sciences: essays on the history and politics of knowledge*. Oakland: University of California Press.

Cummings, B. (2014). "Kenyans protest after woman is beaten and stripped in public." *The Guardian*, 17 November.

Davies, H., S. Goodley, F. Lawrence, P. Lewis and L. O'Carroll (2022). "Uber broke laws, duped Police and secretly lobbied governments, leak reveals." *The Guardian*, 11 July.

De Smedt, J. (2009). "'Kill me quick': a history of Nubian gin in Kibera." *The International Journal of African Historical Studies* 42(2): 201–220.

del Nido, J. M. (2021). *Taxis vs. Uber: courts, markets, and technology in Buenos Aires*. Redwood City: Stanford University Press.

Dewey, O. F. (2016). "BRT as a tool for negotiated re-regulation," in J. C. Munoz and L. Paget-Seekins (eds.), *Restructuring public transport through bus rapid transit* (pp. 51–72). Bristol: Policy Press.

Diallo, F. D. (2022). "Conflicted translations: an analysis of the bus rapid transit policy adoption process in Cape Town". *Territory, Politics, Governance* 1(19).

Di Nunzio, M. (2019). *The act of living: street life, marginality, and development in urban Ethiopia*. Ithaca: Cornell University Press.

Doherty, J. (2017) "Life (and limb) in the fast-lane: disposable people as infrastructure in Kampala's boda boda industry." *Critical African Studies* 9(2): 192–209.

East African Women's League (1962). *They made it their home*. Nairobi: East African Standard Limited.

Edelman, M. and A. Haugerud (2004). *The anthropology of development and globalization*. Oxford: Blackwell.

Elkins, C. (2005) *Imperial reckoning: the untold story of Britain's gulag in Kenya*. New York: Macmillan.

Erturk, I., J. Froud, S. Johal, A. Leaver and K. Williams (2007). "The democratisation of

finance? Promises, outcomes and conditions." *Review of International Political Economy* 14: 553–575.

Farzan, A. N. (2018). "BBQ Becky, Permit Patty and Cornerstone Caroline." *Washington Post*, 19 October.

Elyachar, J. (2010) "Phatic labor, infrastructure, and the question of empowerment in Cairo." *American Ethnologist* 37(3): 452–464.

Felski, R. (1989). *Beyond feminist aesthetics: feminist literature and social change*. Cambridge, MA: Harvard University Press.

Ference, M. (2021). "'You will build me': fiscal disobedience, reciprocity and the dangerous negotiations of redistribution on Nairobi's *matatu*." *Africa* 91(1): 16–34.

———. (2023). "'Compliments from the Housewives': contesting white public space in late-colonial Nairobi." *The Journal of African History* 64(2): 229–247.

Ferguson, J. (2015). *Give a man a fish: reflections on the new politics of distribution*. Durham: Duke University Press.
Fernando, P. and G. Porter (2002). *Balancing the load: women, gender and transport*. New York: Zed Books.
Firth, R. and A. Robinson (2016). "For a revival of feminist consciousness-raising: horizontal transformation of epistemologies and transgression of neoliberal TimeSpace". *Gender and Education* 28(3): 343–358.
Florence, N. (2014). *Wangari Maathai: visionary, environmental leader, political activist*. Woodstock: Lantern Books.
Fourchard, L. (2023). "In the shadow of the state: the making of garage laws in Lagos." *Swiss Journal of Sociocultural Anthropology* 29: 85–101.
Foucault, M. (1991). *The Foucault effect: studies in governmentality*. Chicago IL: University of Chicago Press.
Fraser, N. (1990). "Rethinking the public sphere: a contribution to the critique of actually existing democracy." *Social Text* 25/26: 56–80.
Fredericks, R. (2018). *Garbage citizenship: vital infrastructures of labor in Dakar, Senegal*. Durham: Duke University Press.
French, J. D. (2000). "The missteps of anti-imperialist reason: Bourdieu, Wacquant and Hanchard's *Orpheus and Power*." *Theory, Culture & Society* 17(1): 107–128.
Furedi, F. (1973). "The African crowd in Nairobi: popular movements and elite politics." *The Journal of African History* 14(2): 275–290.
Gal, S. and K. A. Woolard (2014 [2001]). "Constructing languages and publics authority and representation," in S. Gal and K. A. Woolard (eds.), *Languages and Publics* (pp. 1–12). New York: Routledge.
Ganti, T. (2014). "Neoliberalism." *Annual Review of Anthropology* 43: 89–104.
Gettleman, J. 2014 "Transit cards to replace cash on Kenyan minibuses are a hard sell." *New York Times*, 15 July.
Gieryn, T. (2000). "A space for place in sociology." *Annual Review of Sociology* 26(1): 463–496.
Gill, L. (2009). "The limits of solidarity: labor and transnational organizing against Coca-Cola." *American Ethnologist* 36(4): 667–680.
Gill, L. and S. Kasmir (2008). "Forum: solidarity." *Dialectical Anthropology* 32(175).
Ginsburgh N. and W. Jackson (2018). "Settler Societies." *A Companion to African History* 18: 77–91.
Githinji, P. (2006). "Bazes and their shibboleths: lexical variation and Sheng speakers' identity in Nairobi." *Nordic Journal of African Studies* 15(4).
Githiora, C. J. (2018). *Sheng: rise of a Kenyan Swahili vernacular*. Woodbridge: James Currey.
Gladys, M. M. (2006). "Road safety in Kenya." Doctoral dissertation, University of Nairobi.
Goffman, I. (1963). *Stigma: notes on the management of spoiled identity*. New York: Simon & Schuster.
Gorman, D. (2014). Organic union or aggressive altruism: imperial internationalism in East Africa in the 1920s. *The Journal of Imperial and Commonwealth History* 42(2): 258–285.
Graeff, J. (2008) "The organization and future of the matatu industry in Nairobi, Kenya." Working Paper. Report for the Center for Sustainable Development – Earth Institute. New York.

Grossack, M. M. (1956). "Psychological effects of segregation on buses", *Journal of the Arkansas Academy of Science* 9(14).

Grossman-Thompson, B. (2020). "'In this profession we eat dust': informal and formal solidarity among women urban transportation workers in Nepal." *Development and Change* 51(3): 874–894.

Gupta, A. and J. Ferguson (1992). "Beyond 'culture': space, identity, and the politics of difference." *Cultural Anthropology* 7(1): 6–23.

Habyarimana, J. and W. Jack (2015). "Results of a large-scale randomized behavior change intervention on road safety in Kenya." *Proceedings of the National Academy of Sciences* 112(34): E4661–E4670.

Hall, E. (1963). "A system for the notation of proxemic behavior." *American Anthropologist* 65(5): 1003–1026.

Hart, K. (2009) "On the informal economy: the political history of an ethnographic concept." Working Papers CEB 09-042.RS, Universite Libre de Bruxelles.

Harvey, D. (2007). *A brief history of neoliberalism*. New York: Oxford University Press.

Harvey, P. and H. Knox (2015). *Roads: an anthropology of infrastructure and expertise*. Ithaca: Cornell University Press.

Haugerud, A. (1995). *The culture of politics in modern Kenya*. Cambridge: Cambridge University Press.

Heinze, R. (2018) "Fighting over urban space: *matatu* infrastructure and bus stations in Nairobi, 1960–2000", *Africa Today* 65(2): 3–22.

Herzig, P. (2006). *South Asians in Kenya: gender, generation and changing identities in diaspora*. Münster: LIT Verlag.

Hirschkind, C. (2006). *The ethical soundscape: cassette sermons and Islamic counterpublics*. New York: Columbia University Press.

Hirst, D. and D. Lamba (1994). *The struggle for Nairobi*. Nairobi: Mazingira Institute.

Ho, K. (2009). *Liquidated: an ethnography of Wall Street*. Durham: Duke University Press.

Huchzermeyer, M. (2011). *Cities with slums: from informal settlement eradication to a right to the city in Africa*. Cape Town: University of Cape Town Press.

Isaac, M. (2019). *Super pumped: the battle for Uber*. New York: WW Norton.

Jackson, W. (2013). "Dangers to the Colony: loose women and the 'poor white' problem in Kenya." *Journal of Colonialism and Colonial History*, 14(2).

Jensen, O. B. (2009). "Flows of meaning, culture of movements – urban mobility as meaningful everyday life practice." *Mobilities* 4(1): 139–158.

Jerkins, M. (2018) "Why white women keep calling the cops on black people." *Rolling Stone*, 17 July.

Jones, P. S. (2020). "Nairobi: the politics of the capital," in N. Cheeseman, K. Kanyinga and G. Lynch (eds.), *The Oxford Handbook of Kenyan Politics*. Oxford University Press.

Kabeer, N. (1999). Resources, agency, achievements: reflections on the measurement of women's empowerment. *Development and Change* 30(3): 435–464.

K'akumu, O. A. and W. H. Olima (2007). "The dynamics and implications of residential segregation in Nairobi." *Habitat International* 31(1): 87–99.

Kamau, A. and T. Wright (2022). "Tackling gender-based violence and sexual harassment in the public transport sector: the role of key actors," in T. Wright, L. Budd and S. Ison (eds.), *Women, Work and Transport* Vol. 16 (pp. 37–51). Leeds: Emerald Publishing.

Kanogo, T. (1987). *Squatters and the roots of Mau Mau, 1905-63.* East African Publishers.

Kanter, R. M. (1975). "Women and the structure of organizations: explorations in theory and behavior." *Sociological Inquiry* 45(2–3): 34–74.

Kaplan, D. (2018). *The nation and the promise of friendship: building solidarity through sociability.* Cham: Springer.

Kelley, R.D. (2017). "The rest of us: rethinking settler and native." *American Quarterly* 69(2): 267–276.

Khayesi, M. and F. M. Nafukho (2016). *Informal public transport in practice: matatu entrepreneurship.* Oxford: Routledge.

Khosa, M. M. (1992). Routes, ranks and rebels: feuding in the taxi revolution. *Journal of Southern African Studies* 18(1): 232–251.

———. (1997). "Sisters on slippery wheels: women taxi drivers in South Africa." *Transformation* (33): 18–33.

Kießling, R. and M. Mous (2004). "Urban youth languages in Africa." *Anthropological Linguistics* 303–341.

Kiberenge, K. (2022). "The night swearing in that blotted Kibaki's rich legacy." *The Nation*, 22 April.

Kilimo, M. J. (2022). "'You can't do politics without money': female politicians, matronage, and the limits of gender quotas in Kenya." *Africa* 92(2): 210–229.

Kimeu, G. (2023) "Who's that busker on the streets of Nairobi? Only the world-famous cellist Yo-Yo Ma!" *The Guardian*, 13 June.

King, K. (1996). *Jua kali Kenya: change & development in an informal economy, 1970-95.* Columbus: Ohio State University Press.

Kinyanjui, N. (2019). *African Markets and the Utu-Ubuntu Business Model. A perspective on economic informality in Nairobi: a perspective on economic informality in Nairobi.* Oxford: African Books Collective.

Kiplagat, S. (2017) "Matatu driver, tout sentenced to death for stripping woman." *The Nation*, 28 June.

Klopp, J. M. (2008). "Remembering the destruction of Muoroto: slum demolitions, land and democratisation in Kenya." *African Studies* 67(3): 295–314.

———. (2012). "Towards a political economy of transportation policy and practice in Nairobi," in *Urban Forum* (23)1: 1–21.

———. (2021). "From 'para-transit' to transit? power politics and popular transport." *Advances in Transport Policy and Planning* 8: 191–209.

Klopp, J. and W. Mitullah (2015). "Politics, policy and paratransit: a view from Nairobi," in R. Behrens, D. McCormick. and D. Mfinanga (eds.), *Paratransit in African cities: operations, regulation and reform.* Abingdon: Routledge.

Klopp, J. M. J. Harber and M. Quarshie (2019). "A review of BRT as public transport reform in African cities." *VREF Research Synthesis Project Governance of Metropolitan Transport* 30.

Korongo, C. (2009). "Noise rules here to stay." *Capital News*, 9 December.

Krippner, G. (2005) "The financialization of the American economy." *Socio-Economic Review*, 3: 173–208.

Kumar, A. and F. Barrett (2008). "Stuck in traffic: urban transport in Africa." *Africa Infrastructure Country Diagnostic Background Paper*. Washington DC: World Bank,

Kusenbach, M. (2003). Street phenomenology: the go-along as ethnographic research tool. *Ethnography* 4(3): 455–485.

Kusimba, S. (2018). "'It's easy for women to ask!': gender and digital finance in Kenya." *Economic Anthropology* 5: 247–260.

Lamont, M. (2013). "Speed governors: road safety and infrastructural overload in post-colonial Kenya, c. 1963–2013." *Africa* 83(3): 367–384.

Lamont, M. and R. Lee (2015). "Arrive alive: road safety in Kenya and South Africa." *Technology and Culture* 56(2): 464–488.

Larkin, B. (2013). "The politics and poetics of infrastructure." *Annual Review of Anthropology* 42: 327–343.

———. (2008). *Signal and noise: media, infrastructure and urban culture in Nigeria*. Durham: Duke University Press.

Latour, B. (2005). "From realpolitik to dingpolitik or how to make things public," in B. Latour and P. Weibel (eds.), *Making things public: atmospheres of democracy*. Cambridge, MA: MIT Press, pp. 14–41.

Latour, B. and C. Venn (2002). "Morality and technology". *Theory, Culture & Society* 19(5–6): 247–260.

Lee, R. (2012). Death in slow motion: funerals, ritual practice and road danger in South Africa. *African Studies* 71(2): 195–211.

Lee, B. and E. LiPuma (2002). "Cultures of circulation: the imaginations of modernity." *Public Culture* 14(1): 191–213.

Leys, C. (1975). *Underdevelopment in Kenya: the political economy of neo-colonialism*. London: Heinemann; Nairobi: East African Publishers.

Link, B. G. and Phelan, J. C. (2001) "Conceptualizing stigma." *Annual Review of Sociology* 27(1): 363–385.

Lonsdale, J.and B. Berman (1979). "Coping with the contradictions: the development of the colonial state in Kenya, 1895–1914." *The Journal of African History* 20(4): 487–505.

Low, S. and D. Lawrence-Zúñiga (2003). "Locating culture," in S. Low and D. Lawrence-Zúñiga (eds.), *The anthropology of space and place: locating culture*. Oxford: Blackwell.

ltwstu (2017). "Land and labor regimes: Tania Li and R. Alan Covey in conversation." *Comparative Studies in Society and History (CSSH)* 16 April.

M'Inoti, K. (1997). "The Kipande: a colonial debate revisited." *Economic Review* (Nairobi) 218: 19–20.

Maathai, W. (2007). *Unbowed: a memoir*. New York: Anchor.

Macharia, K. (2007). "Tensions created by the formal and informal use of urban space: the case of Nairobi, Kenya." *Journal of Global South Studies* 24(2): 145–162.

Mahmood, S. (2004). "Women's agency within feminist historiography." *The Journal of Religion* 84(4): 573–579.

Mahoney, D. (2017). *The art of connection: risk, mobility, and the crafting of transparency in coastal Kenya*. Oakland: University of California Press.

Mains, D. (2019). "Under construction," in *Under Construction: Technologies of Development in Urban Ethiopia*. Durham: Duke University Press.

Mains, D. and E. Kinfu (2017). "Governing three-wheeled motorcycle taxis in urban Ethiopia: states, markets, and moral discourses of infrastructure." *American Ethnologist* 44(2): 263–274.

Manning, P. (2022). Flânerie in text and city: the heterogeneous urban publics of the Georgian Feuilleton." *Journal of Linguistic Anthropology* 32(3): 585–606.

Mays, J. and S. Piccoli (2018). "A white woman, Teresa Klein, called the police on a black child she falsely said groped her." *New York Times*, 12 October.

Mazrui, A. (1995). "Slang and code switching: the case of Sheng in Kenya." *Afrikanistiche Arbeitspapiere* 42: 168–179.

McCormick, D. and W. Mitullah (2013). "Paratransit business strategies: a bird's-eye view of matatus in Nairobi." *Journal of Public Transportation* 16(2): 135–152.

McIntosh, J. (2016). *Unsettled: denial and belonging among white Kenyans*. Oakland: University of California Press.

McMichael, P. (2000). *Development and social change, a global perspective*. London: Sage Publications.

Mills, M. B. (1999). *Thai women in the global labor force: consuming desires, contested selves*. New Brunswick: Rutgers University Press.

Mirowski, P. (2013). *Never let a serious crisis go to waste: how neoliberalism survived the financial meltdown*. New York: Verso Books.

Mitullah, W. (2020). "Gender Mainstreaming and the Campaign for Equality," in N. Cheeseman, K. Kanyinga and G. Lynch (eds.), *The Oxford Handbook of Kenyan Politics*. Oxford University Press.

Mitullah, W. and Onsate, S. (2013). "Formalising the Matatu Industry in Kenya: Policy Twists and Turns." Institute for Developing Studies Policy Brief, University of Nairobi.

Mohanty, C. T. (2003). "'Under Western eyes' revisited: feminist solidarity through anticapitalist struggles." *Signs: Journal of Women in Culture and Society* 28(2): 499–535.

Mamoulaki, E. (2017). "Anthropology, history and academic ethnocentrism: biases and limitations in recognizing and understanding solidarity." *Etnofoor* 29(2): 39–58.

Murray-Li, T. (2017). "The price of un/freedom: Indonesia's colonial and contemporary plantation labor regimes." *Comparative Studies in Society and History* 59(2): 245–276.

Mutongi, K. (2006). "Thugs or entrepreneurs? Perceptions of *matatu* operators in Nairobi, 1970 to the present." *Africa* 76(4): 549–568.

———. (2017). *Matatu: a history of popular transportation in Nairobi*. Chicago IL: University of Chicago Press.

Myers, G. (2003). *Verandahs of power: colonialism and space in urban Africa*. Syracuse University Press.

———. (2015). A world-class city-region? Envisioning the Nairobi of 2030. *American Behavioral Scientist* 59(3): 328–346.

Nyabola, N. (2018). *Digital democracy, analogue politics: how the internet era is transforming politics in Kenya*. London: Bloomsbury.

Nyabuga, G. (2007). Media corporatism: whither journalistic values? *Networking Knowledge: Journal of the MeCCSA Postgraduate Network* 1(1).
Njoroge, M (1970). "The Pirates." *Nation Magazine*, 13 March.
Ogot, B. A. and W. R. Ochieng (eds.) (1995). *Decolonization & independence in Kenya, 1940–93*. Athens: Ohio State University Press.
Olemo, D. (2016). "Exploring the major causes of road traffic accidents in Nairobi County." Report. University of Nairobi.
Ombuor, R. (2017). "Kenyans of Asian descent become nation's 44th tribe." *Voice of America*, 28 July
Ommeh, M., McCormick, D., Mitullah, W., Orero, R., and Chitere, P. (2015). "The politics behind the phasing out of the 14-seater matatu in Kenya." University of Nairobi Digital Repository.
Omulo, C. (2022). "Artur brothers raid on Meida: scandals during Kibaki's tenure." *Daily Nation*, 1 May.
Ong, A. (2006). *Neoliberalism as exception: Mutations in citizenship and sovereignty*. Durham, NC: Duke University Press.
———. (2010). *Spirits of resistance and capitalist discipline: factory women in Malaysia*. New York: SUNY Press.
Oonk, G. (2013). "South Asians in East Africa, 1800–2000: an entrepreneurial minority caught in a 'Catch-22'." *Tijdschrift voor sociale en economische geschiedenis* 2103(10): 59–81.
Ortner, S. B. (1997). *Making gender: the politics and erotics of culture*. Boston, MA: Beacon Press.
Osborn, M. (2008). "Fuelling the flames: rumour and politics in Kibera" *Journal of Eastern African Studies* 2(2): 315–327.
Osse, A. (2016). "Police reform in Kenya: a process of 'meddling through'." *Policing and Society* 26(8): 907–924.
Oyěwùmí, O. (1997). *The invention of women: making an African sense of Western gender discourses*. Minneapolis: University of Minnesota Press.
Parsons, T. (1997). "'Kibra is our blood': Sudanese military legacy in Nairobi's Kibera location, 1902–1968." *International Journal of African Historical Studies* 30(1): 87–123.
———. (2003). *The 1964 army mutinies and the making of East Africa*. Westport CT: Praeger.
———. (2004). *Race, resistance, and the Boy Scout movement in British colonial Africa*. Athens: Ohio University Press.
———. (2011). "Local responses to the ethnic geography of colonialism in the Gusii highlands of British-ruled Kenya." *Ethnohistory* 58(3): 491–523.
———. (2012). "Being Kikuyu in Meru: challenging the tribal geography of colonial Kenya." *The Journal of African History* 53(1): 65–86.
———. (2014). *The second British Empire: in the crucible of the twentieth century*. Washington DC: Rowman & Littlefield.
Paulsen, K. (2010) "Placemaking," in Ray Hutchison (ed.), *Encyclopedia of Urban Studies* (pp. 599–603). London: Sage.
Peterson, D. R. (2004). *Creative writing: translation, bookkeeping, and the work of imagination in colonial Kenya*. Portsmouth: Heinemann.
Plano, C. (2022). "Improving paratransit service: lessons from transport

management companies in Nairobi, Kenya and their transferability." *Case Studies on Transport Policy* 10(1): 156–165.
Poggiali, L. (2016). Seeing (from) digital peripheries: technology and transparency in Kenya's silicon savannah. *Cultural Anthropology* 31(3): 387–411.
Porter, G. (2008). "Transport planning in sub-Saharan Africa II: putting gender into mobility and transport planning in Africa." *Progress in Development Studies* 8(3): 281–289.
———. (2011). "'I think a woman who travels a lot is befriending other men and that's why she travels': mobility constraints and their implications for rural women and girls in sub-Saharan Africa." *Gender, Place and Culture* 18(01): 65–81.
Porter, G. and N. Omwega (2022). "Experiences of women workers in the African road transport sector," in T. Wright, L. Budd and S. Ison (eds.), *Women, work and transport* (Vol. 16, pp. 55–69). Leeds: Emerald Publishing.
Rajab, R. (2014). "Matatu graffiti should be allowed, Uhuru says." *The Star*. 6 November.
Rasmussen, J. (2010). "Mungiki as youth movement: revolution, gender and generational politics in Nairobi, Kenya." *Young* 18(3): 301–319.
———. (2012). "Inside the system, outside the law: operating the *matatu* sector in Nairobi." *Urban Forum* 23(4): 415–432.
Reed, R. C. (2018). "Transportation turned performance art: Nairobi's matatu crews." *The New York Times*, 14 April.
Relph, E. (1976). *Place and placelessness*. London: Pion.
Rice, X. (2008). "We told them to come out of the church, but they locked the door ... so we burned them." *The Guardian*, 2 January.
Richardson, T. (2005). "Walking streets, talking history: the making of Odessa." *Ethnology* (1): 13–33.
Rizzo, M. (2017). *Taken for a ride: grounding neoliberalism, precarious labour, and public transport in an African metropolis*. Oxford University Press.
Robinson, J. (2006). *Ordinary cities: between modernity and development*. London: Routledge.
Rodgers, D. and B. O'Neill (2012). "Infrastructural violence: introduction to the special issue." *Ethnography* 13(4): 401–412.
Rodima-Taylor, D. (2022). "Platformizing Ubuntu? Fintech, inclusion and mutual help in Africa." *Journal of Cultural Economy* 15(4): 416–435.
Rodman, M. (1992). "Empowering place: multilocality and multivocality." *American Anthropologist* 94(3): 640–656.
Roe, E. M. (1991). "Development narratives, or making the best of blueprint development." *World Development* 19(4): 287–300.
Roitman, J. (2005) *Fiscal disobedience: an anthropology of economic regulation in Central Africa*. Princeton NJ: Princeton University Press.
Rosberg, C. and J. Nottingham (1966). *The Myth of "Mau Mau": nationalism in Kenya*. New York: Meridian Books.
Salon, D. and E. M. Aligula (2012). "Urban travel in Nairobi, Kenya: analysis, insights, and opportunities." *Journal of Transport Geography* 22: 65–76.
Salon, D. and S. Gulyani (2019). "Commuting in urban Kenya: unpacking travel demand in large and small kenyan cities." *Sustainability* 11(14): 3823.

Samper, D. (2002) "Talking *Sheng*: the role of a hybrid language in the construction of identity and youth culture in Nairobi, Kenya". PhD dissertation, University of Pennsylvania.

Samuels, D. W., L. Meintjes, A. M. Ochoa and T. Porcello (2010). "Soundscapes: toward a sounded anthropology." *Annual Review of Anthropology* 39: 329–345.

Schiller, N. (2019). "Urban Media as Infrastructure for Social Change," in Z. Krajina and D. Stevenson *(eds.), The Routledge companion to urban media and communication* (pp. 204–214). New York: Routledge.

Scott, J. C. (1998). *Seeing like a state: how certain schemes to improve the human condition have failed.* New Haven, CT: Yale University Press.

Shadle. B. (2015). *The souls of white folk: white settlers in Kenya, 1900s–1920s.* Manchester: Manchester University Press.

Shell, J. (2015). *Transportation and revolt: pigeons, mules, canals, and the vanishing geographies of subversive mobility.* Cambridge MA: MIT Press.

Sheller, M. J. and Urry (2006). "The new mobilities paradigm." *Environment and Planning A* 38(2): 207–226.

Siddiqi, D. M. (2020). Logics of sedition: re-signifying insurgent labour in Bangladesh's garment factories. *Journal of South Asian Development* 15(3): 371–397.

Simone, A. (2004) "People as infrastructure: intersecting fragments in Johannesburg." *Public Culture* 16(3): 407–429.

Smith, C. (2019). *Nairobi in the making: landscapes of time and urban belonging.* Woodbridge: James Currey.

Snyder, R. (1999). "Neoliberalism: the politics of reregulation in Mexico." *World Politics* 51(2): 173–204.

Sopranzetti, C. (2014). "Owners of the map: mobility and mobilization among motorcycle taxi drivers in Bangkok." *City & Society* 26(1), 120–143.

Spear, T. and R. Waller (eds.) (1993). *Being Maasai: ethnicity and identity in East Africa.* Athens: Ohio University Press.

Spencer, J. (1985). *The Kenya African Union.* Boston: Routledge & Kegan Paul.

Sperber, A. (2020). Uber made big promises in Kenya: drivers say it's ruined their lives. *NBC News*, 29 November.

Spinney, J. (2007). "Cycling the city: non-place and the sensory conception of meaning in mobile practice," in D. Horton, P. Rosen and P. Cox (eds.) *Cycling and the city.* Burlington, VT: Ashgate.

Stanley, A. (2015). "Review: 'Sense 8' the Wachowski's Netflix series, connects young and cute." *New York Times*, 3 June.

Stasik, M. and S. Cissokho (2018). "Introduction to special issue: bus stations in Africa." *Africa Today* 65(2): vii–xxiv.

Swainson, N. (1980). *The development of corporate capitalism in Kenya, 1918–77.* Oakland: University of California Press.

Theoharis, J. (2015). *The rebellious life of Mrs. Rosa Parks.* Boston, MA: Beacon Press.

Thieme, T. (2018) "The hustle economy: informality, uncertainty and the geographies of getting by." *Progress in Human Geography* 42(4): 529–548.

Thieme, T., M.E. Ference and N. van Stapele (2021). Introduction, "Harnessing the 'hustle': struggle, solidarities and narratives of work in Nairobi and beyond". *Africa* 91(1): 1–15.

Thrift, N. (2004). "Driving in the City." *Theory, Culture & Society* 21(4–5): 41–59.

Throup, D. (2020). "Daniel arap Moi and one-party Rule (1978–1991)," in. N. Cheeseman, K. Kanyinga and G, Lynch (eds.), *The Oxford handbook of Kenyan politics*. Oxford University Press.

Travers, A. (2003). Parallel subaltern feminist counterpublics in cyberspace. *Sociological Perspectives* 46(2): 223–237.

Tsing, A. (2011) *Friction: an ethnography of global connection*. Princeton: Princeton University Press.

van der Zwan, N. (2014). "Making sense of financialization." *Socio-Economic Review* 12(1): 99–129.

van Stapele, N., T. G. Diphoorn, M. Ruteere and P. Mutahi (2019). "'Ready to shoot' vs 'ready to loot!' the violent potentialities of demonstrations in Kenya," in M. Ruteere and P. Mutahi (eds.), *Policing protests in Kenya*. Nairobi: Centre for Human Rights and Policy Studies.

Velasco, C. (2022). "Monopoly and competition: The Kenyan commercial banks at the end of the colonial period (1954–1963)." *Business History* 64(6): 1071–1087.

Vokes, R. and K. Pype (2018). "Chronotopes of media in sub-Saharan Africa." *Ethnos*.83(2): 207–217.

Wa-Mungai, M. (2013) *Nairobi's "matatu" men: portrait of a subculture*. Nairobi: Contact Zones.

Wa-Mungai, M. D. A. Samper (2006). "'No mercy, no remorse': personal experience narratives about public passenger transportation in Nairobi, Kenya." *Africa Today* (1): 51–81.

Waitt, G., T. Harada and M. Duffy (2017). "'Let's have some music': sound, gender and car mobility." *Mobilities* 12(3): 324–342.

Wambua, S. (2009). "Disciplining the Reckless Matatu Driver." *The Nation*, 9 October.

Wamue, G. (2001). "Revisiting our indigenous shrines through *Mungiki*", *African Affairs* 100(400): 453–467.

Warner, G. (2014). "Viral videos show Kenyan women assaulted for wearing miniskirts." *NPR* Morning Edition, 28 November.

Warner, M. (2002). "Publics and counterpublics." *Quarterly Journal of Speech* 88(4): 413–425.

Webber, G. R. and P. Giuffre (2019). "Women's relationships with women at work: barriers to solidarity." *Sociology Compass* 13(6): e12698.

Weiss, E. and C. McGranahan (2021). "Rethinking pseudonyms in ethnography: an introduction," in C. McGranahan and E. Weiss (eds.), *Rethinking pseudonyms in ethnography*. American Ethnologist (web).

Weitzberg, K. (2020). "Biometrics, race making and white exceptionalism: the controversy of universal fingerprinting in Kenya." *The Journal of African History* 61(1): 23–43.

Weitzberg, K., M. Cheesman, A. Martin and E. Schoemaker (2021). "Between surveillance and recognition: rethinking digital identity in aid." *Big Data & Society* 8(1).

White, L. (1990). *The comforts of home: prostitution in colonial Nairobi*. Chicago: University of Chicago Press.

Wikman, A. and C, Muhoza (2019). "Women are changing the narrative in East Africa's public transport sector." Stockholm Environment Institute (SEI) Features, 13 May

Williams, J. L., A. A. Malik and S. McTarnaghan (2020). Gender-based violence on public transportation: a review of evidence and existing solutions. URBANLINKS policy brief. USAID.

Wipper, A. (1975). "The *Maendeleo ya Wanawake* organization: The co-optation of leadership." *African Studies Review* 18(3): 99–120.

Wolfe, P. (2006). "Settler colonialism and the elimination of the native." *Journal of Genocide Research* 8(4): 387–409.

Wood, A. (2015). Multiple temporalities of policy circulation: gradual, repetitive and delayed processes of BRT adoption in South African cities. *International Journal of Urban and Regional Research* 39(3): 568–580.

Wright, T. (2016). *Gender and sexuality in male-dominated occupations: women working in construction and transport.* New York: Palgrave Macmillan.

Wrong, M. and M. Williams (2009). *It's our turn to eat: the story of a Kenyan whistleblower.* London: Fourth Estate.

Yeoh, B. (1996). *Contesting space: power relations and the urban built environment in colonial Singapore.* Oxford: Oxford University Press.

Zuboff, S. (2019). *The age of surveillance capitalism: the fight for a human future at the new frontier of power.* London: Profile books.

Unpublished Theses

Abiero-Gariy, Z. C. (1989). "Public transport problems in Nairobi: a study of the management and operations of Kenya Bus Services (KBS) Limited." Doctoral dissertation, University of Nairobi.

Aduwo I. G. (1990) "The role, efficiency and quality of service of the *matatu* mode of public transport in Nairobi: a geographical analysis". MA thesis, University of Nairobi.

Bonna, R.J.M. (1985). "Rent control in middle income housing – a case study of Buru Buru housing estate, Nairobi." MA Thesis, University of Nairobi.

Farrell, L. (2015). "'Hustling NGOs': coming of age in Kibera Slum, Nairobi, Kenya." Doctoral Thesis, Boston University.

Feliciano, T. (2024). "Dancing in the heart of the empire." Doctoral Thesis, City University of New York.

Nyakundi, F. N. (2020). "Huduma Namba: Kenya's transformation into an informational state." University of Washington.

Osinde, K (1986). Sheng: an investigation into the social and cultural aspects of an evolving language. BA Thesis, University of Nairobi, Kenya.

van Stapele, N. (2007) "'*Kudé? kudedi!*' try or die: ethnicity, class and masculinity in a Kenyan slum." MA thesis, Erasmus Universiteit.

Web Sources

Flone Initiative (2020). Flone Initiative Annual Report. Retrieved from: https://womenandtransportafrica.org

Nairobi Commuter Rail. https://krc.co.ke/the-nairobi-commuter-rail

INDEX

Page numbers in italics refer to figures and tables.

Abiria card   113
Abuka, Victor   115
Allied Transport Workers Union   46
Anderson, David M.   106
Anthony (*matatu* worker)   104–5, 145
anti-languages   20
archival research   36
Artur brothers   73
askari (guards)   155
Augé, Marc   70
automobility culture   70

Bakhtin, Mikhail   70
bangh (marijuana)   109
Basi Go   193–94
Basso, Keith   78
Battacharya, Jit   193
BebaPay card   111–13, 115, 116
Bedi, Tarini   80
Bena (*matatu* worker)   108–9
Berman, Bruce   108
Biaya, Tshikala   75–76
biological determinism   180
Blom-Hansen, Thomas   82
bodaboda (motorcycle taxis)   163, 165, 178
Bolt   180
Bonna, R.J.M.   69
Botswana   163
Buru Buru
  as commuter hub   69
  Express Connection and   125–26
  joyriding in   68–70

matatu minibus taxis in   23–24
  River of God (ROG) and   127–28
bus rapid transit (BRT) systems   14, 119–20, 122, 190–92, *191*

Camp, Garrett   181
card readers   114–16, *116–17*, 128–29
Carol (*matatu* worker)   179
cars   18, 44
Casey, E. S.   75
cashless transportation cards   15, 111–17, *114*, *116–17*, 128–29
catcalling   173, *175*
Central Business District (CBD)   121, 122–24, 125
ChapChap   182
Chappell, Ben   85
China   190
Christianity   77, 78–79, 127–28, 138, 145
chronotope   70
Chun, C. E.   63, 96
Citi Hoppa   123, 126–27
Citi Shuttle   123
civil rights movement   54
Clinton, Hillary   190n1
Cody, Francis   10–11, 169
Colombia   120, 190
Colvin, Claudette   54
consciousness raising (CR)   163, 178–80
Cooper, Frederick   39
counterpublics
  concept of   72

counterpublics (*continued*)
   joyriding and   71, 72–73, 83–84, 86–87
   women as *matatu* workers and   21–23, 162–63, 168–77
   See also publics
COVID-19 pandemic   32, 34, 153, 182
Cowan, Liz   190n1

Daily Nation (newspaper)   97, 98, 115, 122
detribalization   43
development narratives   119–20, 188
Diamond Trust Bank   116
disability   22–23, 154–55, 160–61, 166
Doherty, Jacob   90, 105
domestic space   51–52
Double M   123, 125–27

East African Rifles (later King's African Rifles, KAR)   58
East African Standard (newspaper)   59–60, 61, 84
East African Women's League (EAWL)   51–52
economic capital   4, 9, 14–16. *See also* target system
Economist (magazine)   8
electric vehicles   193–94, *193*
elimination logics   41–42
Elizabeth (*matatu* worker)
   on electric vehicles   193–94
   Flone Initiative and   34
   on masculinity   150–51
   paradoxes of empowerment and   137, 154–60
   passengers with disability and   22–23, 154–55, *156*
   photograph of   77
   on solidarity   167
   on women as *matatu* workers   138–40
Elyachar, Julia   105
Embassava   138, 140, 154, 166–67, 193–94

Emergency. *See* Kenya Emergency (1952–1960)
empowerment   136–37, 154–60
Engsh (language)   21
Equity Bank   116
Ethiopia   88
Eunice (Uber driver)   183–85
Express Connection (previously Double M)   123, 125–27
EZ (*matatu* worker)   79

feminist research and activism
   consciousness raising (CR) and   163, 178–80
   on counterpublics   21–23
   on intersectional stigma   148
   Maathai and   3, 5, 73, 135
   #mydressmychoice movement and   135–36, 162, 173, 180
   post-structuralism and   141
   Western vs. African perspectives and   163, 180
   See also Flone Initiative
Ferguson, James   86
financialization   119–20, 129
fiscal disobedience   89, 100–104, 110
Flone Initiative
   aims and initiatives of   22, 33–34, 136, 160–61, 162–64, 175–77, 188
   bus rapid transit (BRT) system and   190, *191*
   consciousness raising and   178–80
   "Report It Stop It" campaign and   170, *171–72*, *174–75*
   solidarity and   167–68
   See also Women in Transportation (WIT)
Foucault, Michel   78, 118
fourteen-seater phase-out   121–22
Fraser, Nancy   177

Gal, Susan   71
gangs   90–91, 94–96, 100–101, 142–43. *See also* Kamjesh; Mungiki
gender-based violence (GBV)   133–34, 135–36,

149–50, 162–63. *See also* sexual harassment and violence
George (*matatu* worker)   93, 145–46, 148
Gettleman, Jeffrey   7–8, 15, 111–13, 130
gin   52, 58, 59, 66–67, 72, 168, 194
githaka ituika (generational turnover of land)   108
Githiora, Chege   19
Githu, Samuel   65
Gladys (*matatu* worker)   104, 146, 148
Global Gender Index   135
go-along ethnography   29–30
Goffman, Erving   142
Goldman Sachs   120
Google   111–13, 115, 116, 129
governmentality   11–12, 118
graffiti   2, 11
Green Belt Movement (GBM)   24
Grossack, Martin   54–55
Gupta, Akhil   86

Habermas, Jürgen   21, 72, 169
Hakim (*matatu* worker)   77–78
Hart, Keith   9
Haugerud, Angelique   72, 99
Havelock, W. B.   62
Heinze, Robert   95, 107
Housewives (European settler women)
  "Ladies Only" bus stops and   59–61
  one-class, one-fare bus policy (1956) and   38–43, *39*, 48–54, 55–58, 65–66
Hustwit, Gary   190n2

I Call It Culture (Matatu) (emails)   148–50
informal transportation   9–10
Institute for Transportation and Development Policy (ITDP)   120, 190
International Monetary Fund (IMF)   119
interpenetration   44

intimacy
  automobility culture and   70
  colonial bus and   39–43, 48–49, 54–55, 57
  matatu minibus taxis and   81–82, 194
  publics and   169
  urban transportation and   11–12
Isaacs, Gregory   3

Jackson (*matatu* worker)   7, 92, 106, 107–8
James (member of transport police)   101, 103–4
Jensen, Ole B.   78
Jesse (*matatu* worker)   99
Jones, Peris S.   17
Joseph (*matatu* worker)   138
Joshua (*matatu* worker)   138–39
Joyce (*matatu* worker)   78–79, 83, 124–25
joyriding. See *manyangas*

Kalanick, Travis   181
Kamau (*matatu* worker)   77
Kamjesh   91, 95, 108–10
Kanjo (guards)   155
Kaplan, Danny   165
Kelley, Robin   41–42
Kenya Bus Service (KBS)
  cashless transportation cards and   113, 116
  Central Business District (CBD) and   123–24
  end of service by   10
  "Ladies Only" bus stops and   59–61
  Nubian women with home-brewed gin on   52, 58, 59, 66–67, 72, 134–35, 168, 194
  one-class, one-fare bus policy (1956) and   38–43, *39*, 48–54, 55–58, 65–66
  origins and history of   44–46
  pirate taxis and   7, 62–66, *64*, 96–97
  role of   18, 189
  safety and   12

Kenya Commercial Bank
    (KCB)   113, 116
Kenya Emergency (1952–1960)
    githaka ituika (generational
        turnover of land) and   108
    Kikuyu veterans as taxi drivers
        and   46
    Nubian women and   58
    Operation Anvil and   40, 48
    pirate taxis and   65
Kenya Transport and Allied Workers
    Union (KTAWU)   97
Kenya Welfare Association   44
Kenyan National Archives
    (KNA)   36
Kenyan Television Network
    (KTN)   84
Kenyatta, Jomo   12, 19, 48, 97, 98
Kenyatta, Uhuru   85
Kibaki, Mwai   13, 84
Kießling, Roland   20
Kikuyu people
    githaka ituika (generational
        turnover of land) and   108
    Makadara and   61–62
    veterans as taxi drivers and   10,
        45–46, 48, 66–67, 168, 189
    See also Kenya Emergency
        (1952–1960)
Kinfu, Eshetayehu   88
kipande system   17, 43–44
Kirby, A. F.   62
Klopp, Jaqueline   10, 119, 122
kombi taxis   82

Land and Freedom Army   10, 48
Langat, Steve   83–84
Larkin, Brian   11
Latour, Bruno   10–11
Lee, Benjamin   71
Legal Notice 23 (2014)   114
Legal Notice 161. *See* Michuki Rules
    (2004)
LiPuma, Edward   71
Lonsdale, John   45, 108
lowriding   85
ltwstu   142

Lucas (SACCO secretary)   140
Lucia (*matatu* worker)   138

Ma, Yo-Yo   155–56, *157–58*, 187, 194
Maathai, Wangari   3, 5, 24, 73, 135
MADCOWA (Matatu Drivers
    and Conductors Welfare
    Association)   26–27, 30
Maendeleo wa Wanawake (Women
    for Development)   163n1
Maina (*matatu* worker)   88–89,
    107–8
Mains, Daniel   88
Makadara   48, 61–66
manspreading   170, *171*
manyangas
    aesthetics of   73–76, *77*, 86–87,
        170
    as counterpublics   71, 72–73,
        83–84, 86–87
    Ma and   155–56, *157–58*, 187,
        194
    music and sound in   69–70, 74,
        81–83
    naming of   76–80
    placemaking and   71–73
    as political space   168
    practice of joyriding and   68–70
    risk and   75
    in *Sense8* (television
        series)   80–81
    women and   138–41
Mariga, Thuo   96
marijuana (*bangh*)   109
Martin (*matatu* worker)   79–80
Mary (Flone Initiative
    member)   178–80
Mary (*matatu* worker)   138–39
Maryam (*matatu* worker)   80, 82–83
masculinity   6, 136–37, 141–50, 166
Mastercard   115–16
matatu minibus taxis
    aesthetics of   2–4, *4–5*, 73–76, *77*,
        86–87, 170
    Central Business District (CBD)
        permits and   121, 122–24
    cost of   73–74

Index

decriminalization (1973) of 12, 19, 98
electric vehicles and 193–94, *193*
ethnographic approach to 4–5, 8–9, 23–24, 25–30, 32–36
future planning of Nairobi and 187–88
gender-based violence (GBV) and 134, 135–36. *See also* #mydressmychoice movement
illegality as redistribution and 88–90. *See also* gangs; police
joyriding and. See *manyangas*
masculinity and 6, 136–37, 141–50, 166
naming of 3, 76–80, 82
noise pollution and 85
number of vehicles and workers in 1, *2*, 7, 181, 186
origin of name 18–19, *19*
origins and history of 97–100, 194–96
as publics 71–72, 86–87, 168–77. *See also* counterpublics
regulation of 6, 83–85, 120–25. *See also* Michuki Rules (2004)
reputation of 1, *3*, 7–8, 24–26. *See also* stigma
risk and 4, 24–30, 89–90
seatbelts and. *See* seatbelts
skwads (one-off trips) and 87, 91–95, 109–10
target system and. *See* target system
women as *matatu* workers and 178–80
youth culture and 75–76, 81–82
Matatu Owners Association (MOA) 116
Matatu Today (magazine) 79, 101
Matatu Vehicle Owners Association (MVOA) 98
Matatu Welfare Association (MWA) 115

Mau Mau rebellion. *See* Kenya Emergency (1952–1960)
McIntosh, Janet 53
mental health 54–55
Michuki, John
    Artur brothers and 73n2
    NARC government and 13, 84
    regulation of *matatu* sector and 83–85, 121. *See also* Michuki Rules (2004)
    "shoot to kill" orders and 104, 108
Michuki Rules (2004)
    ethnographic approach to 24
    implementation and impact of 13–14, 32, 84, 120–21
    Mwangi and 125, 126–27
    seatbelts and 117–18, 126
    on yellow stripe on vehicles 46
Mina (*matatu* worker) 179
minibus and midibus taxis (MBTs) 9–10. See also *matatu* minibus taxis
Mirowski, Philip 112, 189
Mitchell, Phillip 47
mlami (White person) 31–32, 35
mlengo (out of turn on the board) 28–29, *29*
Moi, Daniel arap
    authoritarian regime of 12–13
    Maathai and 135
    role of *matatu* and 10, 71, 72–73, 98–99, 168
Mombasa, Reginald 44
Montgomery Bus Boycott 54
Moses, Robert 181
motorcycle taxis
    in Ethiopia 88
    in Kenya 163, 165, 178
    in Uganda 90, 105
Mous, Maarten 20
M-PESA (digital money transfer technology) 15, 112, 113, 115
"Msupa Wa Nganya" (Beautiful *Manyanga* Girl) (song) 175–77
multiracialism 40, 47, 49–50, 59–61

Mungiki 90–91, 95, 104, 105, 106–10, *107*
music and sound
 Flone Initiative and 22, 175–77
 joyriding and 69–70, 74, 81–83, 140
 matatu aesthetics and 2, 3–4
 Moi's authoritarian regime and 10, 71, 72–73, 98–99, 168
 noise pollution and 85
 political speeches and 10, 12–13, 71, 72–73, 98–99, 168
 River of God (ROG) and 128
Mutongi, Kenda 5, 121, 144, 168–69
Mwai (SACCO chairman) 140
Mwangi, Ed 8
Mwangi, John 8, 125–26
Mwangi, Mary 8, 125–27
Mwaura, Naomi 22, 135–36
My 1963 card 113–14, *114*, 115
#mydressmychoice movement 135–36, 162, 173, 180
Myers, Garth Andrew 187
mzungu (White or foreign person) 31, 131–32

Nairobi, Kenya
 African population in 44, 48
 British colonial administration in 17–19, 43–44
 multiracialism in 40, 47, 49–50, 59–61
 Nubians in 57–59
 South Asians in 40, 48, 131–33
 See also urban transportation in Nairobi; *specific neighbourhoods*
Nairobi City Council (NCC)
 Central Business District (CBD) permits and 123
 Kenya Bus Service (KBS) and 49
 passengers with disability and 155
 pirate taxis and 97, 98
Nairobi Commuter Rail 10

Nation (magazine) 7, 97–98
The National Archives (TNA) (formerly Public Records Office, PRO) 36
National Environmental Management Authority (NEMA) 85
National Integrated Identity Management Scheme (NIIMS) 128
National Rainbow Coalition (NARC) government 13, 84
National Transport and Safety Authority (NTSA) 33, 162
National Transportation Safety Association (NTSA) 114, 127
National Youth Service (NYS) 100
Native Registration Amendment Ordinance 43
Native Reserve system 17, 43–44
neoliberalism
 bus rapid transit (BRT) systems and 192
 development narratives and 120, 188
 financialization and 119–20, 129
 governmentality and 11–12, 118
 infrastructures and 187–88
 matatu minibus taxis and 6, 88
 reregulation and 112, 116–17, 120–25, 129–30, 188, 189
Nepal 134, 151
New York Times (newspaper) 7–8, 15, 81, 111–13
Ngoza, Paul 20
Njoroge, Martin 97–98
noise pollution 85
Nubian, use of term 57–59
Nubian women
 home-brewed gin on KBS buses and 52, 58, 59, 66–67, 72, 134–35, 168, 194
 Housewives and 39, 40–42, 59–61
 Kikuyu women married to Sudanese ex-soldiers as 59
 settler violence against 56–57
Nyabola, Nanjala 162

Nyayo Bus 100, 121
Nzuga, Kipende 31

Obama, Barack 2–3
Odinga, Raila 84
Omwega, Nyaboke 160
Ong, Aihwa 124
Operation Anvil (1954) 40, 48
Oyewùmí, Oyèrónke 163

paratransit 9–10
Parker, Mary 47
parking 18, 44
Parks, Rosa 54
Pepea card 113
Peter (ROG executive
 member) 127–28
phatic labor 105
pirate taxis
 meaning and morality of 169
 origin and history of 7, 18–19,
  61–66, *64*
 police and 19, 88, 95–98
 risk and 12
placelessness 70
placemaking 71–73, 86–87
police
 bribes from *matatu* minibus taxis
  to 90–91, 94–96, 100–101,
  142–43
 pirate taxis and 19, 88, 95–98
 relationship with *matatu*
  operators 101–4
 "shoot to kill" orders and 104,
  108
 women as *matatu* workers
  and 152–54
political speeches 10, 12–13, 71,
 72–73, 98–99, 168
popular transportation 9–10
Porter, Gina 160
post-structuralism 141
private taxis 164–65. *See also* Uber
Public Officers and Ethics Act
 (2006) 101
public sphere 72
publics

 concept of 10–11, 71–72, 169–70
 matatu minibus taxis as 11, 71–72,
  86–87, 162, 168–77
 See also counterpublics

Rachel (*matatu* worker) 151–52
Rasta George (*matatu* worker)
 on gangs 106
 on masculinity 143, 145–47
 on Michuki Rules 121
 on police 102–4
 on *skwads* 93–94
 solidarity and 8–9
redistributive labor 9
Relph, Edward 70
"Report It Stop It" campaign 170,
 171–72, 174–75
reregulation 112, 116–17, 120–25,
 129–30, 188, 189
Rhea (*matatu* worker) 139–40
Richardson, Tanya 83
risk
 manyangas and 75
 matatu minibus taxis and 4,
  24–30, 89–90
 pirate taxis and 12
rites of passage 142–43
River of God (ROG) 114–15, 127–28,
 138
Rizzo, Matteo 105, 120, 192
Robert (*matatu* worker) 78
Rodima-Taylor, Daivi 112, 117
Rodman, Margaret C. 75
Roe, Emory 119–20
Roitman, Janet 89, 95, 100
Ruth (*matatu* worker) 151, 152–54

SACCOs. *See* savings and credit
 co-operatives (SACCOs)
Safaricom 113–14, *114*
safety
 matatu minibus taxis and 12
 seatbelts and 13, 117–18, 126
 Sheng (language) and 20
 See also gender-based violence
  (GBV)
Samper, David A. 25

Sarah (Flone Initiative member) 178–80
savings and credit co-operatives (SACCOs)
  cashless transportation cards and 114–15
  electric vehicles and 193–94
  Flone Initiative and 163–64
  police payoffs and 95
  publics and 72
  role of 33, 90, 121, 124–25
  women and 6, 34, 137–38, 159, 166–67, 185
seatbelts 13, 117–18, 126
second-wave feminism 163
Sense8 (television series) 80–81, 156
settler colonialism 41–42, 56–57. *See also* Housewives (European settler women)
sex workers 134–35
sexual harassment and violence
  I Call It Culture (Matatu) (emails) on 149–50
  #mydressmychoice movement and 135–36, 162, 173, 180
  "Report It Stop It" campaign and 170–73, *171–72*, *175*
  urban transportation and 134
Shadle, Brett 57
Shell, Jacob 72
Sheng (language)
  placemaking and 71, 73, 86–87
  solidarity and 20–21
  uses of 3–4, 19–21, 80, 105, 137, 142–43
  women and 150
  words for White and foreign people in 31–32
Sidian Bank 182
Signal and Noise (Larkin) 11
Simone, Abdoulique 94, 105
skwads (one-off trips) 87, 91–95, 109–10
Smedt, Johan de 58
Smith, Constance 188
Snyder, Richard 116–17

social media 180
solidarity
  colonial bus and 39–43, 55
  concept of 165
  illegality as redistribution and 89, 110
  Sheng (language) and 20–21
  skwads and 93–94
  Steve's accident and death and 8–9, 30
  women and 34, 136–37, 142, 159–61, 162, 164, 165–68, 179–80, 184–86, 188, 194
Sonya (*matatu* worker) 151
Sopranzetti, Claudio 25
soundscapes 81–82. *See also* music and sound
South Africa 14, 82, 133, 190–92
South Asians 40. 48, 131–33
speed governors 117
Sperber, Amanda 182–83
Standard Gauge Railway (SGR) 187
Stanley, Alessandra 81
Star (newspaper) 74
Steve (*matatu* worker)
  accident and death of 8–9, 30
  on masculinity 144, 146–48
  on Michuki Rules 121
  on police 102–4
  on risk 25–30
  on seatbelts 118
  on *skwads* 92–94
stigma
  matatu minibus taxis and 6, 8, 30, 98, 136, 141–42
  skwads and 91
  women as *matatu* workers and 136–37, 142, 148, 152, 160
subversive mobility 72
Sudanese soldiers 57–59
surveillance capitalism 128–29, 188
Susan (Flone Initiative member) 178–80
sustainable urban transportation 187–88

swanking taxis 82
symbolic capital 4, 9, 16

Tanzania 105, 120, 192
target system 15–16, 90–95, 139–41
Taxify 164–65, 180
taxis
 in Ethiopia 88
 Kikuyu veterans as drivers 10, 45–46, 48, 66–67, 168, 189
 in South Africa 14, 82, 133, 190–92
 in Tanzania 105
 in Uganda 90, 105
 See also *matatu* minibus taxis; pirate taxis
technologies of the self 78
tempos 134, 151
Tent of the Living God 106
Theuri, Patrick 79
TLB (Transport Licensing Board)
 Central Business District (CBD) permits and 123
 origins and history of 18, 44–46
 pirate taxis and 65, 97
 regulation of *matatu* sector and 6. See also SACCOs (savings and credit co-operatives)
 role of 33
 TNA (The National Archives) (formerly Public Records Office, PRO) 36
Tony (*matatu* worker) 73–74, 89, 101–2
touts 7, 15, 91, 102
transport management companies (TMCs) 6, 122–24, 125–26
*tuk tuk*s 134
Turning Tables 175–77

Uber 163, 164–65, 178, 180–85, 189
Uber Files 181
Uganda 90, 105
unemployment 76, 94, 122
United States 54, 66
United Transport 97

urban ethnography 11–12
urban transportation
 financialization of 119–20, 129
 gendered work practices and 133–34, 148
 as male-dominated sector 6, 133–34
urban transportation in Nairobi
 bus rapid transit (BRT) system and 120, 122, 190–92, *191*
 cars and parking 18, 44
 future of 187–94, *191*, *193*
 gendered work practices in 134–36
 Kikuyu veterans as taxi drivers and 10, 45–46, 48, 66–67, 168, 189
 motorcycle taxis and 163, 165, 178
 private taxi business in 164–65. See also Uber
 as sustainable 187–88
 transport monopoly agreement (1934) and 18, 88, 97, 120–21
 See also Kenya Bus Service (KBS); *matatu* minibus taxis; pirate taxis
Urbanized (Hustwit, 2011) 190n2

Van Damme, Jean-Claude 80
Visa 116
Vision 2030 (National Development Plan) 16–17, 127, 187–88, 190

Waitt, Gordon R. 74
Wamama Wa Mathree ("Mothers of the *Matatu*") (play) 22
Wambua, Sammy 7
Wa-Mungai, Mbugua 25, 80, 137, 144
Warner, Michael 72
Waruhiru, Senior Chief 48
White, Louise 134–35
Wilson (*matatu* worker) 94, 103–4, 147–48

Winnie (*bodaboda* driver) 178
Wolfe, Patrick 41, 55, 61
women
   future of transportation and 190–94, *191*
   gendered work practices in Nairobi and 134–36
   male *matatu* workers and 144–51, 162–63. *See also* sexual harassment and violence
   as *matatu* workers 6, 33–35, 132–33, 136–41, 142, 150–60. *See also* Elizabeth (*matatu* worker)
   private taxis and 164–65
   savings and credit co-operatives (SACCOs) and 6, 34, 137–38, 159
   solidarity and 34, 136–37, 142, 159–61, 162, 164, 165–68, 179–80, 184–86, 188, 194
   transportation as male-dominated sector and 133–34
   as Uber drivers 163, 164–65, 178, 183–85
   See also feminist research and activism; Housewives (European settler women); Nubian women; sexual harassment and violence
Women in Transportation (WIT)
   aims and initiatives of 22, 136, 159
   annual conferences and 34, 152–54, 163–64
   bus rapid transit (BRT) system and 190, *191*
   Elizabeth (*matatu* worker) and 154–55
   "Report It Stop It" campaign and 170, *171–72*, *174–75*
Woolard, Kathryn A. 71
World Bank 9, 119, 120, 127, 192
Wright, Tessa 168

Yeoh, Brenda S.A. 48
youth culture 75–76, 81–82

Zachary (fomer SACCO chairman) 140
Zakah 2, 11
Zohari Leasing 182
Zuboff, Shoshana 129, 189
Zwan, Natascha van der 119

Printed in the United States
by Baker & Taylor Publisher Services